REPUBLIC OR EMPIRE

REPUBLIC OR EMPIRE

American Resistance

to the Philippine War

By DANIEL B. SCHIRMER
Preface by Howard Zinn

SCHENKMAN PUBLISHING COMPANY, INC.
Cambridge, Massachusetts 02138
Distributed by General Learning Press

Schenkman books are distributed by
General Learning Press
250 James Street
Morristown, New Jersey 07960

The author has requested that royalties from the sale of this book be assigned to the Massachusetts Vietnam Veterans Against the War.

Copyright © 1972
Schenkman Publishing Company
Cambridge, Massachusetts

Library of Congress Catalog Card Number: 74-189100
Printed in the United States of America

ALL RIGHTS RESERVED. THIS BOOK, OR PARTS THEREOF, MAY NOT BE REPRODUCED IN ANY FORM WITHOUT WRITTEN PERMISSION OF THE PUBLISHER.

Acknowledgments

I am indebted to numerous individuals and institutions for help in my work on this book:

The Louis M. Rabinowitz Foundation, Inc. made a grant of financial assistance.

Professors Robert V. Bruce, Herbert Moller, Robert E. Moody, Arnold A. Offner and Howard Zinn, all of Boston University, were generously helpful (although the author claims full responsibility for interpretation of events described).

Of great assistance were the staffs of the Boston Public Library (especially Microtext), Boston University's Mugar Library, Congregational Library, Harvard University's Widener Library (especially the Documents and Microtext Division), Houghton Library, and Baker Library, the Library of Congress, the Massachusetts Historical Society, the Massachusetts State Library, the National Archives, the New England Deposit Library, the New York Public Library, and the Yale University Library.

The Massachusetts Historical Society granted permission to quote from papers in its possession, and Harvard College Library did so with respect to papers in Houghton Library. The *New Republic* gave permission for the use of material that first appeared in its pages.

Max Gordon and the editorial staff of the Schenkman Publishing Company helped with editing. I was also helped in many ways by many friends, including Marta Abramowicz, Herbert Aptheker, Kurt Baum, Jean and Leo Berman, Robert Brandfon, William Charney, Joan Colebrook, Horace B. Davis, Joan and Carl Fenichel, Philip Foner, Selma, Alex and David Ganz, George Gloss of the Brattle Book Shop, Virginia and Earl Gove, Grace and Max Granich, William B. Hixson, Jr., Jane Hodes, Francis and Otis Hood, Ella and Eugene Jackson, Benjamin Landey, Eric Levenson, Arthur MacEwan, Phyllis MacEwan, Jerry Markowitz, Henry Mins, Steve Nelson, Barbara and Paul Rosenkrantz, Robert Rubin, Mark I. Solomon, and Dirk J. Struik.

The members of my family, Peggy, Audrey, Abbie and Joe Schirmer were a constant aid.

Contents

	Preface	ix
	Foreword	1
1	Massachusetts Anti-Imperialism: The Background	7
2	Countervailing forces and Early Contests	19
3	The Venezuelan Crisis	33
4	The Spanish War: "The Political Economy of Barbarism"	45
5	Faneuil Hall and Aguinaldo	65
6	Aging Abolitionists, Rejuvenated Racism	83
7	The New England Anti-Imperialist League	93
8	Opposition to the Treaty	105
9	The Treaty Passes	121
10	Against the Philippine War	135
11	Atkinson and the Volunteers	149
12	The Rise of Monopoly and Finance	161
13	An Organization Formed, A Republic Smashed	171
14	Forging an Anti-Imperialist Coalition	187
15	The Victory of Imperialism	205
16	Against Atrocities: The Last Campaign	225
17	The Dissolution of the Movement	241
	Afterword	255
	Notes	261
	Index	289

Preface

How poor was our historical education is shown by the fact that when the war in Vietnam became obviously ugly, we did not think immediately of the crushing of the Filipino insurrection at the start of this century. Nor did we, when the movement against the Vietnam war became powerful, recall an earlier anti-imperialist movement that took shape during the war with the Philippines. This book turns our eyes firmly back to those dramatic and shameful years.

Daniel Boone Schirmer, in these pages, redresses that odd imbalance of treatment in our usual history courses, where the war with Spain, a brief, victorious military romp — "a splendid little war," as some called it — is the central event in foreign policy in that period, and the taking of the Philippines a shadowy anti-climax. Here, we face the fact that the war against Spain in Cuba took several months and the casualties were small; the war against the Filipino *insurrectos* took several years and the casualties were enormous (perhaps 600,000 died on the island of Luzon alone, of war and pestilence).

It is rare that a history teacher can resist telling how, after praying all night, President McKinley got the word from God that he had better take the Philippines, to "civilize and Christianize" the natives. It is also rare that a history teacher dwells on what happened after that: how the Filipinos did not get that same message from God, how they resisted the Americans replacing the Spanish as their rulers, how they fought bitterly for three years and longer, until too many villages had been destroyed, too much land ruined, too many people killed, too many leaders put into prison.

This book tells us that story, and much more that is missing in orthodox histories. It tells the story of the Anti-Imperialist League, centered in Massachusetts, of its tough battle against American domination of the Philippines, of the odd assortment of men associated in that battle: journalists like Samuel Bowles, intellectuals like William James, labor leaders like Samuel Gompers, middle-class reformers like Edward Atkinson, wealthy industrialists like Andrew Carnegie, and Boston Brahmins like Charles Francis Adams. Mr. Schirmer has his own interpretation of why the League lost that battle and fell apart.

Most histories, in the interest of professional propriety, or prudence, avoid declaring their connections with present controversial issues. That is a timidity we cannot afford in an era when we need every kind of factual and historical sustenance we can get to be active, engaged citizens, resisting the mendaciousness of official sources, the orthodoxy of traditional textbooks. Daniel Boone Schirmer will have none of that. One feels, even as he wends his way soberly, meticulously, through the facts about the war in the Philippines then, that he is aware of the war in Indochina now, and the frightening recapitulation of history taking place.

The parallels between the Philippine and Indochina wars are striking: the trumped-up "incidents" to justify launching the war (a land version of the Gulf of Tonkin affair); the euphemisms for imperial expansion (McKinley called his policy "Benevolent Assimilation"); the ignoring of peace overtures from the other side; the desperation over the popular support for the guerrillas, and the subsequent turning to terror tactics against the population; the incessant promises of victory just around the corner; the look beyond the battlefield to the markets of China; the growing disgust of American soldiers with the war; the token court-martials with token punishments for officers accused of atrocities; the racism of soldiers in the field and financiers in the stock exchanges, as our armies searched and destroyed "the niggers" of the Philippines.

Mr. Schirmer has dug deeply into the primary sources: the newspapers, the government reports, the letters and papers of the participants. He combines careful scholarship with a lively sense of narrative, and always, an undercurrent of urgency which tells us: this is not just history, not just a colorful reproduction of past events; this is about us, our country, our violence and our hypocrisy, our movements of protest, our political maneuverings and moral anguish, our despair, our bit of hope that history, which so often repeats itself, also, sometimes, leaps in a new direction.

HOWARD ZINN

I wish to offer . . . tribute . . . to Massachusetts . . . for fostering more than any other state the spirit of liberty and independence for the Filipinos.

Martin P. De Veyra, Jr., Filipino speaker at the memorial meeting for George S. Boutwell, Faneuil Hall, April 18, 1905.

I think it will not be denied that the country at large has recognized Boston as the centre of the opposition to this unhappy war.

Edwin D. Mead, *The Principles of the Founders*, 1903.

Foreword

> *The* Republican *firmly believes in the American principles of government and society. It does not doubt that through democracy are the people to attain the largest measure of happiness and well-being . . . It is opposed to imperialism and militarism, to the domination of wealth and aristocracy. It sees in the purchase and conquest of the Philippine Islands new evidence of the unceasing effort of incorporated and syndicated wealth to conduct national affairs at the expense of the great body of the people. (Prospectus of the* Springfield Daily Republican, *January 6, 1900.)*

The Vietnam War is only the last, most prolonged and most brutal of a series of United States interventions in the affairs of other peoples. The invasion of Cuba sponsored by United States authorities failed at the Bay of Pigs, but intervention has been more effective on other occasions, as in the Dominican Republic, Guatemala, British Guiana, Iran and the Congo. Nor is the list complete; other colonial peoples (and some European as well) have felt the effects of aggressive American intrusion upon their domestic politics, whether or not in the form of outright violence. In most of the countries concerned such activities have apparently been in response to what Washington authorities have seen as a threat to existing social and political conditions from revolution, or drastic reform.[1]

This suggests that of late the United States has been directing its foreign policy toward increasingly frequent and intensive efforts to stem the tide of reform and revolution sweeping the world as a result of the dynamics of nationalism and social change. Such efforts, in their most overt and violent form, go by the name of counter-insurgency. Even now in the Panama Canal Zone the United States Southern Command maintains a multi-million dollar headquarters to promote counter-insurgency, where thousands of troops sent to Vietnam received training. In the past few years this mission has, as well, conducted hundreds of operations all over South America (perhaps the most highly publicized of these was the capture in Bolivia of the Cuban revolutionary Che Guevara). An officer in command at this headquarters adds, "After Vietnam, our experience will be useful against subversion in Latin America and elsewhere."[2]

Nevertheless, the once colonial nations of Africa, Asia and South America are in a period of sustained revolt and reformation. Influenced by the massive Russian and Chinese revolutions of this century, they tend to turn to socialist methods and goals as they seek to assert their national identity and reconstruct their national life. In the most notable case of Vietnam — the Soviet Union, Peoples' China and other socialist countries have supplied economic and military assistance.

Oppressive intervention in other peoples' affairs is nothing new to American history, especially in its ultimate form of a war of conquest. With its inception and for more than a hundred years thereafter the United States waged relentless war against the American Indians, expelling them from their land. In the middle of the nineteenth century the United States government, under the direction of Southern slaveholders, made an aggressive war on Mexico, seizing much of her territory.

Present-day policies of counter-insurgency and intervention, however, have their source in events that occurred at the opening of the twentieth century. Then the United States defeated Spain in war and stripped her of colonies in the Caribbean and the Pacific, taking Puerto Rico outright, giving Cuba nominal independence, and annexing the Philippines after first suppressing a nationalist revolution in those islands by force. What particularly distinguishes modern foreign policy from the Mexican War and the Indian wars for most of their span is that it is the product of another era in American history and comes in response to decisively different social pressures. Modern foreign policy is associated with the rise of the large-scale corporation, industrial and financial, as the dominant economic force in the country, exerting a most powerful influence upon the government of the United States. The Spanish-American War and the war to subdue Aguinaldo and the Philippine insurgents were the first foreign wars conducted as a consequence of this influence, the first wars of modern corporate America. The United States suppression of the Philippine national revolution was the progenitor of the Vietnam War; it represented the beginning of counter-insurgency.

Turning toward intervention in the affairs of colonial peoples and a policy of imperialism with the Spanish War and what followed, the United States assumed, for the first time, the burden of militarism as a sustained feature of national life. It entered the international arms race, which has continued intermittently throughout the twentieth century and at present assumes monstrous proportions. The crisis of the Spanish War initiated the elevation of the role of the military in American society and politics which has gone so far today; it gave a first impetus to those connections between the military and corporate interests which comprise what is now called the military-industrial complex.

The emergence of both corporate dominance and modern interventionist foreign policy was observed with conflicting feelings by Americans at the time. Writing a prospectus for his paper in the year 1900, Samuel Bowles, editor and owner of the *Springfield Republican,* recognized the war against the Philippine independence movement as a turning point in the national life, marked by the overbearing domestic influence of "incorporated and syndicated wealth," by "imperialism and militarism," by emulation of the policies and methods of European monarchies. All this represented to Bowles a significant break with our "traditional policies in government and foreign relations" which had been previously typified, as he saw it, by democracy and abstention from the militarism and long-standing rivalries of European states. In short, Bowles opposed the Philippine War as the expression of the new policies of imperialism and militarism which, in his view, corporate wealth was fastening on the country.

Millions of his fellow citizens, in Massachusetts and the country at large, shared Bowles' feelings and beliefs. In consequence an organized movement of resistance arose of those Americans who opposed the foreign policies of the McKinley Administration and called themselves anti-imperialists.

Historians have dealt one-sidedly with this crucial moment in American history. The war with Spain has received considerable attention. The picture it presents of pathetically ineffective Spaniards, canned beef scandals, overweight and bumbling American generals, the strident Roosevelt charging about with his Rough Riders, above all the quick victory, which gave Cuba a semblance, at least, of freedom, amuses and flatters; it does not disturb the national complacency.

There is a great difference in the treatment of the Philippine War. Its outbreak was "clouded by obscurity" wrote Charles Beard, but in truth the war as a whole has been neglected by American historians.[3] This is in spite of the fact that the Philippine War lasted longer than the war with Spain, was more costly in lives and treasure and had more significant results. Whereas the American victory over Spain in the Caribbean affirmed and enlarged an already established influence in South America, the conquest of the Philippines thrust United States power toward the Asian mainland in a new and unprecedented manner. This aftermath of the Spanish-American War was decisive in giving that war its essential character as one of imperial advantage.

In the Philippine War the United States used its armed might to crush a smaller people struggling for independence, and the anti-imperialists denounced it at the time, with great moral fervor, as one of the most shameful pages in American history. The anti-imperialists, too, have suffered from historical neglect. Nations have a way of turning from what is unsavory in their past, to stifle the voices of conscience.

At this writing American forces have been fighting in Vietnam for more than seven years to reassert an Asian influence first sought in the Philippine War (using military emplacements on those islands won in that war as "invaluable rear installations"), and the American conscience has been touched again.[4] Condemning the war as immoral and contrary to the national interest, blacks, the young, intellectuals, church people and certain trade unionists have joined in a strong movement of opposition. This opposition forced the retirement from the Presidency of the American held most responsible for the war and played a part in bringing on negotiations to end it. Even as the

Philippine War foreshadowed the Vietnamese War, the domestic opposition in both cases rose in response to the struggle waged by a people resisting Washington's domination. The forerunners of today's troubled Americans were the anti-imperialists of that earlier time, and their thought and experience take on a contemporary relevance in the face of problems that seem much the same, though more virulent, perhaps, for being seventy years unsolved.

Here is a study of that important nodal point in American affairs: the period during which the country conclusively turned to a modern imperial course. It deals especially with the American anti-imperialists and therefore of necessity gives attention to the Philippine War they so vigorously opposed. It is written with particular reference to those men from Massachusetts who took leading parts on both sides of the question. From the standpoint of the anti-imperialists such a vantage ground is essential for any real understanding since it was generally acknowledged at the time that the national leadership of the anti-imperialist movement centered in Massachusetts, especially in Boston, and more especially in an organization called the New England Anti-Imperialist League. As far as the proponents of the Philippine War, of imperialism and militarism, are concerned, Massachusetts politics had a national aspect in that one of the most influential promoters of the new foreign policy was the Massachusetts Senator, Henry Cabot Lodge, who dominated the Republican Party of that state and was particularly representative of her industrial interests. The duality and tension of this seminal crisis in American life developed with greatest clarity in Massachusetts politics, and they, in turn, had a significant effect on the national course of events.

1

Massachusetts Anti-Imperialism: The Background

The anti-imperialist movement had its beginnings in Massachusetts. On June 15, 1898, Boston citizens gathered in Faneuil Hall to protest the course of the Spanish-American War, the first such meeting in the country. November of the same year saw the establishment of the New England Anti-Imperialist League in the office of a Boston businessman, the first such organization. There was basis for the leadership of this city and state.[1]

Only some thirty years before the founding of the Anti-Imperialist League the nation had been convulsed by the Civil War, the climax of years of anti-slavery agitation and organization in the Northern states. Boston and Massachusetts had played a leading part in this agitation and during the war itself made an outstanding contribution to the Northern victory. Most of the men who stepped forward to organize the anti-imperialist movement in Boston had been ardent supporters of the anti-slavery struggle and the Union cause in the years before. Several had served in the Union armies, but whether they had seen active service or not, the Civil War remained the supreme event of their lives. The massive blows of Lincoln's armies that overthrew an obsolescent and reactionary social system stayed vivid in their memories. When they saw the United States, so recently made secure by military victory over black slavery at home, pushed into a foreign war to enslave another colored people, they felt the nation, and themselves, betrayed.

The importance of the anti-slavery and Civil War experience as motivation for the New England anti-imperialist leadership is attested to by their writings and speeches, so often charged with deep-felt allusion to the remarkable events of that earlier time. Thomas Wentworth Higginson, who served with black troops in the Civil War, believed that the influence of another and prior democratic revolution was a source of anti-imperialism, as well. It was often noted that the leadership of the anti-imperialist movement was, for the most part, elderly or aged. Higginson ascribed this to the fact that "the older men were brought up in the period when the revolutionary traditions lingered among us."[2] Indeed the nation's oldest political tradition was anti-imperialism, for the United States had been born in a war against British imperial rule. Again, in this struggle Boston had been a leading center, and Massachusetts the seat of initial conflict. The New England leaders of the anti-imperialist movement were very conscious of this heritage. When the issue arose, Charles Francis Adams, whose great-grandfather had signed the Declaration of Independence, thought that he had no choice but to speak out for Philippine independence.[3] So it was with others.

Adams and Higginson were Boston Brahmins; that is, they came from upper-middle class families that represented the city's established mercantile wealth with its ministerial and professional adjuncts. Anti-imperialists like Edward Atkinson, Charles Eliot Norton, Charles Russell Codman, Gamaliel Bradford, Robert M. Morse, Winslow Warren, Erving Winslow, David Greene Haskins, Jr., Moorfield Storey, Josiah Quincy and Robert Treat Paine, Jr., all sprang from Pilgrims and Puritans, Revolutionary soldiers and statesmen, merchants, ministers, magistrates and lawyers. A small group of men of this type initiated the New England Anti-Imperialist League. (The anti-imperialists, of course, did not speak for the Boston Brahmins as a whole; many of these supported McKinley and the policies of the Republican Party.)

While the bulk of the leaders of the New England Anti-Imperialist League were not Brahmins, they were overwhelmingly middle and upper-middle class. Some sixty New Englanders served as officers of the League in the years of its greatest influence, from 1898 to 1904. These were lawyers, preachers, businessmen, editors, educators and one trade union official. But the initial Brahmin core was ever dominant in the leadership.

The anti-imperialist sentiment of Boston's middle class, however, was affected by more than the political traditions of the two great liberating upheavals of the country's past. It also had economic and social roots. These roots of Boston anti-imperialism are clearly visible in the case of Henry Lee, the banker, regarded by many at the time of his death in November 1898 as Boston's first citizen. Of revolutionary and Brahmin stock, an anti-slavery activist before this cause became popular, Lee ended his days an anti-imperialist.[4]

In the spring of 1898, after the McKinley Administration had plunged the United States into a war with Spain, Henry Lee lay old and sick, his illness caused in part, he felt, by his distress at what he considered to be an inexcusable war. Unable to use a pen, he dictated an appeal to his friends, "Ought not we to meet and protest in a most solemn manner this armed intervention, a measure contrary to justice, contrary to our country's best traditions. . . . "[5]

It was not Lee's call that brought about the first meeting to protest the Spanish-American War. His experience in the world of business, however, casts light on the motivations of Boston's middle class anti-imperialists. Graduating from Harvard in 1838, Lee entered his father's mercantile house which he took over four years later and ran until 1852. Then, as his contemporary Boston biographer wrote, "It was quite time to retire from this commercial business. The protective tariff had slowly but surely destroyed the foreign commerce by which the merchants and ship-owners had hitherto lived and prospered." The region was turning to new pursuits, to cotton mills, and the textile towns of Lawrence and Lowell were growing rapidly. Such a transformation did not appeal to Lee, and he resented the economic policy that had effected it, "for his father's belief in free trade had descended to him, and he remained a stalwart free trader to the end of his days." Carrying "his hostility to these upstart factories" so far that he would never invest in their stocks, he turned instead to banking. The firm he joined — Lee, Higginson and Company — soon took the lead in this field of business in the city.[6]

Lee's "hostility to these upstart factories" suggests that Boston's middle class anti-imperialism was influenced by mercantile dissatisfaction with the shifting balance of power in the state and nation, as the growth of industry shoved commercial interests to one side economically and politically. This discontent came into focus after the Civil War in the struggle over the tariff. Boston's merchants, at the side of their fellows in New York and elsewhere, called for free trade to protect their interest in imports, while Massachusetts industrialists joined their brethren in other states in calling for high tariffs to protect the home market. To his chagrin, Henry Lee saw "greedy, unscrupulous, rapacious manufacturers" come to lead the Republican Party after the Civil War, and the Republican Party dominated the national government for most of the time, so that the mercantile interests lost out on the matter of the tariff.[7]

The political thrust of mercantile discontent had been carried after the Civil War not by the merchants alone, but also by a group of Boston liberals, many of whom were later prominent in the anti-imperialist movement. Linked as they were to the city's older mercantile wealth by manifold family ties and social connections, these lawyers and professionals quite naturally shared its hostility to the new-rich industrialists and their policies. They first gained political identity after the Civil War as Liberal Republicans, challenging the dominant party leadership; after their support of the Democrat Cleveland in the 1884 elections they were known as Mugwumps.

In addition to free trade, the Boston liberals were concerned with sound currency and civil service reform. Sound currency was important to the holders of inherited wealth, who felt threatened in these years by the popular agitation for cheap money (the free coinage of silver). The demand for civil service reform arose from the evidence of corruption at all levels of government after the Civil War. The country's new industrial entrepeneurs caused more than one scandal by their efforts to buy what they wanted politically, offending puritan sensibilities.

When the Boston Merchants Association took a stand against the Spanish-American War and the annexation of the Philippines it was thus capping a long history of mercantile opposition to policies promoted pre-eminently by the country's manufacturing interests.[8] The anti-imperialist activity of Boston's middle class liberals was the climax of years of reform effort around the issues of tariff, sound currency and civil service. In fact the New England Anti-Imperialist League organized in 1898 was the offspring of the Massachusetts Reform Club established in 1882 to further their Mugwump program.

If, however, the anti-imperialist leadership had rested on its accustomed social base in Boston, there would have been no organized anti-imperialist movement of the popular dimensions that were achieved. The leadership, instead, sought to stimulate anti-imperialist sentiment and activity in all segments of society.[9] They found especially responsive those for whom conditions of life left something to

Charles Eliot Norton, Harvard professor, first to speak out against the Spanish War.

Gamaliel Bradford, Mayflower descendant, initiator of the anti-imperialist movement.

George E. McNeill, trade union anti-imperialist, life-long proponent of labor reforms.

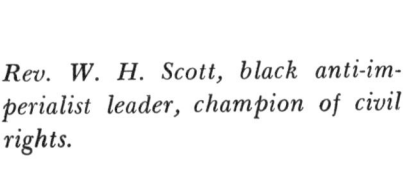

Rev. W. H. Scott, black anti-imperialist leader, champion of civil rights.

Patrick A. Collins, leading anti-imperialist of Irish descent, Mayor of Boston, 1901-1905.

George Sewall Boutwell, Abraham Lincoln's friend and associate, president of the anti-imperialist league.

F. B. Sanborn, anti-imperialist journalist, previously close supporter of the abolitionist, John Brown.

Edward Atkinson, Boston businessman, outspoken opponent of the Philippine War.

Moorfield Storey, Boston lawyer of national standing, leader of campaign against United States atrocities in the Philippines.

be desired as the United States entered the corporate era.

Responding to the surge of industry, labor organization had grown after the Civil War, first as the Knights of Labor, then as the more stable American Federation of Labor. The nineties had seen labor unrest reach a peak in the steel workers' strike at Carnegie's Homestead plant and that of the railroad workers at Pullman and Chicago. Firmly wed to their own conservative individualism, the Mugwumps had looked with disfavor on the development of trade union organization. But when they started to organize against imperialism they turned at once to a Massachusetts labor leader of national reputation, George E. McNeill, veteran of many union drives and strikes among the state's shoe and textile workers. From the outset he took a leading part in their work. Then they persuaded Samuel Gompers, president of the American Federation of Labor, to join the anti-imperialist league. Both men were active in promoting its point of view among trade unionists, bringing the American Federation of Labor into the campaign against imperialism, particularly in its initial phase.

The organized labor movement in Massachusetts was composed in large part of Irish-Americans, who had come to Boston in great numbers before the Civil War. Struggling to better their position as one of the state's most exploited and disadvantaged groups, they also sought representation through the Democratic Party and constituted that party's main source of popular strength in the urban areas of Massachusetts (whereas a number of Yankee lawyers and merchants in Boston constituted its state leadership).[10] Patrick A. Collins, the outstanding Irish Democrat in the state, and perhaps in the nation, soon became a militant leader of the anti-imperialist league. Brought to Boston as an infant at the time of the potato famine, he made his way to a seat in Congress in the eighties and a diplomatic appointment in Cleveland's second term. Collins symbolized the antagonism Irish-Americans felt for the policies of empire, and in particular for the friendship the McKinley Administration began to display toward Great Britain, Ireland's ancient oppressor.

Farm discontent with the government policies shaped by the industrialists was shown by the rural support for William Jennings Bryan's anti-trust, free silver campaign in the presidential elections of 1896. Farm interests were represented in the leadership of the New England Anti-Imperialist League by Herbert Myrick, publisher of the *New England Homestead* and editor of a national chain of farm journals with a circulation of over a million. He was responsible for putting the National Grange on record against imperialism in November 1898 and he editorialized in his papers along the same lines.[11]

As McKinley pursued empire abroad, the conditions of black citizens in the United States worsened under pressure of a white supremacist offensive launched from the South. Black residents of Boston condemned the foremost Negro leader of the time, Booker T. Washington, for offering insufficient resistance to the attack on black rights, and began to organize a movement to counteract Washington's influence. One of those most prominent in challenging Washington's policies was the Reverend William H. Scott. Outstanding as a black anti-imperialist, Scott was elected a vice president of the League in 1901.

A sign of middle class disaffection with the growing concentration of industrial wealth and power was the Social Gospel movement in the Protestant Church, an attempt to democratize the church and bring it closer to the urban poor. The Reverend Charles F. Dole preached the Social Gospel from a pulpit in a Boston suburb, condemning war, imperialism and militarism as violations of the Christian doctrine of the brotherhood of man. Impelled perhaps by like considerations, other members of the Protestant clergy in New England also served as elected leaders of the anti-imperialist league. (Especially active, also, was the rabbi of a Boston reform temple, Charles Fleischer. Although none of the New England Catholic clergy participated in the anti-imperialist movement, several did so elsewhere.)

Intellectuals gathered around the anti-imperialist movement as they had around anti-slavery. The philosopher-psychologist William James expressed himself as freely on this issue as Emerson had on the other. James' friend, Charles Eliot Norton, literary man and esthete, was equally outspoken. Both James and Norton taught at Harvard; Harvard's president, Charles William Eliot, on occasion lent his name to the anti-imperialists, and a great many of the Boston anti-imperialist leaders were alumni of that university. "Harvard and the slums" was the taunt thrown at the Mugwumps; it also described the basic components of the local anti-imperialist movement.[12]

Certain Massachusetts newspapers gave the anti-imperialists most influential support through the daily expression of their point of view. Aiding in this way were the *Boston Post,* geared to the city's

Democracy, labor and the Irish, and the *Pilot,* the lay weekly of Catholic opinion that had rallied Boston's Irish to the Union in the Civil War. Addressing themselves more to middle class and Mugwump readers were the *Boston Herald* and the *Boston Evening Transcript,* both advocates of the anti-imperialist viewpoint in the early days of the movement. The *Transcript,* especially, was the paper of Brahmin Boston, and no Boston newspaperman was closer to the anti-imperialist leadership than its editor, Edward H. Clement.

The *Springfield Republican,* however, in the western part of the state soon became the recognized spokesman of Massachusetts anti-imperialism. The Republican's editor and owner, Samuel Bowles, was a vice-president of the league, and its special Boston correspondent, F. B. Sanborn, was a league officer also. Bowles' father had established the *Republican* as a paper with a nation-wide influence and subscription by his unswerving support for Lincoln during the Civil War. After his father's death in 1877, Samuel Bowles maintained the paper's quality and prestige, while espousing Mugwump reform.

Well-to-do descendant of a family originating in the Boston of Puritan times, Bowles was a Brahmin transplant. Editing a paper in Springfield, a town of flourishing, tariff-hungry industries, he championed free trade, and his independence caused consternation in the circles of corporate finance. President Mellen of the New Haven railroad, a Morgan protege, is said to have asked a member of the board of directors whether there was no one in his vicinity who could control the *Springfield Republican.* "I should like to know who he is," came the reply. "I'll resign in his favor for the railroad will need his services."[13] Bowles was as zealous for anti-imperialism as his father was for anti-slavery.

In the mid-nineteenth century Boston had won a national reputation as the city of reform, especially for its leading role in the Abolitionist movement. In addition feminism, pacificism, transcendentalism and utopian socialism had flourished in the city and its environs. Just as most reformers of every sort had supported the anti-slavery cause as the central issue, so at the end of the nineteenth century Boston citizens active in diverse movements of reform supported anti-imperialism as the cause decisive for the future of the country. This was true of Abbie Morton Diaz and Robert Treat Paine, leaders of the long-established feminist and pacifist movements, as it was of Josiah Quincy and Edwin D. Mead, who were active in the newer movement of urban reform. Mugwump reformers, labor reformers, black reformers, religious reformers gave their support to anti-imperialism. Many alienated from existing social conditions for one reason or another in the decades after the Civil War, saw in the United States conquest of the Philippines an even more compelling reason for estrangement. The anti-imperialist movement thus emerged as a climactic moment in the history of post-Civil War reform, when, once again, Massachusetts men and women stood at the center of the national stage.

The anti-imperialist movement undertook to reverse the policy urged by "incorporated and syndicated wealth," and put into practice by the party which this wealth controlled. Brahmin liberals had promoted such a challenge to the ruling political party before in the movement of Mugwump reform. But this time the issue at stake went deeper than the fight against high tariffs and political corruption. Their disagreement with the ruling party involved fundamental aspects of foreign policy, determining the United States' role in the world at large; it opposed the government in its ultimate, war-making function. Anti-imperialism was a more radical venture than Mugwump reform; it did not command the same near-unanimous support from Brahmin Boston. Some members of the Massachusetts Reform Club had been opposed even to discussing it at meetings.[14] This suggested that the anti-imperialists could expect less support from the well-to-do generally. The militant Boston liberals thus sought allies in other social groups and classes to an extent they had not done before. Whereas the Massachusetts Reform Club had been an exclusive society for Boston gentlemen, the Anti-Imperialist League, in the composition of its leadership at least, reflected efforts to set on foot a loose coalition of diverse social forces.

Putting aside their upper-class aversion to organized labor and Boston's Irish population, the Brahmin anti-imperialists turned to them as important participants in the common cause. Their bitter disagreements with currency-reforming Silver Democrats, Silver Republicans and Populists they likewise set aside; they included even the Socialists, whose views most of them abhorred. They made special appeals to blacks and women. They worked to influence and unite with anti-imperialists in Democratic, and, so far as they could, Republican ranks. They sought out anti-imperialist clergymen, intellectuals, farmers' representatives. They worked to bring the press into the anti-imperialist fold. The elected leadership of the Anti-Imperialist League gave evidence of this policy in all save one respect: it included no women. Evidently even the pressing need for anti-imperialist unity could not subdue this stubborn prejudice.

The Massachusetts anti-imperialists set afoot, and gave decisive leadership to, a movement that involved millions in discussion and debate and left an impress on the national politics of the day. They could not have done this, however, if anti-imperialist sentiment had not existed in the country independently of them. This sentiment stemmed from the democratic aspects of the country's past. It received impetus as well from widespread dissatisfaction with the growing power of the great new economic formations — the corporations, trusts and monopolies. The anti-imperialists helped to turn this democratic tendency, this social discontent, against the foreign policy of the McKinley Administration. They undertook to bring together disparate sections of the population in a more or less unified political movement on the basis of a common mood.

The policy of anti-imperialist unity was a matter of conscious determination and forethought. It was given expression by the Secretary of the New England Anti-Imperialist League, Erving Winslow. Descendant of the Pilgrim John Winslow, member of the Massachusetts Reform Club, Winslow was the only Secretary the League had throughout its existence. As a commission merchant in the city from 1868 until his retirement to work full-time as a volunteer for the Anti-Imperialist League (with some help from its founder Gamaliel Bradford), he had been part of Boston's mercantile establishment. Other men may have been more influential spokesmen and publicists, but Winslow was the chief organizer of the Anti-Imperialist League. In November 1899, in his report to the first annual meeting of the League, Winslow projected the policy of anti-imperialist unity:

> Until the battle is fought out our purpose should be to maintain an absolute independence of all lesser issues . . . Those who dispute about standards of value while the foundation of the Republic is undermined will be listened to as little as those who wrangle about the small economics of the household while the house is on fire . . . As individuals, we reserve the right, when this question is settled, to go our several ways, but . . . we must in our organization stand shoulder to shoulder, Republican, Democrat, Socialist, Populist, Gold-man, Silver-man, and Mugwump, for the one momentous, vital, paramount issue, Anti-Imperialism and the preservation of the Republic.[15]

2

Countervailing Forces and Early Contests

In the initial phases of modern American imperialism both imperialists and anti-imperialists believed that the demand of industry for new foreign markets inspired an aggressive and interventionist foreign policy. The need to export manufactured goods was seen as the prime cause of imperial policy in the first instance; the export of capital appeared only as a factor of potential importance. This was especially the case in Massachusetts, because the industries of that state faced special problems on the home market.

In January 1896 the *Home Market Bulletin,* a magazine published by Massachusetts manufacturers, carried what amounted to a manifesto of the new imperial outlook in the form of a speech by a leading Philadelphia Republican and newspaper publisher, Charles Emory Smith. Smith, who had served as minister to Russia, had delivered the speech before the New York Chamber of Commerce.* Reproducing it in its entirety, the *Bulletin* declared the speech to be "good" and of "economic value." Smith reminded the New York businessmen that in their lifetime they had seen the United States "pass and outstrip all the old nations hoary with the moss of a thousand years." In the past England had been "the industrial bee-

---

* Smith's views were of special significance for he was to be a direct agent in the policies of the McKinley Administration. In 1898, when relations with Spain became acute, Smith took a place at the President's side "in very close conference" as "special advisor," and on April 23, when Postmaster General Gary (who disapproved of the war with Spain) resigned, Smith assumed that position in the Cabinet, not to lick stamps, but to help with the conduct of the war. (*Boston Evening Transcript,* April 21, 23, 1898.)

hive of the world," and "in 1860 the product of our manufacture was little more than half of hers. In 1890 it more than doubled her output . . . Our expansion in industries was more than twice that of England, France and Germany put together." Because the United States "afforded an unrivalled market among ourselves, we have thus far had little concern about foreign commerce." Then Smith boldly sounded the message of change. "Now," he declared, "like Alexander we sigh for new worlds to conquer." Although the past twenty years had seen the United States outstrip England, France and Germany in the expansion of foreign commerce, this was but the beginning. In the years ahead, "Our spirit, if not our flag will rule the hemisphere." American capital would construct an Isthmian Canal to link the Atlantic and the Pacific, "and New York wresting the financial sceptre from London, will stand . . . the focus and emporium of the world's wide commerce between the Orient and Occident." In the coming century the United States would achieve its grand destiny, "when the rivalry of nations shall culminate in the unchallenged primacy of the American Republic."

Smith's speech emphasized an all-important truth: the United States, since the Civil War, had advanced to a new place among the nations of the earth. While in 1860 the United States had ranked fourth among the nations in the value of manufactures, by 1894 it stood first in the world.[1] In Massachusetts this rapid industrial growth had been reflected in the post-war expansion of cotton textile production, the state's leading industrial interest. In 1870, more than forty-four million dollars were invested in this industry; in 1895, more than one hundred and seventeen million dollars were so invested.[2]

At the close of the century textile production as a whole (with cotton textile leading) was the dominant element in the economy of Massachusetts, with boot and shoe production next in order of importance.[3] These economic interests, with their allied organizations, trade journals and newspapers, constituted the decisive Massachusetts advocates for the new departure in foreign policy. The state's Republican Party provided McKinley's imperialism with its center of political support; for, as Henry Lee had occasion to observe, in this party the manufacturing interests were the leading element. In addition there was, of course, sympathy for McKinley's foreign policies among rank and file Republicans and among citizens of the state at large, who felt this to be a question of patriotic necessity, while certain members of the Protestant clergy in Boston looked upon the Philippine war as a means of promoting missionary activities.[4]

To further their common interests the Massachusetts cotton textile industrialists had organized the New England Cotton Manufacturers Association, and the boot and shoe manufacturers had similarly organized. These industries had trade journals; the *Boot and Shoe Recorder* was published in Boston, as was the *Textile World;* the *Textile Record,* published in Philadelphia, had a New England agency at Boston.

Representing not only the textile manufacturers of Massachusetts but the state's industrial interests in general was the Home Market Club. Just before his death in 1887, George Draper, founder and owner of an important textile machinery firm at Hopedale, Massachusetts, had organized this association to further the cause of the protective tariff. The biggest industrialists in the state were members, as were manufacturers throughout the country. It had become one of the most important high tariff associations in the United States. The *Home Market Bulletin* was its monthly publication.[5]

Eben S. Draper, son of the founder of the Hopedale firm, who continued with his two brothers in its ownership and direction, was also a director of the *Boston Journal,* the most consistent and ardent of the Boston dailies in its support of McKinley's foreign policies. The *Boston Globe* was another important daily paper that gave these policies support.

Failure of the home market provided the stimulus for the full development of imperial policies in the United States. The great economic depression which had begun in 1893 and which was not yet over provided background for Charles Emory Smith's observation that the United States was now turning to the expansion of foreign markets. Seeing the depression as a crisis of overproduction, many businessmen had become convinced that the domestic market was no longer sufficient to absorb the vastly expanded output of American industry; new markets abroad must be found. If the expanded production of goods gave the United States potential advantage over her international rivals in relation to world markets, it at the same time rendered the home market inadequate to the needs of the great new productive machine. The growth of American industry made the conquest of foreign markets not only an inviting possibility, but a hard-felt necessity.[6]

Massachusetts industry in particular felt the need for foreign markets. As an older, more established industrial region, New England was at a competitive disadvantage on the domestic market with the more recent industrial plant of the South and West. Hence the depression of 1893 lingered on in Massachusetts even after the rest of the country began to show signs of recovery. Early in 1898 the chairman of the Massachusetts Republican Club found the state of the cotton industry still something to deplore, even while conditions generally were more favorable.[7]

The expansion of foreign trade as a relief from Southern and Western competition had been urged at meetings of both New England shoe manufacturers and cotton textile men even before the McKinley Administration initiated military policies designed, in the main, to promote new foreign markets. In January 1896, C. A. Lamson, former United States Consul to Brazil, addressed the Boston Shoe Associates, urging them to go after South American trade to counter-balance competition from the West. In October 1897, the New England Cotton Manufacturers Association heard a similar plea to the "old New England" firms to go after the export trade to offset Southern underselling. And at the Association's next meeting (just before Commodore Dewey's victory over the Spanish fleet at Manila Bay), the Director of the Lowell Textile Institute made the point again, with a new emphasis on China as a market for New England textiles.[8]

If mercantile Boston's opposition to McKinley's policies was a reflex of its displacement in the scheme of things by industrial capital, the support Massachusetts industrialists gave to these same policies was heightened by the pressure they felt as a result of the growth of industry elsewhere in the country. Significantly, Massachusetts Senator Henry Cabot Lodge, acting from what a friendly biographer called "his position as representative of New England industries," was a major figure in urging the policies of imperialism and expansion upon the McKinley Administration.[9] He was, in fact, one of a small number of men who bore great individual responsibility for the turn in United States foreign policy around 1900.

Descended from Boston merchant families of wealth and position, Senator Lodge began his political career as a Liberal Republican; only later did he break with his reform-minded peers in Boston to become a leading imperialist. After graduation from Harvard in 1871 he organized the Commonwealth Club, "for the purification of politics," with some of his liberal friends (including Moorfield Storey, later the prominent anti-imperialist).[10]

In 1872 the Liberal Republicans of Boston joined forces with New York City reformers to break away from the party machine. At a convention in Cincinnati they hoped to nominate Charles Francis Adams, Sr., as an independent presidential candidate, in opposition to the re-election of President Grant, whose administration was charged with corruption. A group of political bosses outmaneuvered them at Cincinnati, and the convention selected Horace Greeley as presidential nominee, a candidate altogether unsatisfactory to the reformers.

Nonetheless the activities of the Boston liberals in 1872 foreshadowed the anti-imperialist movement. One of their chief complaints against Grant had been his first-term attempt to annex Santo Domingo, an outlying tropical island with a black population and "large promise of wealth."[11] Charles Sumner, Massachusetts leader of the anti-slavery struggle, had conducted a successful Senatorial opposition to Grant's imperial adventure, but the episode had shaken the confidence of Boston's Liberal Republicans in Grant, while it demonstrated their anti-imperialist inclinations.

Lodge played no significant part in the reform activities of 1872. But in 1876 he had a prominent role in the proceedings of a second conference of Liberal Republicans to nominate an independent candidate. Although nothing came of this effort, not even a Greeley, Lodge helped to organize the conference and served as its secretary. Joining fellow-reformers, Lodge broke away from the Republican Party and voted for Samuel J. Tilden, the Democratic presidential candidate, in the ensuing election.

Not long after this Lodge showed signs of diverging from the political thinking of his Boston associates in the reform movement. Delivering Boston's Fourth of July Address in 1879, Lodge sounded themes not usually heard from Boston's well-to-do liberals. He extolled the military strength displayed in the Northern victory and the astonishing industrial development since that time as the basis for a new assertion of American power in the world.[12] The following year he refused membership in the Cobden Club, an English free trade society, on the grounds that he did not believe in free trade. In 1882, in a Memorial Day address to the residents of Nahant, the seashore resort north of Boston where his family had a summer home, he delivered an economic challenge to the countries of Europe. "We have beat them in the production of the great staples, the necessities of life," he declared. "We are certain to beat them in the long run in manufactures and commerce." As a corollary he called for "the reconstruction of our navy."[13]

But not until the presidential elections of 1884 did Lodge break with his Brahmin associates in the reform movement. The Liberal Republicans bolted the Republican Party and supported Grover Cleveland, a reform Democrat, for president. Lodge stayed with the Republican candidate, James G. Blaine, who personified what the Republican reformers hated most in contemporary politics. Charges of corruption had been brought against him which he was never able to disprove. There was evidence that he had used his influence in the Senate to secure legislation favorable to a certain railroad corporation in return for purchase of stocks and bonds at a favorable price. All this was widely aired in Boston since Blaine had been a Senator from Maine and had conducted his business with Bostonians. Some of the incriminating documents eventually fell into the hands of Moorfield Storey, who made them public.[14]

More than any other political figure in the period after the Civil War, Blaine had directed public attention to the foreign markets available to United States industry in South America and the Pacific, had asserted United States industry's potential superiority in international competition, and had called for naval rearmament to protect United States interests in the markets of the world. As Secretary of State in the Garfield Administration he had brought these ideas into play in what was described as "a vigorous foreign policy."[15]

Boston's Mugwumps were primarily repelled by Blaine's odor of corruption, but their hostility to his trail-blazing imperialism followed closely. Early in the 1884 election contest the *Boston Herald* denounced Blaine for his "new departure" in foreign policy, declaring that he intended to dictate the terms of trade and political life to the nations of the Western Hemisphere, even at the point of a gun. This would be a "war policy," which would delight "the hearts of the speculative capitalists who are so warmly attached to the Republican candidate." But, thought the *Herald,* the "chance of finding a market for our products would not compensate . . . for the useless slaughter of tens or hundreds of thousands of our young men."[16]

Liberal Republicans from Massachusetts, Lodge included, had gone to the Republican convention in 1884 pledged to oppose Blaine's nomination. When this effort failed, Lodge announced his support for the successful nominee. Theodore Roosevelt, a young aristocratic reformer from New York City, joined his friend Lodge in this political about-face. Since the elections of 1884 aroused Boston's liberals intensely, Lodge's break from the ranks caused sharp anger and animosity. Moorfield Storey, the old friend of the Commonwealth Club, never spoke to Lodge again, an extreme example of a general social ostracism. The resulting isolation drew Lodge to his fellow apostate, Roosevelt, and sealed a personal and political friendship that was to have important consequences.

Lodge's break with his reform friends put the issues of the election into focus in Massachusetts, and meetings held in the course of the campaign further defined them. On June 13, just after Blaine's nomination, the leaders of the Massachusetts Reform Club held a rally where they registered their dissatisfaction with it so vehemently that participants were reminded of the anti-slavery days. Colonel Charles Russell Codman, a Civil War veteran who was chairman, condemned Blaine's high tariff policies as a sop to industrial monopoly. The resolution of the day urged the Democrats to nominate a reform candidate. It was offered by Thomas Wentworth Higginson and seconded by Charles W. Eliot.[17]

(Once before Eliot had followed Higginson in an even more militant endeavor. Thirty years previously, in the decade before the Civil War, when the fugitive slave Anthony Burns had been captured in Boston by Southern slave-catchers and turned over to the city authorities for safekeeping, Higginson had led an unsuccessful attempt to free Burns from his prison cell by force. When Higginson and an unknown black had made a rush upon the doors of the Boston Court House where Burns lay jailed, Charles W. Eliot — not then a university president — followed in support.)[18]

At the close of the campaign, a banquet to honor Blaine was held in New York City at Delmonico's restaurant, attended by Jay Gould, Russell Sage, Cyrus W. Field, Jr., John Jacob Astor, the Rockefeller associates H. M. Flagler and H. H. Rogers and others of such financial importance that the affair became known as the "Millionaires' Dinner." In his speech Blaine told his hearers that while New York was often regarded as a city important for its commerce, its real importance lay in its standing as the second largest manufacturing city in the world. He claimed that the city's wealth had grown from just under two billion dollars at the time of the Civil War to over six billion dollars in 1884, "under the influence of the industrial and financial system" for which the Republican Party was "proudly responsible."[19]

On the day that Blaine dined with the New York millionaires, Boston businessmen held a rally for Cleveland at Faneuil Hall. With General Francis A. Osborn (the Civil War officer who eventually became Anti-Imperialist League Treasurer) in the chair, speakers charged that Blaine's policies had driven commerce from their city. They recalled Blaine's corporate connections and warned Bostonians that to elect him would be to "invite these corporations to ride roughshod over you." The *Boston Evening Transcript* hailed the meeting as an indication of "the strength of the mercantile opposition to Mr. Blaine's candidacy here." The editor compared the rectitude of Boston's merchants with "the stock-jobbing ringsters of New York who opened their purses to Blaine."[20]

The Mugwump revolt of 1884, which the Boston meeting of June 13 did much to spark, won wide support in that city. Most of the major Boston papers (the *Transcript, Herald, Globe, Post, Advertiser, Pilot*) were anti-Blaine, only the *Journal* speaking for him. Taking on nationwide proportions, the Mugwump movement gained conservative adherents (even J. P. Morgan, the New York financier of the trust movement, drew the line at Blaine). The Republican candidate was too flagrant a corruptionist, and Cleveland was elected.

In the men and the issues involved, the drama of 1884 forecast the anti-imperialist struggle fourteen years later. On both occasions Boston middle class liberals provided important leadership. Nearly half of the Bostonians who later became elected leaders of the Anti-Imperialist League signed the call to the June 13 rally which instigated the Mugwump revolt. The key Brahmin group in the anti-imperialist leadership was virtually unanimous in its support of Cleveland. The issue of political corruption took precedence in 1884 over that of imperialism, but in both struggles corporate dominance of the national life was called in question.

Blaine's defeat was the high point of the Mugwump movement; what followed was anti-climactic. Cleveland's accomplishments as a reform President were not spectacular. The Mugwumps could be fairly well satisfied with his record on civil service matters, but after his second election in 1892 his efforts at tariff reform were frustrated and his foreign policy was shockingly ambiguous.

Lodge was defeated for Congress in 1884, rebuffed, in the main, by the votes of the shoe-workers of Lynn. Lodge's former Mugwump friends took special pains to assist the workingman who ran on the Democratic ticket and won the Congressional seat from the young blue-blood. Theodore Roosevelt thought the outcome "simply cruel."[21] Lodge was, however, rewarded for his partisan loyalty when he was elected to Congress from the same district in 1886 for two terms thereafter. In Congress Lodge's main activity, from the standpoint of his emergence as an outstanding imperialist, was his championship of naval rearmament as a member of the House Naval Affairs Committee.

Militarism was assuming a place as an integral element in the imperialist program, and at this stage it took the form of a more powerful navy. Blaine had early drawn attention to the close relationship between military power and economic expansion abroad when he declared, in January 1879, "We want a navy, but we want something for it to do. We want a navy to protect commerce, but we want a commerce in advance for the navy to protect."* Lodge soon joined Blaine in sounding this note. The Navy itself was pressing the case through Captain Alfred Thayer Mahan, whose book, *The Influence of Sea Power on History*, published in 1890, became a handbook for men like Lodge.[22]

In 1890 Congressman Lodge was influential in securing the passage of an appropriation for three "sea-going coastal battleships." These ships were the first step toward putting into effect Mahan's plan for a unified and mobile high seas fleet that could take the offensive. The navy had traditionally concentrated on coastal defense. The unusual legislative description of these ships as "sea-going coastal battleships" (Lodge's inspiration) linked this radically new naval policy to what was accustomed in the past presumably with the intent of quieting public apprehension. In the same way, speaking on

---

* This was an imperialist axiom that was to be re-emphasized by John D. Long, Secretary of the Navy during the Spanish and Philippine wars. Speaking at a meeting of the National Association of Manufacturers held in Boston in April 1900, Long said: "The best and largest function of the navy is to serve commerce in its distribution of our manufactured products." (*Boston Evening Transcript*, April 27, 1900.)

the floor of the House, Lodge pitched his argument for the enabling legislation on the needs of coastal defense, warning: "Our two great sea coasts on the Atlantic and the Pacific . . . are . . . entirely undefended . . . One English battleship could pillage and destroy anywhere on the long line of either of these coasts."[23]

The threat of British attack posed by Lodge reflected what was then a dominant consideration for the proponents of budding American empire. Great Britain was the main rival of the United States for the markets of the world.* Lodge very pointedly told Congress, "If the government built battleships it reduced the fighting force of the British Navy."[24]

Lodge found no favor with the *Boston Evening Transcript* for his stand. Early in April 1890 during the Congressional debates on the navy, the Brahmin journal objected to the proposed battleships on technical grounds; they would be top-heavy, unseaworthy, etc. At the end of the month the editor dealt with the political issues involved, writing that those who would force heavy armaments on the government in fact proposed to dislodge the United States from its unique and favored position among nations, as a country hitherto without that burden. "These clamorers for a large supply of the panoply of war" forgot that the United States had held aloof from the imperial rivalries of Europe and that, unlike the nations of the Continent, our country had no colonies. Moreover the editor looked forward to the use of arbitration rather than gun powder in the settlement of international disputes; future hopes as well as past policies argued against such armaments.[25] Congress voted otherwise, however.

In 1892 Congressman Lodge used his influence in the Republican organization of Massachusetts to get his friend of the textile machinery firm, Eben S. Draper, elected state chairman of the party. Draper helped Lodge secure the nomination and election to the United States Senate.[26] Lodge was now, without question, the leading figure in the Republican politics of the state. His opponents charged that his power came from control of a political machine. While his solid base in the Republican party state organization was undoubtedly important, another related source of strength was the close rapport he

---

* It was, for example, with British shovel manufacturers that Lodge's shovel-making Massachusetts friend Oliver Ames had to compete for the mastery of the South American market. (*Boston Evening Transcript*, September 19, 1899.)

developed with the men most entrenched in the economy of the state, whose spokesman he became.

As Senator, Lodge quickly made clear his social orientation. Speaking on the Senate floor, in April 1894, against Cleveland's proposed tariff reduction, he declared industrial capital to be superior to mercantile capital, more important to the national economy and more deserving of consideration. The main concern of national policy, he said, should be to do what was best for industry. "Our first object should be to hold our own market, because it is the largest and the best . . . our next object should be to increase our outside market by any possible device."[27]

Consciously seeking to represent the industrial interests of his state, Lodge became a prominent figure nationally. To serve the needs of industry he called for trade expansion and naval rearmament, thereby nurturing the military-industrial complex in its early form. Moreover, in the years immediately ahead, the Senator was to devote his best efforts to increasing outside markets, "by any possible device," including war.

After his intercession on behalf of the navy, Lodge plunged into the campaign for Hawaiian annexation, again fostering antagonism to Great Britain. Followed closely by the Venezuelan crisis and the Spanish and Philippine wars, the attempt to annex Hawaii was an early and important episode in the burst of aggressive activity that marked the maturation of United States imperialism. Here, as in his efforts for naval and trade expansion, Lodge followed the lead of Blaine.

In August 1891, from his Bar Harbor summer home, Blaine wrote President Harrison that there were three places of value that the United States should acquire: Hawaii, Cuba and Puerto Rico. Only in the case of Hawaii was the question imminent, thought Blaine, and he hoped that the United States would decide to act affirmatively.[28] Blaine had good reason to believe that the acquisition of Hawaii might be imminent. In 1889 Harrison appointed Blaine's old Maine friend, J. L. Stevens, United States Minister to Hawaii. Stevens' views on the disposition of the Hawaiian Islands were suggested when it was later said in his defense that he had "a partiality for white folks," and believed that "the islands belonged to us, and our title would be perfected some day."[29]

In Hawaii Stevens encouraged annexationist sentiment among the

American sugar planters and the old missionary families. Although a minority in relation to the Asian population that included the native Hawaiians, the white settlers had appropriated most of the land. The Americans, a majority among the white settlers, controlled two-thirds of the islands' capital.[30] Apprehensive of Hawaiian Queen Liliuokalani's policies, and suffering from economic depression brought on by a change in United States sugar tariff policy, many white businessmen had come to look upon annexation by the United States as guarantee of a friendly government and prosperity.[31] Consequently these elements on January 16, 1893 staged a revolution under the protection of United States troops ordered ashore by Minister Stevens from the cruiser *Boston,* and set up a provisional government. Stevens recognized the government and declared Hawaii a protectorate. He advised the State Department that the "Hawaiian pear is now fully ripe and this is the golden hour for the United States to pluck it," warning of possible British annexation if the United States did not act.[32]

Accordingly the Harrison Administration readied a treaty of annexation for approval by the United States Senate. But a change of administration took place, with Grover Cleveland assuming the presidency again. Cleveland was opposed to colonial annexation and withdrew the treaty from the Senate. The matter of Hawaii was left unresolved, but not unheeded. Blaine died in 1893, but others kept the issue alive.

In Congressional debates of February 1894, Representative William F. Draper of Massachusetts, elder brother of Lodge's ally Eben, declared that if the United States aimed at commercial supremacy in the Pacific, its trade must have assurances of naval protection, "and a first necessity is the acquisition of bases for its protectors." Hawaii should be annexed to provide a naval base. Nor was that all. The United States needed other bases – one in Samoa, one at the mouth of the projected Isthmian canal, and another at the straits of Magellan. "With these bases, a properly organized fleet . . . will hold the Pacific as an American ocean, dominated by American commercial enterprise for all time."[33] Draper was senior partner in an extensive manufacturing establishment, the prosperity of which depended on the growth of the textile industry and its access to wide markets.

Beginning in January 1895 Senator Lodge made a series of four speeches in support of annexation. Borrowing heavily from Mahan,

Lodge said that no nation could be really great without sea-power, and that sea-power depended not alone on a powerful navy, but on naval bases as well, "strong places where a navy can be protected and refurnished."[34] He gave classic definition to the over-all imperial design, in which Hawaii was but a first step, and which later events would bring to completion. Draper hammered away at this theme, and it was winning general acceptance in imperialist quarters, but Lodge gave it form that was clear, concise and regally conclusive:

> We should take all outlying territory necessary for our own defense, to the protection of the Isthmian canal, to the upbuilding of our trade and commerce, and to the maintenance of our military safety everywhere. I would take and hold the outerworks as now we hold the citadel of American power.[35]

Lodge's main thrust was against Great Britain; his main complaint against Cleveland. By refusing to annex, Cleveland presented a priceless opportunity to the nation's greatest competitor. Dramatically bringing a map of the Pacific to the Senate floor, Lodge pointed to Britain's already extensive possessions in this area, and demanded that the United States grab Hawaii before Britain did. Great Britain had "always opposed, thwarted, and sought to injure us," and Lodge did not shrink from the threat of war. If it came to this, Britain's great territory of Canada "would pass from her never to return."[36] Lodge had painted Britain as an awesome menace when he wanted battleships; now when he wanted Hawaii, he made her appear less fearful. In both cases, however, Lodge tweaked the nose of mercantile Boston, which, because of trade and family connections, was profoundly Anglophile.

James H. Blount, Cleveland's special commissioner to Hawaii, after investigation on the spot in 1893, had come to the conclusion that the majority of the people of the islands, "overwhelmingly Asiatic," were opposed to annexation, while the whites, especially the Americans, were for it.[37] With Blount's report before him, Henry Cabot Lodge urged United States annexation of the Hawaiian Islands against the wishes of the colored majority, and in the interests of a white, property-holding minority, mainly of American descent. He urged this even at the risk of war.

War came. It was not with the rival that Lodge envisioned, and it involved the subjugation of another colored people. But Lodge was instrumental in bringing it on.

He acted thus, in part at least, because of his sense of history. Boston Brahmins tended to be highly conscious of the American past, and this was as true of the empire-builder Lodge as it was of many of his anti-imperialist opponents (both Lodge and leading anti-imperialists were active members of the Massachusetts Historical Society). Arguing for Hawaiian annexation in 1898, Lodge wrote, "We have a record of conquest, colonization, and territorial expansion . . . unequalled by any people in the 19th century."[38] In truth the United States did possess two conflicting historical traditions. There was the tradition of liberation and democracy, and there was the tradition of conquest and domination. Samuel Bowles and his fellow-anti-imperialists plainly saw themselves as heirs to the first tradition as they invoked, again and again, the American Revolution and the anti-slavery crusade. Henry Cabot Lodge just as plainly saw the imperialist policies he recommended as the contemporary expression of the second tradition. Quite rightly he believed the war to subjugate the Philippines was in direct line with the wars to appropriate the lands of the American Indians and to conquer Mexico. With equal justice Lodge could have pointed to the slave-owners and the Confederate cause as precedents for the policy of empire. He wisely left the enunciation of this truth, which would not have been well received by Massachusetts voters, to his imperialist brethren in the South.

3

The Venezuelan Crisis

Rejection of Hawaiian annexation won Cleveland renewed support and praise from his Boston Mugwump friends. Charles Francis Adams told him, "I remember no stand taken by a government so morally sound," and Gamaliel Bradford wrote the *Transcript,* "It seems to be stamped with the honest desire to do right."[1] All the greater was the reformers' shock at what appeared to be the President's unaccountable behavior in the next crisis of foreign affairs, the Venezuelan boundary dispute. Here Cleveland threatened war against Great Britain, the Boston Mugwumps' second home, and established his second administration as an important link between Blaine and McKinley in the development of imperialist policy.

However shocking to some, it became obvious that Cleveland, despite his stand on Hawaii, was in accord with much of the imperialist program. He opposed colonial annexation, its extreme feature. This drew him toward the anti-imperialists. But in his first administration he sponsored the up-building of the United States Navy and military intervention in Panama and Ecuador; in his second he declared an interest in the active pursuit of foreign markets. When he menaced his nation's main competitor with military force to secure dominance in South America, he brought these previously manifested aspects of his policy sharply into play. Then, as an imperialist of sorts, he broke with his Mugwump friends and sided with their opponents.

Certain political advantages can be noted in Cleveland's Venezuelan policy. It turned aside charges of surrender to Great Britain leveled against him on the Hawaiian issue. It cast him in the role of defender of a colonial people against the British Empire and so had popular appeal. Dominant, however, in the formulation of this policy was the domestic economic situation. The year 1893 marked the beginning not only of Cleveland's second term, but of the industrial crisis as well. Then men in business and government began to look abroad to relieve the glut of goods. The markets of South America were near at hand, but dominated by the British.

Cleveland suggested the economic pressures at work in the message to Congress that renounced Hawaiian annexation. Keeping his eyes firmly on his free-trade and mercantile supporters, he rather ponderously backed into the question of foreign trade by way of tariff reform: a lower tariff on imported raw materials would increase the sale of American manufactured goods abroad by cheapening their price. So would prosperity and employment be enhanced.[2]

Not quite a year later Cleveland spoke at the launching of the *St. Louis,* the "largest . . . steamship ever built in the Western Hemisphere." Here he left no doubt about his concern for an increase in foreign trade. He told his audience that he was proud of the part he had played in "the great work of creating an American Navy" in his first term, but that "I shall deem myself especially fortunate if in time to come it can be said that I have done something during the present incumbency in aid of the freedom and extension of American commerce."[3] The President started to do so very shortly.

In December 1894, about a month after this last speech, Cleveland used his annual message to notify Congress that he intended once more to bring about the arbitration of the Venezuelan boundary dispute, which had been an occasion of United States-British rivalry in South America. Here Great Britain had been pressing for a boundary adjustment that would take territory from Venezuela and give it to the neighboring British colony of Guiana. The United States had persistently indicated her sympathy for Venezuela's resistance to British claims, on the former's direct appeal to Washington, and there the situation had hung fire for years. In 1887, during his first term, Cleveland had suggested arbitration at the instance of Venezuela, only to be brushed aside by Great Britain.

But in 1894 Cleveland decided to revive the Venezuelan question and in the following year to pursue it with great vigor. If the economic crisis provided the new background in internal affairs to these decisions, it was the intensification of imperial rivalries on the world scene that provided the new consideration externally. An opening seemed to offer itself in the difficulties Great Britain faced as the result of heightened international tensions. This had been pointed out to the Cleveland Administration in 1893 by Thomas Francis Bayard, the American Ambassador to Great Britain, shortly after his appointment. Then he had informed the State Department from London that "Great Britain just now has her hands very full in other quarters of the globe. The United States is the last nation on earth with whom the British people or their rulers desire to quarrel." Bayard believed the time ripe for a settlement of the Venezuelan boundary dispute.[4]

This was to prove the opportunity Cleveland had hoped would come to him. Of most assistance in taking advantage of it was Richard Olney, whose prompt dispatch of Federal troops to Chicago had crushed the railroad strike of 1894. After Olney left the Attorney General's office to become Secretary of State in June, 1895, things began to happen. Olney was a Yankee Democrat from Boston whose vocation in private life seemed to have prepared him well for the role he was to assume in government. The *Boston Evening Transcript* described him as "one of the most conservative of New England's lawyers . . . who has had more millions of corporation capital, spread throughout the country, depending on him for safe council than perhaps any lawyer of his generation."[5] With years of experience in the legal defense of railroads and other industrial concerns behind him, Olney, in public office, turned quite naturally from an aggressive policy directed against railroad labor's challenge to corporate interests at home to an aggressive policy directed against their main rival abroad.

Olney enjoyed what seemed to be complete rapport with his Chief Executive on matters of foreign policy. Like Cleveland he questioned the wisdom of colonial acquisition in Asia only to support most energetically other elements of the imperialist program, so that in the development of the Venezuelan crisis, the relationship between the Cleveland Administration and Lodge, the bellwether of the imperialists, took on an apparent pattern of stimulus and response, pressure and counter-pressure.

In February 1895, not long after Cleveland's message which reopened the Venezuelan question, Congress passed a joint resolution endorsing the President's suggestion of friendly arbitration. Senator Lodge, however, did not let the matter rest here: while in full cry on the Senate floor against Cleveland on Hawaiian annexation, Lodge, in the March *Forum,* lighted on what he saw as the failure of the

Cleveland Administration to support Venezuela as just one more example of what he called "Our Blundering Foreign Policy." He called on the United States to repudiate Cleveland and join in the general imperialist scramble then at such high pitch: "The great nations of the world are rapidly absorbing all the waste places of the earth . . . As one of the great nations of the world, the United States must not fall out of the line of march."[6]

Lodge followed this with an article in the June *North American Review* that put emphasis on British rivalry in South America and the need to put United States intervention in the boundary dispute under the shelter of the Monroe Doctrine. Referring to the fact that Britain's territorial demands included control of the great Orinoco river system and a rich and adjacent mining district, Lodge revealed some of the specifics in the relationship of the Venezuelan crisis to "the extension and freedom of American commerce" that President Cleveland wished to further. Warning that France and Germany would follow Great Britain in the territorial division of South America, and declaring that the United States was not ready to give up her "rightful supremacy" in the Western Hemisphere, Lodge rose to a resounding and portentous conclusion: "The supremacy of the Monroe Doctrine should be established and at once — peaceably if we can, forcibly if we must. It will be the duty and privilege of the next Congress to see that this is done."[7] Lodge threatened the British rival with war, and the Cleveland administration with Congressional action to that end.

On July 25, 1895, about a month after Lodge made his threat, the new Secretary of State notified the British government that any pressure on Venezuela would be regarded by the United States as a violation of the Monroe Doctrine; peaceful arbitration under United States auspices was the only way to settle the controversy. Olney warned that the United States would not permit European nations to partition South America as they had Africa. He asserted United States hegemony in the Western Hemisphere, echoing Lodge right up to the last bellicose threat: "Today the United States is practically sovereign on this continent, and its fiat is law upon the subjects to which it confines its interposition."[8] President Cleveland called the message Olney's "twenty-inch gun," but Britain did not trouble to reply to this pronouncement until late in November. Then she again brushed off any suggestion of arbitration.

In the fall the Republican Party of Massachusetts ran a successful gubernatorial campaign that endorsed the militant enforcement of the Monroe Doctrine as Lodge proposed. Not all regular Republicans approved this program, however; outstanding in his opposition was the old Free Soiler, George S. Boutwell.[9] But it was the Boston Mugwumps who, at this time, really opened up the debate over foreign policy. They seemed to sense the approaching crisis and so mounted a challenge to imperialist policy on Hawaii and Venezuela. A symposium in the November *Century* revealed Theodore Roosevelt to be an adherent of his friend Lodge's foreign policy views. Roosevelt's article was answered by William E. Russell, a young Boston Democrat of reform persuasion, who recalled Grant's ill-fated Santo Domingo adventure and denounced Republicans for the revival of "a defeated and almost forgotten Jingoism."[10] Writing also for a national audience in the November *North American Review*, Edward Atkinson, a prominent Mugwump, called for the public disgrace of those promoting hostilities with Great Britain, singling out Lodge as a prime Jingo. (At the same time Atkinson betrayed the Anglophilism characteristic of Brahmin Boston when he said that British rule was beneficial to colonial peoples even though they resisted its somewhat "rough and tactless" methods.) [11]

Lodge got support, however, from the annual meeting of the Home Market Club, held late in November and attended by many leading industrialists. Main speaker was Charles Emory Smith. His Boston speech followed by two days the one he had given before the New York Chamber of Commerce that the *Home Market Bulletin* thought important to reprint. If in New York Smith outlined the long-range perspectives of the imperialist policy-makers, in Boston he itemized their current agenda,

> We shall not lower our flag where it is peacefully and rightfully placed; that's Hawaii [applause]; we shall not look with indifference upon the outrage of any independent nation among our neighbors by any European assailant; that's Venezuela [applause]; we shall give our sympathies to oppressed people who are struggling for freedom, and . . . who . . . see their best happiness and prosperity under our aegis; that's Cuba [applause].

The *Bulletin* reported that Smith's words "electrified" the members of the Home Market Club.[12]

As if to counter this boost for imperialist policy from industrial capital, the Massachusetts Reform Club held a largely attended meeting early in December at which Atkinson spoke. After paying his respects to blatant Jingoists like Senator Lodge, he criticized "men of pure intentions who attained position and influence in the late great struggle for existence" but who now gave dangerous, passive support to Jingoism.[13] His audience understood that he was aiming at George Frisbie Hoar, the senior Senator from Massachusetts, Atkinson's associate in the Union cause during the Civil War.

After his magazine article and Reform Club speech, Atkinson received significant letters of support. The President of the Boston Merchants Association, J. R. Leeson, thanked him for his timely address "upon the subject of lunatics at large with chips on their shoulders." J. Sterling Morton, Secretary of Agriculture in Cleveland's cabinet sent congratulations and made an interesting observation about those in Congress who were talking up war, "These new jingoes say . . . war is prosperity."[14]

On December 17 the Young Men's Democratic Club of Massachusetts (the reform wing of the party) held a meeting at which speakers denounced the Jingo talk and identified it with the manufacturing interests, "who are to profit by a war."[15] But on the same day Cleveland delivered a message to Congress on the Venezuelan issue that embodied an ultimatum and a threat of war. He recommended an American commission to make a finding on the disputed boundary, and threatened Britain with the use of force to secure compliance. As he made his threat, Cleveland released the Olney dispatches from State Department files. Now the tough Olney-Cleveland line of policy was brought into public view.

Cleveland's war-like ultimatum caused consternation in the ranks of his Brahmin supporters in Boston. Charles Francis Adams wrote in his diary, "I fairly rubbed my eyes over it. Could it be that I was dreaming?" Edward Atkinson dashed off an anguished appeal to Secretary of Agriculture Morton, "What does it mean? For God's sake let me know." But the Mugwumps quickly recovered their balance. Their opposition gained new intensity and breadth, so that Boston was, as Olney's biographer wrote, "of all American cities, the one in which his Venezuelan policy . . . aroused most critics."[16]

From the Mugwump standpoint the main change in the situation was now the need to oppose not only the Republican Jingoes but also the Democratic President of the United States, whom they had hitherto looked upon as their great champion. No time was lost in telling Cleveland this. Three days after the President gave his message to Congress Edward Atkinson wired him that his "closest friends and most earnest supporters" in Boston were shocked by the position he had taken and were doing all in their power to defeat his policy. Atkinson also sent a similar message to Senator Hoar. But even as the Boston man was urging the contrary upon him, the Senator was telling a meeting at Plymouth, "We must not back down."[17]

The junior Senator from Massachusetts received the Cleveland message "bubbling over with delight," and wrote his mother in triumph, "I first alone in the wilderness cried out about Venezuela last June and was called a jingo for my pains. I am no longer lonely — jingoes are plenty enough now."[18] Two days after Cleveland's message the Boston meeting of the Middlesex Republican Club bore out Lodge's comment. Those present greeted Rev. E. A. Horton with "tremendous applause and old war-time yells" as he called for the country to take a strong stand.[19]

Not all those who knew the "old war-time yells" felt this way, however. Dana Estes, the Boston publisher who had served in the Union forces from the first days of war until forced out by a disabling wound, met Colonel Charles R. Codman in downtown Boston on the morning of December 20. To Codman Estes suggested a public meeting in Faneuil Hall to counteract the Jingo excitement. He followed this encounter with a letter to his former comrade-in-arms, writing, "I have, like yourself, seen enough of war and its effects to induce me to use every effort in my power to prevent the spread of any desire for war with any country." Then Estes wrote Atkinson to get his support for such a meeting.[20]

Nor was Rev. Mr. Horton's stand endorsed by all of Boston's Protestant ministers. The Sunday after Cleveland's message many (including Charles Fletcher Dole) made the threatening aspect of Anglo-American relations the subject of their sermons, and "the sentiment was practically unanimous for peace." Only recently Rev. William H. Scott and other black citizens had held a protest meeting against Southern lynching to which certain white ministers had lent support. Now one of these, Rev. C. G. Ames, cautioned Northerners who criticized the South for lynching lest they should "join in a similar act of unreason on a national scale."[21]

Sentiment in Boston's mercantile and financial community was strong against the threat of war. At a meeting of the New England Free Trade League, William Lloyd Garrison, Jr., the abolitionist's stock-broker son, warned that war with Britain would be "a needless war against our nearest kin and most important customer." The *Transcript* reported that there seemed to be a general feeling among financial men against war-like demonstrations in the Venezuelan matter, and many favored sending a petition to Washington to that effect. The war talk was causing a disturbance in the price of stocks.[22]

Three days after the Cleveland Administration had revealed its hand a group of Harvard professors and students wrote a letter to the *Crimson,* the undergraduate paper, urging all members of the University to write Congress against the President's Venezuelan policy. When Theodore Roosevelt, then Reform Police Commissioner in New York City, read this he wrote Lodge to ask his opinion about sending the *Crimson* "a smashing letter . . . saying a word for Patriotism and Americanism." Privately Roosevelt told Lodge he hoped the fight would come soon: "The clamor of the peace faction has convinced me that this country needs a war." But in his public letter to the *Crimson* Roosevelt praised Cleveland's policy as the way to peace, condemning those who opposed it for "stock-jobbing timidity, the Baboo kind of statesmanship, which . . . would in the end most assuredly invite war."[23]

Roosevelt's letter, which described Cleveland's critics as traitors, opened a controversy in the *Crimson*'s columns. Among those who answered him was Professor William James, who strongly defended the right to dissent when the federal executive was taking the country on a "career . . . pregnant with calamity for civilization." Where Roosevelt had concluded his letter with a ringing appeal for the building of "a really first class navy," James hit at this proposal as "the next obligatory step in the novel national career sprung upon us so abruptly by the President," and made an equally spirited counter-appeal: let the students begin the fight "at this very point . . . doing what little they can towards bringing the threatened increase of armament to naught."[24]

Organized labor in Boston entered the discussion caused by the threat of war. The *Labor Leader,* a paper founded by George E. McNeill and edited by his disciple, Frank Foster, demanded, "Wherefore war? . . . That Military gentry may flash their new fighting equipment? That brass band statesmen may blow their loud bazoo? . . .

That gold-hoarders may fatten on the necessities of the country? . . . Only this, and nothing more." Recollecting that British workers had stood for peace with the United States during the Civil War when Tory England wanted to intervene on behalf of the slave-holders, the paper called upon American workers now to do likewise. "The labor movement is international."[25]

At a meeting of the Boston Central Labor Union on the first Sunday in January 1896, Foster introduced a resolution that condemned the militaristic spirit of the President's message and declared that in "the mighty wars to come the power of the trade unionists will be found in united, not opposing lines." The meeting adopted the resolution by a vote of 48 to 25; then it instructed the Secretary of the Central Labor Union, Edward O'Donnell (who had been an early member of Karl Marx's First International) to forward a copy of the resolution to the British Labor Congress. But a minority of the Central Labor Union who supported Cleveland made great protest, so that Foster urged the submission of the matter to trade unions in the Boston area for referendum vote, and thus the business was disposed of.[26]

The Boston Central Labor Union's resolution asserted that the real purpose of the war hysteria was to divert attention from the greater issue of social reform, and the problems of the economic crisis were suggested. But that same Sunday another labor gathering in nearby Lynn gave more radical expression to popular discontent with the war threat, unemployment and hard times. A large congregation of trade unionists and businessmen heard Rev. Herbert Casson preach against Cleveland's policies at the Social Gospel, Labor Church of which he was pastor. Casson said that if ever war was justifiable it was when a people were robbed of their earnings and starved in the midst of a plenty they had themselves produced. If there was to be any fighting, let it be against the corporation kings who had monopolized everything save hunger and cold. "If you must fire a gun, point it at the industrial feudalism of America."[27]

In Boston, in the winter of 1895-96, the Venezuelan crisis stirred into active opposition elements that were later to come together in the anti-imperialist movement against the Spanish and Philippine wars. There were a few important exceptions in this expression of anti-imperialist sentiment that the later crisis would see removed. The Boston *Pilot,* which certainly spoke for much of the city's Irish population, criticized Atkinson for his opposition to Cleveland. An outstanding individual, Thomas Wentworth Higginson, also saw Venezuela as a small nation threatened by the British Empire.[28] But for a few weeks many voices — Brahmin, merchant, banker, labor, Protestant, intellectual — raged against the threat of a Jingo war.

Then, as suddenly as it had begun, the crisis ended, leaving suspended plans for a protest rally in Faneuil Hall, financiers' remonstrances and labor referenda. James Ford Rhodes, the wealthy Cleveland industrialist who had retired to Boston to write history, described how this crisis came to an end. On the evening of January 2, 1896, Rhodes asked his friend, General Francis A. Walker, President of the Massachusetts Institute of Technology, what way there was out of the situation when each nation had practically given the other an ultimatum. "One or the other must crawl," Walker replied, "but the news in tonight's paper shows the resolution of the difficulty." This was the report of Dr. Jameson's raid.[29]

Jameson's raid upon the Boers, the Dutch settlers of South Africa, was inspired by the British imperialist Cecil Rhodes with certain mining properties in view. The Boers, however, repelled Jameson and the raid ended in defeat, after which the German Emperor sent the Boers a congratulatory telegram. The Kaiser's telegram put the Venezuelan affair in new perspective for the British government. Rivalry with Germany in Africa and elsewhere proved decisive, as Bayard had originally surmised; and circumstances like those which led Cleveland to initiate the Venezuelan crisis governed its conclusion by Great Britain. Cleveland and Olney won their gamble, which had seemed to bring the nation to the brink of war. Great Britain agreed to arbitrate the Venezuelan boundary dispute. By this act of submission Great Britain virtually acknowledged the political hegemony of the United States in the Western Hemisphere.

This expansion of overseas political hegemony opened the door to another and more stubborn problem for United States imperialism: the dislodgement of Great Britain from economic domination of South American markets. In the *Transcript* of December 21 and 24, there appeared two articles from a special correspondent in Jamaica, British West Indies, that went right to the point. British textiles dominated the Jamaican market, while United States textiles were only a small portion of Jamaican imports, and this was the case in South America generally. If New England cotton goods manufacturers wished to increase their sales in South America and dislodge British textiles from supremacy, they would have to improve their marketing methods. The writer outlined the reforms needed, including the establishment of American banking facilities in South America.

Most interesting was the manner in which he related this economic question to the aggressive policies then current, saying that it sounded very masterful for the United States to advance the claim of "America for the Americans," as suzeraine of this hemisphere. "But where is the good of a thing if one does not utilize it?"

Sounding this very plain call to put political hegemony to economic advantage, the writer was enthusiastic about the outlook. While the British were preparing for the United States economic offensive they now expected to take place, the possibility did exist for American manufacturers to break the British monopoly of the South American market. A great future lay before the citizens of the United States. Having developed the Northern continent, they must now extend their enterprise to the Southern. "The most apparent beginning lies in the extension of commerce. The extension of railway and other industrial enterprises, now in but an incipient stage, will follow as a matter of course." First manufactured goods, then finance and investment — alluring prospects beckoned from the south.

Massachusetts textile manufacturers gave serious attention to the economic follow-up of the Venezuelan crisis at the semi-annual meeting of the New England Cotton Manufacturers Association in September 1896. Dr. W. P. Wilson, of the Philadelphia Museums (an institution recently organized to promote exports), devoted an address to the question of trade with Venezuela and South America. Dr. Wilson contended that while England now had the lion's share of the cotton goods imported into Venezuela, and the United States only one-sixth of her rival's portion, "Every condition in Venezuela is in favor of your having all of this trade."

The Philadelphia Museums, continued Wilson, had been in active communication for more than a year with the Chamber of Commerce at Caracas, Venezuela, and "That Chamber has been vigorously working for us, as we expect every chamber in South America to work." Venezuela had agreed to an exhibition of American manufactured goods, which the National Association of Manufacturers was now preparing.[30]

" . . . Every condition in Venezuela is in favor of your having all of this trade . . . That Chamber has been vigorously working for us, as we expect every chamber in South America to work . . . " The political victory scored by United States imperialism over its British rival brought certain advantages. In this relation the *Boston Evening Transcript* remarked that "Olney's recent stand against British aggression has given him strength in the very quarters where Cleveland has always been particularly weak."[31] As the President had hoped, something had been done for trade.

Senator Lodge had predicted as much when he had told Massachusetts Republicans in November 1895 before the Venezuelan crisis came to a head, "These South American countries are waiting, eager to open their markets, to draw closer relations with us."[32] The promises he had made for imperialist policy seemed coming true. Lodge was doing his work well as the "representative of New England industries." But it was up to the manufacturing interests to realize on the opportunities so gained; the Senator had other things to do.

Britain's concession of United States hegemony in South America was the first major political victory won by modern United States imperialism. As such it was a decisive step taken by the latter on its way to the hegemony of the imperialist world. That, however, lay in the more distant future. There was another accession of power that was nearer to hand. An aggressive foreign policy had forced Great Britain, the main rival of the United States in South America, to give way, thus clearing the path for confrontation with Spain, a lesser rival with desirable estate. Imperialists in the United States now turned their attention to this new problem. Again Henry Cabot Lodge led the rest.

4

The Spanish War: "The Political Economy of Barbarism"

"War is prosperity" said Congressional Jingoes at the time of the Venezuelan crisis, proposing a novel and arresting cure for the country's economic distress. But there was no war with Britain, and the remedy had to be postponed. Very shortly, however, a war with Spain put the Jingo nostrum to the test.

It was a Cuban revolt and Spain's harsh repression of it that enabled American imperialists to bring the pressure against their Spanish rival that led direct to war. The economic crisis of 1893 was world-wide in its effects and so brought hardship and then, in February 1895, insurrection to Cuba, one of Spain's last colonial possessions in the Western Hemisphere. The Spanish General Weyler laid waste the countryside and herded the Cuban people into camps under military guard where want, filth and disease were rampant. This *reconcentrados* policy aroused much feeling for Cuba among the American people. In Massachusetts sympathy for Cuban suffering under Spanish imperial rule provided a popular base for the interventionist policies sponsored by the state's powerful economic interests and the Republican leader Lodge. The Senator and his associates, in other words, testified to the power of the anti-imperialist tradition in the United States when they took advantage of it to launch themselves in full career, and American imperialism came to the fore under the banner of anti-imperialism.

In March 1896 Senator Lodge made a speech to the Republican State Convention. After paying tribute to the victory the United States had won over Great Britain in the recently resolved Venezuelan crisis, Lodge turned to the next order of business, the Cuban question. The United States, the Senator said, took ninety per cent of Cuba's products, but that island took hardly anything from us, owing to Spanish laws. Moreover Cuba lay athwart the Gulf, commanding the entrance to the proposed Nicaraguan canal. Her market would be ours and the control of the Gulf removed from all danger, if Cuba were free, for "she would have to rely on us for support."[1] The editor of the *Home Market Bulletin* was enthusiastic about Lodge's speech, especially the part relating to Cuba, and he reprinted this in the next issue. With a new declaration of support from Massachusetts industrialists, Lodge continued on his way. In April Congress overwhelmingly passed a resolution favoring recognition of Cuban belligerency. But Cleveland ignored it, to maintain the neutrality he had adopted when the Cuban revolt first began.

Senator Lodge's activities in the Venezuelan crisis had brought him recognition with his accession to a place on the Senate Foreign Relations Committee, which was to be the center of the war party in Congress. Beside this he helped write the Republican Party's national platform in June 1896, particularly the foreign policy planks; these declared that Spain had lost control of Cuba, was unable to protect the lives or property of American citizens there, and that accordingly the United States should use its good offices to bring peace and independence to the island.

Foreign policy was lost sight of in the elections. The popular discontent caused by the economic crisis intervened and the campaign centered on Bryan and his issues of domestic concern, free silver and the trusts. McKinley was elected, and the massive campaign funds that his advisor, Mark Hanna, the millionaire Midwestern industrialist, was able to raise from the great corporations helped no little.

After the elections, Senator Lodge supported a Congressional resolution recognizing the independence of Cuba, virtually declaring war on Spain. The Cleveland Administration in its last days of office again ignored the act of Congress, and for the moment Lodge could only acquiesce. Roosevelt was dissatisfied, however, and complained that Lodge might at least have been more war-like in his response to Cleveland's snub.[2] Nonetheless, the passage of the resolution for Cuban independence indicated heavy support in Congress for those elements pressing forward as the war party.

The Congressional action stirred things up in Mugwump and mercantile Boston, and contention with Lodge ensued. Since the country had not yet fully recovered from the economic crisis, and the textile industry was still depressed, it is not surprising that the question of business prosperity entered into this discussion. In December 1897 Charles Francis Adams (who, like Estes and Codman, had seen Civil War action) wrote Lodge condemning the Congressional resolve on Cuba, "I regard war not as a sort of football, but as a serious thing." Adams went on to say that the only remedy he saw for matters at present was a return to prosperity, for, he had observed, when people were employed and prosperous they ceased to be Jingoes.[3]

Lodge, however, had by now developed notions about the relationship of war to business prosperity quite contrary to those of Adams. Where Adams saw the return of prosperity as a means of overcoming the war danger, Lodge saw war as a means of attaining prosperity. These ideas Lodge expressed to a Boston cotton broker named Weld, who wrote him complaining that belligerent law-makers in Congress were ruining business and knocking down the price of stocks just when the economy was beginning to revive a little. Lodge replied:

> From the purely business standpoint business would not suffer from a fight with Spain. On the contrary our mills would make more goods, our railroads carry more freight, but these are the things that constitute business and not the stock market prices.[4]

Re-asserting the social orientation of his 1894 tariff speech, Lodge claimed priority for manufacturing interests. The difference was that in the present correspondence he put forward war rather than high tariff as the policy goal to be desired "from the purely business standpoint."

The projection of war as a means of overcoming the market difficulties of industry was a new development in the imperialist program, but, given the assumption that industrial profitability was the highest national good, it took its place with complete consistency. Blaine had proposed a military machine as a necessary adjunct to the acquisition of foreign markets for American industry. Now Lodge saw the military machine, extended in war, as an important new market for industry *per se*. He advocated, for industrial capital, the desirability of war as a means of profit in itself, the very concept Adams deplored.* Another, most powerful link between the military establishment and the industrial community was coming to the fore,

---

* Nor was Adam alone in this. The *Boston Herald* of March 29, 1898, complained editorially of the Jingoes "who have been wishing, and still are wishing to plunge this country into a war merely for the purpose of having a war."

pushed into view by the long-lingering depression.

As the debate with Lodge indicated, Boston opposition to an aggressive foreign policy did not cease with the coming to office of the new Republican President, although the election tended to change the form of its expression. During the campaign the Boston Mugwumps had been shocked by Bryan's call for a cheapened currency and had broken with the traditional Democrats to support John Palmer as the presidential candidate of a National Democratic Party that had plumped for the gold standard. The campaign these dissidents had waged for the Gold Democrat Palmer helped insure McKinley's election. Their support for sound currency brought the Mugwumps closer to the Republican Party; the New York Mugwump leader Carl Schurz had even campaigned for McKinley on this issue. Partisan considerations alone, therefore, would seem to have indicated an attempt by the new Administration to maintain and strengthen this relationship, to prevent another Mugwump swing away from the Republicans. Shortly after taking office McKinley promised Carl Schurz that there would be "no Jingo nonsense" under his administration, particularly repudiating any attempt to annex Hawaii.[5]

Boston Mugwumps could derive satisfaction as well from McKinley's appointment of a Massachusetts man, John D. Long, to be Secretary of the Navy. Though not a Brahmin, he had cultivated ties with Brahmin reformers by his support of the Massachusetts Peace Society, woman's suffrage and other high-minded Boston causes. A successful lawyer and Republican politician who had been friendly with McKinley when both served in Congress in the 1880's, his pacifist inclinations were well known. For this reason his appointment had infuriated Lodge who had tried unsuccessfully to dissuade McKinley from it.[6] Another important member of the McKinley Administration from New England, Maine's Thomas B. Reed, the Speaker of the House, was opposed to aggressive imperialist policies and not afraid to show it. In the early days of the new regime, therefore, the intimation of McKinley's attitude and first-hand knowledge of the opinions of Long and Reed, gave Boston anti-imperialists a sense of confidence despite the war threat brought into view by Congress.

It was in these terms that the struggle over foreign policy came to the fore again, the election results having thrown back the domestic threat to financial and social stability that Mugwump and Republican alike had seen in the Bryan campaign. Shortly after McKinley took office the Senate passed a resolution endorsing Cuban independence. In the House, Speaker Reed sidetracked this motion, and that body took no action. The Senate, however, had re-established its pressure upon the new administration for war with Spain.

Although the Jingoes were only partially successful in legislative action, Lodge in April 1897 secured them a distinct gain by bringing off the Presidential appointment, after much wire-pulling, of Theodore Roosevelt as Assistant Secretary of the Navy. Not only was Long offset, but the representatives of the war party in Congress secured intimate and effective connection with the Navy and with imperialist-minded men like Mahan in its higher echelons, so that military measures of great importance could be taken to implement the expansionist program.*

The effect of this new combination of forces was first felt in relation to Hawaii. A few days after Roosevelt took office Secretary Long was away from the Navy Department, and, in his absence the Assistant Secretary sent warships to Hawaii to counterbalance the presence of a Japanese cruiser in the harbor of Honolulu.[7] Then Roosevelt wrote Mahan confidentially of his adherence to the Captain's views, especially about the annexation of Hawaii, adding that Lodge was pressing the President to this end "with all his strength." A month later, Roosevelt wrote Mahan that he himself had urged annexation on McKinley and hoped for Presidential action very soon.[8] The next week McKinley submitted a new treaty for the annexation of Hawaii to the Senate.

McKinley's proposal called forth renewed condemnation in Massachusetts, and the revived efforts of anti-imperialists, Democrats, the sugar trust and domestic growers of beet sugar stalled the Hawaiian treaty on the floor of the Senate. The expansionists received their second check since McKinley came to office, to Mugwump satisfaction.

Despite this, the revival of the Hawaiian treaty set the pattern for the events to come which would bring defeat to the Massachusetts

---

* On March 30, 1898, Roosevelt wrote a friend, "I see a great deal of the Lodges . . . also of all the Senate Committee on Foreign Affairs, with whom I am in entire sympathy." (*The Letters of Theodore Roosevelt*, ed. by E. E. Morison, Harvard University Press, Cambridge, 1951-54, II, 805.)

Mugwumps and their hopes for peace. McKinley's anti-Jingo talk, which they applauded, would be nullified in the next months by his ready response to pressure from imperialists in Congress and the military, spearheaded by Lodge and Roosevelt. As for Secretary Long, whatever the weight of his pacifist inclinations, they would be circumvented by his Assistant, who was to dominate the Navy Department.

During the summer McKinley demonstrated his responsiveness to the wishes of the imperialist faction with respect to Spain, although this did not meet the public eye. When he gave his instructions to Stewart L. Woodford, the new United States minister to Madrid, he told Woodford to make clear to Spain that, while wishing to stay at peace with her, the United States would feel bound to intervene in Cuba if the conflict there was not ended soon, and the President plainly cited great Congressional pressure for such an ultimatum.[9]

With Long on extended vacation, Roosevelt prepared the navy for war with Spain. Moreover, the Assistant Secretary of the Navy had important discussions on this topic with McKinley, and made it his business to bring to the President's attention the main features of a plan for war with Spain worked out in the last days of the Cleveland Administration by the Office of Naval Intelligence. Besides naval operations around Cuba and off the coast of Spain, this plan included a strike by the United States Asiatic Squadron at the Spanish fleet in the Philippines. Roosevelt, in a letter to Lodge, implied Presidential assent to this plan; McKinley had been "most kind." Over Long's objections, Lodge and Roosevelt secured from McKinley the appointment of one of their imperialist coterie, George E. Dewey, to command the Asiatic Squadron in the planned offensive.[10]

Massachusetts Mugwumps, at the time did not fully appreciate the shift in the McKinley Administration toward a war with Spain. In June Roosevelt had made a bellicose speech at the Naval War College, boosting racial ideas then gaining prominence, as he proclaimed, "All great masterful races have been fighting races." As if to preserve a balance, the Administration invited Moorfield Storey to address the War College in September, and he came down hard on the other side, declaring, "I can imagine no greater calamity to this country than a successful war."[11] Later that month many of the Brahmin anti-imperialists gathered at the state convention of the Gold Democratic Party, and Storey, who gave the keynote address, spoke for

THE SPANISH WAR: "THE POLITICAL ECONOMY OF BARBARISM" 51

their attitude: "The Executive thus far preserves the attitude of neutrality toward Spain which is required by our traditional policy, but Republican and Democratic Senators vie with each other to precipitate a conflict with that unhappy country." Storey, however, registered disapproval of McKinley's sending a new Hawaiian treaty to the Senate, "for reasons not entirely apparent."[12] Indeed they were not, for they were nothing less than McKinley's accessibility to the imperialists, not yet widely realized, but the nub of the whole affair.

That winter it all came to a head. In December the President used his annual message to Congress to make public the threat of intervention he had already communicated to Spain, pushing to one side the posture of neutrality. Then McKinley and his friend Long made a most critical concession to the war crowd. Early in January Spanish officers rioted in Havana against the autonomy Spain had granted Cuba under American pressure. Seizing upon the incident, interventionists demanded that the Administration send a warship to Havana to protect American lives and property. No American warship had entered a Cuban port for the past three years of the island's strife, for Cleveland had prohibited such visits as too provocative.[13] But on January 24 the battleship *Maine* sailed for Havana under Navy Department orders. While McKinley and Long, who took public responsibility for the action, represented it as a gesture of peace and friendship toward Spain, the *Maine* took up a position in Havana harbor from which both the city and its defenses could be effectively shelled.[14] Roosevelt, who had earlier expressed the desire to use the *Maine* against even so unworthy a rival as Spain, now got his wish. His friends on the Senate Foreign Relations Committee also had reason to be pleased, and it was reported that they received the news of the *Maine*'s orders with "evident satisfaction."[15]

On February 15 an explosion of undetermined origin blew up the *Maine* in Havana harbor, whereupon interventionists raised a great clamor for war, and the next act in the drama took place. Nerves frayed, and exhausted by the access of tension, Secretary Long took time off, "to get away for a while." In his absence and under the eyes of the visiting Senator Lodge, Roosevelt sent Dewey word to be ready for offensive operations in the Philippine Islands, in line with the plans of Naval Intelligence. When Long returned the next day he countermanded many of the orders involving men, materials and ships that Roosevelt had given in his absence. Then he and his

Assistant had "a good laugh" at the younger man's impetuosity. Roosevelt could afford to laugh. Whatever secondary arrangements of the day before Long cancelled, the order to Dewey remained in force. Pushing the lesser ones aside, Long swallowed the largest toad.[16]

While the Secretary of the Navy was having problems with his Assistant, the President was feeling great pressure from Lodge and the Congressional war party, in response to which McKinley also showed a certain reluctance and nervous disarray. Early in March he broke down and wept "like a boy of thirteen" as he complained to an intimate that Congress was trying to drive the country into a war with Spain, while "the Spanish fleet is in Cuban waters, and we haven't enough ammunition on the Atlantic seacoast to fire a salute."[17]

In putting pressure on the President and promoting a war with Spain, Senator Lodge, as in other matters, did not act as an individual alone; his base of support in Massachusetts remained constant. The *Textile Record* for March thought that the United States had been unusually patient in view of the damage the Cuban conflict had done to American trade and property; European powers would have intervened long since. When the textile paper declared, "war will help more than it will hurt productive industry," the roots of Lodge's thinking were to be seen, as they were in the *Boot and Shoe Recorder*'s announcement at the end of March that war "would make a demand for a new line of products." The *Recorder* also believed that, because of the possibilities of trade and investment in Cuba, "any amount of money spent in freeing this island . . . would return an extraordinary profit."[18]

Moreover, Lodge's pro-war pressure represented, at this juncture, the sentiments of those even more powerful in the American economy. In Wall Street, the nation's banking center, at the end of March, the financiers, John Gates, Thomas Fortune Ryan, William Rockefeller, and Stuyvesant Fish were all feeling militant; J. P. Morgan saw nothing to be gained by more talk of arbitration.[19]

But in Boston the war threat brought forth expression of opposition that soon reacher a crescendo. In the last week of March the Boston Chamber of Commerce passed resolutions in favor of the President's efforts to avert war, and the *Transcript* found the Boston banking community almost unanimously of the same opinion. The first week of April saw the Boston Merchants Association, the Twentieth Century Club,* the Boston Bar Association, clergymen of all denominations, eighty-six members of the Harvard faculty led by President Eliot — all declaring against war and for peace.[20]

One thing was clear: in the minds of those Bostonians who opposed the war, the President was identified with peace, for when they spoke out for peace, it was invariably in terms of support for the President's policies. Boston's Secretary of the Navy Long was similarly identified. On March 31, Edwin D. Mead of the Twentieth Century Club wrote Long that the "President's temper and words, and yours, are what we bank on," and he truly spoke for the Mugwump patricians and middle class reformers in Boston who wanted peace.[21]

If opposition to war was rising to a climax, so was pressure for war. On March 27 information reached the State Department that the Spanish government would not stand in the way of United States efforts to feed Cubans suffering from the effects of the *reconcentrados* policy. Republican Jingoes in Congress became alarmed that this concession would relax the mounting hostility between the United States and Spain, with what they felt might be unfortunate effects upon the McKinley Administration. They saw the success of negotiations snatching away the war that seemed just within grasp. They therefore held a conference at which the decision was taken that the President must be warned not to "back down."[22]

On Saturday, April 2, Congressman Barrows of Massachusetts and Rev. Charles F. Dole called upon the Speaker of the House and the President in the interests of peace, and the *Transcript* told the result. They found Speaker Reed firm and resolved to hold the House to a conservative course as long as it should be the Administration's desire. The President they found calm, but taking intense fire from the Jingoes. Up to a week ago, he told them, the pressure upon him had been almost wholly toward the aggressive side, but the peace interest had within the last few days been bringing influence to bear, and that was very gratifying to him.[23]

Precisely a week later Senator Lodge called upon the President. As he left the White House the Senator told the press that the President would be satisfied with nothing less than the complete withdrawal of Spanish forces from Cuba, and he wanted prompt action, without delay; the time had passed for the peace-at-any-price people to have

---

* An organization devoted to municipal reform.

any effect upon him, nor would he turn back. One week for peace, the next for war — as the Congressional war party pushed matters to a head, McKinley's mantle of peace began to wear thin.[24]

The same day that Lodge made his visit to the President the Massachusetts Reform Club held a meeting that stood out as the peak of the opposition in Boston to the coming of the Spanish War. There was division of opinion, with a minority speaking in favor of a war to free Cuba, but the club finally declared for peace after much debate. It was the speech of Moorfield Storey, the Club chairman, that made this meeting the high point of resistance to the outbreak of the Spanish War. Dispensing with the customary assertion of confidence and hope that the policies of McKinley would preserve peace, Storey, with chilling clarity, placed the United States on the very verge of a war with Spain. Such a war, he warned, would be a nodal point in our national development, for with a victory over Spain, "we should be fairly launched upon a policy of military aggression, of territorial expansion, of standing armies and growing navies . . . inconsistent with the continuance of our institutions." Probing the influences making for war, Storey said:

> Some represented in high Federal office think that war will improve business and increase the gains of the rich. I can't refrain from quoting the reply which was made to one of these last week by a Middlesex Yankee of pure blood. He was a manufacturer of woolen goods, and a dealer in wool said to him, "We want war. Just think how it will raise the price of wool, and how it will serve to send your goods up." "Yes," was the answer, "but think how much more the dye stuff will cost. I can't afford to dye my goods in American blood. It comes too high." The man who will send others — husbands, fathers, sons, brothers — to die, in order that his gains may be greater, must be counted with the wretches who visit the battlefield to plunder the slain. He is beneath the contempt of this Club.[25]

The exception Storey made — with Brahmin pride — for the "Middlesex Yankee of pure blood" served only to emphasize the fact that he placed the business interests this woolen manufacturer represented first on the list of the operative causes of the war danger, ahead of the partisan politicians and yellow journalists he also mentioned in that category.

Storey declared the threatening war to be absolutely without excuse. Events lent support to his judgement, so far as concerned the matters the United States government declared to be at issue with Spain. Having previously made concessions on the questions of autonomy and relief for the victims of the *reconcentrados* policy, on March 31 the Spanish government announced the end of that policy altogether and agreed to submit the question of the *Maine* to international arbitration. On April 9 the Spanish government gave way on the question of ending hostilities and agreed to an immediate armistice. At this point the express wishes of the United States government for Cuba had been very largely covered by the Spanish government's concessions. While, so far, Madrid had only conceded Cuban autonomy, not yet independence, Minister Woodford believed that negotiations for independence could be carried to a successful and peaceful conclusion and so indicated when he notified McKinley of Spain's declaration of an immediate armistice.[26] But on the next day, April 11, President McKinley went to Congress and asked for authority to use the armed forces to put an end to the war in Cuba and secure that country a stable government, barely referring to the fact that the Spanish government had already declared an armistice and totally omitting any mention of Woodford's hopes for further negotiation.*

That evening the editor of the *Transcript* itemized the concessions Spain had made in negotiations, declared that country had backed down, and asked what the United States was going to war for. "Do we imply desire to show we can wipe old Spain off the Western Hemisphere?" Two days later he got his answer from an authority when Lodge told the Senate, " . . . if war does come . . . we will meet it so that the curse of Spain shall never rest again on any part of the Western Hemisphere."[27]

On April 20 both houses of Congress gave the President the power to use the armed forces against Spain as he had requested, and once

---

* In the Venezuelan crisis Great Britain gave way before the United States under threat of war, as did Spain in the Cuban. Yet American imperialists went to war against Spain and made peace with Britain. A war was wanted in any case, and perhaps Spain seemed the weaker rival with more desirable real properties to dispose of. This situation made a victim of Minister Woodford. Having taken the President's peaceable declarations and his own diplomatic responsibilities seriously, he felt humiliated — his own country had discredited him just when success and a negotiated settlement seemed within reach. (See David Starr Jordan, *The Days of Man*, World Book Company, Yonkers-on-Hudson, N. Y., 1922, p. 615.)

again Senator Lodge's influential backers in Massachusetts rose up in their places and said "Amen!" The next day the Home Market Club met with President William B. Plunkett in the chair. Plunkett, owner of one of the largest textile mills in Massachusetts, was known as McKinley's closest personal friend in the state, the friendship having its origins in a check for $1,000 Plunkett had sent the Ohio champion of high tariffs to help finance a campaign for Congressional re-election some years past. At the meeting Plunkett paid tribute to his friend, the President, who, he said, would never falter in the prosecution of "necessary war," but would push it vigorously till "the last remnant of Spanish misrule . . . shall be driven from the Western Hemisphere." The shoe manufacturers who met in Boston the same day heard similar sentiments expressed by the secretary of their trade organization and a Protestant minister who improved an occasion already distinguished by patriotic music and decorations.[28]

Senator Lodge and William B. Plunkett, two supporters of the war of more than ordinary significance, both spoke of driving Spain from the hemisphere as a most important objective, and this was a goal suggestive of imperialist rivalries. President McKinley, however, did not talk in these terms. In his message to Congress of April 11 he bore down with greatest emphasis on the side of the popular sympathy that existed for the Cubans, and placed the war on the highest moral ground as a humanitarian crusade: "I speak not of forcible annexation. That by our code of morality would be criminal agression."[29] So President McKinley began to make war in characteristic fashion, readily conceding all the high ground of moral principle to the anti-imperialists, but reserving all the hard decisions of practical effect to the imperialists. It was in this way that he had sidled up to war, all the while making sympathetic gestures to those who wished to maintain peace and completely identifying his intentions with theirs.

In any event the war came. The anti-war forces in Boston had failed to organize or lead any effective opposition to its outbreak. Unduly encouraged, perhaps, by the difficulties the imperialists encountered in the first months of the McKinley regime, in the fall the Mugwumps' reliance on the President and Long had prevented them from realizing the full extent of the war danger; then, when the winter brought the crisis undeniably upon them, they had still looked in the same direction for help. It was very decidedly a case of misplaced confidence. For when face to face with the warmakers and their demands, McKinley was "most kind," and wept in private, while Long gave way with a bluff and manly geniality.

Sympathy for the Cubans had also hindered the growth of opposition to the war's outbreak. Moorfield Storey had described such sympathy as one of the influences making the war possible; certainly this was the case, in the sense that it provided support for the imperialists' approach to war, and when the war actually broke out there came a burst of popular feeling that made things even more difficult for the anti-imperialists.

A few days after war was declared, the number of volunteers for army service at the central recruiting office in Boston was so great that the police had to be called out to keep order, and enrollments were reported in all the armories through the state. Patrick Collins had favored intervention all along, identifying Cuba with Ireland's struggle for freedom, and the press reported that Irish-American working people, particularly the more youthful, thought likewise. The result, after the war's outbreak, was the speedy formation of a regiment of Irish volunteers. A black volunteer regiment was similarly formed (although the general division of opinion was reflected in the city's small black community where many questioned the wisdom of fighting for democracy in Cuba when conditions at home left much to be desired).[30]

The government's commitment to war and the expressions of popular support had effect on some of those who had formerly been outspoken in their demand for the maintenance of peace. Henry Lee Higginson, who had been named after his banker uncle and who took the same vocation, evidently did not share the older man's acute antipathies, for he was notable among those who had a change of heart, writing the *Transcript* to urge all citizens, regardless of previous opinions, to support the government now that war had come.[31]

But not all those in Boston who had opposed the coming of the war subsided so readily. Chief among the stand-outs was Charles Eliot Norton, professor of Fine Arts at Harvard. When there had been a rush of students to enlist at the declaration of war, several professors, among them Norton, had cautioned against disruption of studies by hasty enlistment. Many of the faculty had only recently spoken out for peace, and uneasiness about the war and its necessity may have been behind such counsel. As for Norton, he left no doubt upon that score. He not only cautioned the students in his class against enlistment — he denounced the war. Like that against Mexico, it was "inglorious," "needless" and "criminal." As he concluded his remarks a student rose and, getting permission from Norton to speak, denounced Spanish atrocities in Cuba and peace-at-any-price people at home. Norton was a popular and respected teacher, so that other students attempted to shout the speaker down, whether or not they agreed with their professor's views. Norton checked them, however, and insisted that the man be heard. When the student had finished, Norton replied that Spain was a good example of the unhappy effects of belligerency " . . . Spain had lived by war . . . " and to what ruin it had brought her! The students applauded Norton, and that was all.[32]

But the incident and Norton's remarks were picked up by newspapers throughout the country, and he became the object of considerable condemnation and abuse that lasted, with varying intensity, for the spring and summer months. A Cambridge policeman told the press that Norton should be lynched; a Chicago paper endorsed the suggestion; every day brought Norton hostile letters and postcards, mostly anonymous, a few threatening.[33] All this because Norton was the first person of prominence to make his voice widely heard in a challenge to the government after war had been declared.

Denouncing the war six days after its declaration and at the height of the popular excitement, Norton displayed the moral courage that marked Boston's anti-imperialists at their best. He had the Mugwump hallmarks: Puritan and mercantile background, Harvard education, a record of anti-slavery activity during the Civil War. He displayed other traits common to Boston upperclass dissidents, conceiving, for example, his mission in life to be one of uplift. Profoundly impressed by the civilization and culture of England and the Continent, Norton attempted to bring these to an America obsessed with self-enrichment in a time of booming industry (much as his ancestor, John Eliot, the Puritan divine, had sought to bring the word of God to the Indians in an earlier day), and his Fine Arts chair was the pulpit for his preachments.

Then, again, Norton idealized the mercantile-agrarian society of his boyhood and youth as did other anti-imperialist leaders. He believed that there had never been a community on a "higher and pleasanter

THE SPANISH WAR: "THE POLITICAL ECONOMY OF BARBARISM" 59

level" than New England at the beginning of the nineteenth century, "before the coming of Jacksonian Democracy . . . the invasion of the Irish, and the establishment of the system of Protection"; his country home in Ashfield, Massachusetts, served as an outlet for this nostalgia every summer.[34]

This was the man who became the symbol of resistance to the Spanish-American War in its first days. In part, perhaps, the attention he got from the Jingoes was because he made them such a good target. His outspoken contempt for Philistine America and its emphasis on the material, his unmistakable Anglophile tendencies, all made Norton an easy mark for those who, in the dominant spirit of the times, identified the accumulation of wealth with national virtue.

When Norton compared the Spanish War to the slaveholders' war of conquest against Mexico, he cut through the thick overlay of humanitarian and patriotic sentiment that accompanied the war's initiation to the really operative forces underneath. While in the very first days it was difficult, perhaps, for many to accept Norton's judgement, events soon brought a change. On May 1 the plan worked out by the top circle of the imperialist faction, Roosevelt, Lodge and the naval strategists, came into operation, and Dewey, leading the Asiatic Squadron, smashed the Spanish fleet at Manila Bay in the Philippines. This event and the discussion that followed seemed to lend credence to Norton's strictures and served to shake loose some of those who had originally supported the war for humane or anti-imperialist reasons, causing them to wonder whether something was on foot they had not bargained for. Most striking was the defection of the *Springfield Republican,* because of that paper's influence and prestige.

On May 9 the Springfield paper reported that a recent meeting of the Massachusetts Club, a Republican organization in Boston, had applauded a navy admiral for advocating that the war should not stop until the United States possessed Cuba, Puerto Rico, Hawaii and the Philippines, "to keep and to hold." To talk thus, said the editor, was "to stain the purity of our cause," and he called on President McKinley and Speaker Reed to check such imperialism. Two days later the paper repeated: it had supported the war to free Cuba, not to conquer the Philippines.[35]

There was, in fact, a certain reassessment all around, a consolidation in the ranks of both imperialists and anti-imperialists, so that if the *Springfield Republican* changed sides, it was only to make a switch with Boston's *American Wool and Cotton Reporter,* another journal with an important group of readers in Massachusetts. The conversion of the *American Wool and Cotton Reporter* to the imperial cause, moreover, is of special interest because the process by which it took place presents itself as nothing less than the detailed exploration and verification of the thesis: "War is prosperity."

Early in March, while noting the rapid increase of American textile exports to China in the past year, the editor stoutly declared his was not a Jingo publication, hence it rejected the "grab game" now carried on in Africa and China by England, France, Germany and Russia to get "new markets for their present unsaleable merchandise." A month later, shortly before the declaration of war, the *Reporter* praised McKinley for his efforts to preserve peace. Although aware that "many persons are clamoring for war, because, as they claim, war would impart a favorable aspect to the general business situation," the editor was "not sufficiently convinced . . . to want to see the experiment tried."[36]

On May 19, however, in a leading article entitled "Imperialism," the *Reporter*'s editor announced that he had changed his mind. While imperialism was opposed because it brought with it the government of acquired territory, the enlargement of the army and navy and the possibility of constant hostilities, these objections were overbalanced by the fact that the United States had "extensive commercial interests for which it will soon be necessary to find a wider field than now available."

Evidently the editor was converted to imperialism not only by its aggressive pursuit of foreign markets, but by the war entailed as well. In the next week's issue he spelled this out in an article he called, "The Benefit of War to Commercial and Financial Interests — How the Thing Will Work." Going immediately to the heart of the matter, the editor announced that "One of the most encouraging features of the entire situation is the disposition of the enormous amount of money which is required to carry on the war." It was the American economy's first experience with modern imperialist war; this may explain the editor's tone of rather naive and greedy wonder as he revealed the splendid opportunities the federal government offered the country's industrialists and financiers when it ordered the military machine into actual combat.* First there were the increased expenditures for the construction and repair of battleships, for arms and ammunition, bringing employment to thousands in navy yards, armor plate factories, ordnance and ammunition factories. Why, at the shipyard at Newport News alone, where two years ago only 1,500 men were employed, before the year was out 5,000 would be at work! Involving great expenditures also were provisions for the army, uniforms, food, haversacks, boots and other leather and rubber goods, drugs and medicines, bedding, tents and hospital supplies. Fuel for the army was not to be forgotten, and, as for the navy, " . . . the coal bill alone of a single vessel often amounts to $1,000 in a single week."

The editor finally summed up his findings: "Thus we see that the government in appropriating money for war is really spending most of it in benefiting American industries, and in causing an extraordinary stimulus to business in many branches." Taking no chances, lest his readers fail to see how all this applied to them, the editor recalled, in an adjacent column, that the depressed condition of New England textiles was not due to Southern competition alone, but even more especially to the general loss of purchasing power by the people of the United States. It now appeared, however, that this would once more be such as "to support a stimulus . . . to the cotton manufacturing industry, putting it, so to speak, on its feet."[37]

The experiment had been tried. An unaccustomed and remarkable phenomenon was the result: the war economy. This was bringing prosperity to the industries of the country as a whole and promised the same for New England's cotton textile. Convinced by his own pragmatic standards, the editor of the *American Wool and Cotton Reporter* fell to his knees and said, for all his subscribers to hear, "I believe."

If the imperialists' pursuit of foreign markets, military-strategic advantage and colonial acquisition can be found in the origins of

---

* Even in this area the Civil War cast its long shadow. In the column "Manufactures of Wool," in the *American Wool and Cotton Reporter* for April 14, 1898, before the actual declaration of war, it was written: "If war should be declared, it would turn many of the mills to making cloth for soldier boys . . . Some of the manufacturers this week have been looking over the records of their mills during the time of the late Civil War, and seeing what could be done in the event of another similar state of affairs."

America's war with Spain, then their desire to bring prosperity to industry by means of war can also be seen as a cause of the conflict.

In view, however, of the popular disenchantment with big business hanging over from the depression and Bryan's campaign, the politicians and publicists who labored to secure mass support for the war were not wont to dwell on what the industrial interests saw as the advantages of a war with Spain; rather did they frequently and emphatically denounce the opposition that had existed to the war before its outbreak in the ranks of business, which, in Boston, was particularly to be seen in mercantile, financial and stock exchange circles.* In his speech on Cuban intervention Lodge praised support for the war that existed among "the great mass of our people whose eyes were not blinded by the glitter of too much wealth," and the point was made.[38] This left the promoters of the war with two arguments: war was good for business, and only business opposed the war. The *Boston Evening Transcript* early pointed out this contradiction in the position of the warmongers. On March 24 Senator Thurston of Nebraska made a speech on the Senate floor in which he stressed the industrial prosperity that war might bring. Thurston's speech drew an angry reply from the *Transcript*'s editor:

> Mr. Thurston made light of war, and combatting his own assumption that only "Wall Street" is opposed to it, went on to maintain that war meant more business, and more business meant more money. To this it is sufficient to say that it is barbarous political economy, for it is and has been the political economy of barbarism.[39]

An imperialist war, the violent culmination of the military-industrial alliance, brought prosperity and profit to the manufacturing interests and the banks with which they were allied. Industry discovered in the war an even more remunerative use for militarism than the peacetime protection of foreign trade and investments. The

---

* Some historians have followed, perhaps too readily, this one-sided emphasis. Thus Julius W. Pratt in *Expansionists of* 1898 mentions the *Boston Journal of Commerce* and the *American Wool and Cotton Reporter* as opposed to the war before its declaration. But Pratt neglects to cite the *Textile World* and the *Boot and Shoe Recorder,* both of which supported the war before its declaration, nor does he note the several expressions of interventionist sentiment in the *Home Market Bulletin.*

experience thus gained forged the new link between industry and the military that Lodge and others had foreseen as desirable. The Spanish-American War was the blood-letting rite of initiation to what Boston anti-imperialism called "the political economy of barbarism."

5

Faneuil Hall and Aguinaldo

In December 1897 the *Boston Evening Transcript* commented on the nationalist revolt that had broken out in the Philippine Islands the year before, "In reality the regime against which the Philippine natives and creoles revolted was a good deal like that which drove the Cubans to arms, only as much worse as Manila is further removed from the world's scrutiny than Havana."[1] The editorial showed that there was sympathy in Boston for those who fought for Philippine independence as well as Cuban. This fact had important consequences when American empire-builders supplanted Spanish after the latter's defeat at Manila Bay. Sympathy for Philippine liberation became a powerful source of motivation, a special stimulus to the anti-imperialist movement in the United States (lending further irony to the fact that Cuban nationalism provided American imperialism with the springboard for its launching).

It was the meeting at Faneuil Hall that took the first step toward transforming what had been a matter of individual protest against the Spanish War into an organized movement, and Boston men got this meeting together only after hints in the press that the McKinley Administration was tempted by the Philippines. Later, the open avowal of the Administration's intent to annex those islands led to the organization of the Anti-Imperialist League, and when the Filipinos then showed resistance to the United States occupation of their homeland, further impetus was given to the anti-imperialist movement.

In turn, the movement that the anti-imperialists built in the United States gave political and moral support to Philippine independence, creating difficulties for the American imperialists in the execution of their program. The relationship that came about between American anti-imperialism and Philippine nationalism proved reciprocal in effect, and so it continued, with varying intensity, as long as did the movement that originated at Faneuil Hall. (This relationship was distorted by imperialist spokesmen so as to make it appear that American anti-imperialists were responsible for the Philippine struggle for independence. Such assertions, frequently repeated, suggested a racist underestimation of the Filipinos on the part of those who made them, rather than the reality of the situation. In truth, Philippine nationalism had been a flourishing movement for some time before organized American anti-imperialism saw the light of day, and would seem to have influenced the American anti-imperialists more than the latter did it.)

The occupation of the Philippine Islands by the United States Army did not enter into the discussion Roosevelt held with McKinley in September 1897 about plans for a war with Spain. These had been limited, in relation to the Philippines, to a projected naval strike at the Spanish fleet there based. According to Secretary of War Alger, however, before Dewey attacked the Spanish fleet the McKinley Administration had decided to send an army of occupation to the Philippines, thereby enlarging its military design for the archipelago.[2]

It was the threatened partition of China that put the Philippines in a new perspective for the McKinley Administration. This division had started in 1894 when Japan wrested control of Korea from China by war, had continued in the next two years with the French in their colony of Indo-China pressing her from the South, and Russia bearing down on Manchuria in the North. The fall of 1897 brought the process to a climax: in October Russia took Port Arthur, and in November Germany seized Kiaochow Bay. Towards the end of the year businessmen who had dealings in China came to Washington to urge the maintenance of our treaty privileges in the territories seized by Russia and Germany. Senator Lodge was among the first to recognize the importance of these representations, and on December 24 the partition of China provided the chief topic for discussion at a Cabinet meeting in the White House. The *Transcript* reported one of the participants saying, essentially, that the President intended to keep a watchful eye on the situation in order that full protection might be given to the interests of the United States in China.[3]

That winter Dewey took up his responsibilities as commander of the Asiatic Squadron, and his attitudes reflected the concern and purpose of the Administration in this area. On January 30 Dewey wrote his sister that England, Russia and Germany had all increased their naval forces in the Orient, and the United States was doing likewise. All his ships were in Chinese or Korean waters "looking out for a right to protect American interests . . . What we all want is Chinese trade . . . which we would lose were it not well known that we are ready and will protect it."[4]

The threat to American interests in the Chinese market, which this responsible naval officer had so on his mind, was a matter of concern to members of the Massachusetts business community as well. One of these, Thomas Hammond Talbot, a Boston lawyer, wrote Secretary of the Navy Long a letter early in March that put the Chinese market and the Philippine Islands in the same line of vision. He expressed the hope that the United States would seize and hold the Philippine Islands, since America had a substantial stake in "preventing the closing of portions of China to the world's commerce," and could not "too carefully provide for the great future of these Pacific interests."[5] Writing a month before the Spanish-American War, Talbot suggested a result of that war not originally envisaged by the McKinley Administration. Others made the same association, and further evidence suggests that Talbot's letter was typical of the expansionist thinking that lay behind McKinley's decision to occupy the Philippines.*

In effect the proposal to seize the Philippines was the link between the naval offensive in those islands planned first of all as a result of military considerations, and the share in the Chinese market desired by corporate interests (especially those with the largest stake therein, the leaders of the textile industry and the Standard Oil trust). When the Administration saw the connection and decided to bring it off, the plan to strike down Spanish naval power in the Pacific grew into a plan to hold the Philippine Islands with ground forces; what was

---

* Cushman Davis, Chairman of the Senate Committee on Foreign Affairs and member of the Paris Peace Commission, urged the Senate to ratify the treaty of Philippine annexation because "he, with others, was looking forward to the prospective partition of the vast Chinese market among the European nations, and he foresaw that if the United States did not secure a footing in the Orient, such as they would now have an opportunity to secure through terms of the treaty, they would be most effectually and forever shut off from this vast market." (*Boston Evening Transcript*, January 26, 1899.)

started as a military measure incidental to the displacement of Spanish influence in the Western Hemisphere turned into one directed toward establishing American influence in Asia; and the Philippines were transformed from a collateral to a central concern.

The Philippine nationalists were the first to feel the brunt of this new phase of American military activity in Asia, as they were the ones against whom it was in large measure designed. In 1872 Philippine nationalism had erupted in a quickly suppressed revolt of Filipino soldiers who killed their Spanish officers and called for independence. In 1896 another more sustained and widespread insurrection had begun. This took the form of an armed revolt of the lower classes against the rule of the Spanish religious orders, or friars, who administered the colonial government and owned large feudal estates. The insurrection had as its goals land reform and an end to the white domination Spanish rule imposed on this colored people. In December 1897 the Madrid government had promised reforms; in return for these promises the most prominent nationalists (including the military leader Emilio Aguinaldo) had gone into exile and the revolt had subsided. Spain did not carry out her promised reforms in the Philippines, and in February 1898 armed insurrection again broke out.[6]

It was soon after this, on the eve of the war with Spain, that representatives of the United States government in Asia began to have dealings with the insurgents that were pregnant with result. Sometime in March Dewey sent Captain Wood of the gunboat *Petrel* to confer with Aguinaldo about the possibility of collaboration against Spain in the Philippines, and the next month such conferences were continued.[7]

On March 31, 1898 Dewey made his first written report to the Navy Department (received at Washington only after his victory at Manila Bay), and, while he did not mention the consultation with Aguinaldo, he told authorities that there were five thousand armed Filipino rebels waiting to assist the United States against Spain, and that once Manila was blockaded the Spaniards could be driven from the Philippines either by the insurgents or by United States forces.[8]

This was not the first that Washington had heard of the rebels' willingness to cooperate. In November 1897 Consul Wildman at Hong Kong had forwarded to the State Department an insurgent offer of alliance in the event of a war with Spain. On December 15

Emilio Aguinaldo, leader of the struggle for Philippine independence. "A people which has given proofs of valor and long suffering in time of trouble and danger, and of industry and diligence in time of peace, is not intended for slavery." — Aguinaldo's statement of June 23, 1898.

the State Department had rejected this offer out of hand and told Wildman to have nothing more to do with the insurgents.[9]

As it turned out the State Department's instructions to Wildman were precisely the policy the Administration adopted toward the insurgents when it decided to hold the islands, since it gave the United States a free hand, unencumbered by commitments to local nationalists. At this time, however, it is probable that the McKinley Administration had not yet matured its plans for the Philippines. Perhaps that is why the State Department appears to have neglected to inform other United States representatives in the field of its insurgent policy, with results that were extremely incongruous when Washington's plans for the Philippines took final shape.

Dewey's first report and his initial actions leave little doubt that he was unaware of any settled Administration policy toward the insurgents, and according to Consul Pratt at Singapore, he was similarly in the dark. The latter, therefore, just before the war started, followed up Dewey's contact with Aguinaldo, then in exile on the Chinese mainland, and persuaded him to cooperate with the United States forces against Spain, wiring Dewey of Aguinaldo's assent. Dewey, in turn, wired Pratt of his agreement to this arrangement. Pratt then informed Washington of the projected United States-insurgent collaboration.[10]

On May 19 Aguinaldo was at Cavite, near Manila, brought there by an American warship at Dewey's behest. Cordially received by Dewey, he proceeded to organize an insurgent army under the protection of the guns of the American fleet, taking arms, with Dewey's assent, from the captured Spanish arsenal.[11] Five days after his return to the Philippines Aguinaldo issued a statement to his fellow-countrymen, telling them that the United States, "the cradle of liberty," was "friendly . . . to the liberty of the Filipinos" and came to offer them disinterested protection, believing in their capacity for self-government.[12]

Less than a year after Aguinaldo's statement the United States armed forces were warring against him and his army in an attempt to subjugate the Philippines. Then the anti-imperialists in Massachusetts made the events of this earlier period a matter of controversy. They charged that Dewey, Pratt and others had promised Aguinaldo Philippine independence if he would fight at the side of the Americans against Spain.

The evidence suggests that Pratt indeed made such pledges in writing and by word of mouth.[13] Dewey was careful never to put anything in writing, but it was at this period that he informed Washington that he thought the Filipinos more capable of self-government than the Cubans, and Aguinaldo's statement to his fellow-countrymen indicated that he might have been aware of Dewey's opinion.[14] In any case, as Aguinaldo later said, while the American naval chief made no formal pledge, his attitude and actions were such as to cause the Philippine leader to believe that it was the intention of the United States to set the Filipinos free. A high-placed American observer of these early relationships, General Francis Greene, agreed (also in retrospect) that the actions of Dewey and Pratt were such as to give grounds for insurgent belief in United States recognition.[15]

These were the circumstances that led the anti-imperialists to accuse their government of betraying its Filipino allies, of gaining the military advantage of insurgent support at the price of moral infamy. Their indignation at the plight of the Filipinos, whom they saw as the victims of American breach of faith, strengthened their sympathy for the insurgent cause and their anti-imperialist zeal.

When the Administration at Washington learned from Dewey of the insurgents' presence and willingness to help, and, more disturbing still, from Pratt of the informal United States-insurgent alliance he appeared to have initiated, its response was grimly unfavorable. Having previously decided to send occupying troops to the Philippines, it acted to hasten their dispatch. On May 13 the *Transcript* reported that a series of White House conferences were held in which President McKinley, Secretary of War Alger, Major General Wesley Merritt and other military men of high rank participated. Here it was agreed to send General Merritt with an army of 12,000 men to the Philippines in all possible haste. "Even important plans for beginning an immediate military offensive in Cuba received secondary consideration by the officials of the Army Administration." The reason for this urgency was the Government's "apprehension, based on late advices from Manila that the insurgents will prove almost as troublesome a factor in the situation as the Spaniards."[16]

Thereupon the Administration turned its attention to Dewey and Pratt. The difficulty with Dewey appears to have arisen because the Administration reached the decision to seize and hold the Philippines in the winter of 1897-98, after Dewey left Washington for the scene of action. The script had been changed in his absence and he had responded to the wrong cues (for example, after his victory at Manila Bay Dewey had asked Washington for 5,000 ground troops only, on the basis of fighting the Spanish alone). It was necessary to set him aright, and, all belatedly, Washington cautioned Dewey "not to have political alliances with the insurgents or any faction in the island that would incur liability to maintain their cause in the future."[17]

The State Department then reprimanded Pratt for holding out hope of independence to the Filipinos and ordered him to have no further unauthorized dealings with the insurgents. Apparently believing that it was Pratt who had touched off the whole complication, the Department let him know that the President himself had considered his case and had issued the covering instructions. The President's views, as conveyed to Pratt, were heavy with the overtones of the decision to send 12,000 men: "The United States in entering upon the occupation of the islands . . . will expect from the inhabitants, without regard to their former attitude toward the Spanish Government, that obedience which will be lawfully due from them." The Presidential rebuke to Pratt implied a threat to Aguinaldo.[18]

McKinley's course of action at this moment ran parallel to the thinking of Henry Cabot Lodge and Theodore Roosevelt. Writing a friend on May 18, Lodge saw "all Europe . . . seizing China" and the consequent need to "establish ourselves in the East" so as not to be shut out of Asian markets. Eager to "whip the dagoes" and serve in the war he had helped bring about, Roosevelt, at its onset, had volunteered, leaving Washington to get together his Rough Rider regiment of Eastern club men and Western cow hands. But he wrote Lodge a letter May 16 which concluded with the injunction, "Give my best love to Nannie, and do not make peace until we get Porto Rico, while Cuba is made independent, and the Philippines at any rate taken from the Spaniards."[19]

With Roosevelt away, Lodge had responsibility for keeping the President in line. On May 23 he visited the White House to explain, for McKinley's benefit, the main economic arguments of the imperialists. Lodge ticked off the points. The home market was no longer sufficient to meet the productive capacity of American industry; foreign markets must be secured such as the Philippines would provide. Annex these islands, and their ten million inhabitants would have to buy American goods, and American manufacturers would have so much additional trade. Along with this general lesson, the Senator took it upon himself to give the President direct personal instruction: as formerly McKinley had promoted tariff to insure the home market for American industry, now he must promote an imperial policy to guarantee foreign markets; nothing less was expected of him as the chief representative of American business interests.

"From this theory the President expressed no dissent," concluded the *Transcript*'s report of the interview, and the next day Lodge wrote Roosevelt that "the administration is grasping the whole policy at last." The White House was planning to send no less than twenty thousand men to the Philippines, "the one spot where haste is needed."[20]

Knowledge of McKinley's Philippine hankerings, though pleasing to Lodge, greatly distressed a Boston man, Gamaliel Bradford, and caused him to write a letter which the *Transcript* printed June 3 under the heading "A Cry for Help." After quoting press reports from Washington that a small clique led by Lodge and the *New York Sun* was bent on turning "the great American Republic into a worldwide empire," and that McKinley understood annexation of Hawaii and the Philippines to be a commercial necessity, Bradford made the following impassioned appeal:

> In the name of all the past glories of Massachusetts, I call for help . . . Some months ago I tried to get up a Faneuil Hall meeting to protest against the war, but was met with the excuse that the war feeling might get the upper hand. Other parties tried the same thing later, but gave it up, apparently for the same reason.
> If that is the danger, in God's name let us stand for the right, if the war spirit does prevail! If free speech is to be suppressed in Massachusetts, if Faneuil Hall is to be converted into a silent tomb, if the spirit of Wendell Phillips and William Lloyd Garrison — sorely needed to avert a slavery worse for Massachusetts at least, we had better find it out now. If enough men will join with me to secure the hall, I for one, will stand up and have my say against the insane and wicked ambition which is dragging this country at least to moral ruin.

Bradford's call led directly to the Faneuil Hall meeting.[21]

Before the organized opposition to the Spanish-American War got under way, however, the man who had come to symbolize individual protest spoke out again. On June 7, in an address at a Cambridge

Congregational church, Charles Eliot Norton answered the distortions of his position the pro-war press spread abroad. Norton asserted that he opposed the war not because he scorned the United States but because he loved it. Opposition to the war was, in fact, the duty of the true patriot, for "just in proportion to his love of the ideals for which his country stands, is his hatred for whatever is opposed to them in private conduct or public policy." The Spanish War was the low point in the declining power of American ideals to control the national life that had been in process for "the last thirty years." This was not Norton's only appeal to the zeal of Civil War and anti-slavery times. William Lloyd Garrison had written him a letter of praise for standing by "the moral law" of the abolitionist crusade. Evidently Garrison's letter had awakened a sympathetic response, for in Norton's church speech he exclaimed: "Stop! A declaration of war does not change the moral law. 'The Ten Commandments will not budge' at a joint resolve of Congress."[22]

Norton's talk got a mixed reception from his friends. The next day the *Boston Evening Transcript* hailed the speech as a sign that New England's traditional role of courageous national leadership was once more coming to the fore, "in a country tending too much to a commonplace conformity." This was all very well, but it was not enough for William Lloyd Garrison, whose militancy recalled his father. Though Norton had denounced the war, he had also called for public support of the government in order to bring it to a speedy end. This drew rebuke from Garrison who called for "disobedience to human law when it conflicts with the higher law of righteousness." The government deserved no support at all — that was what adhesion to the moral law demanded![23]

Even as they disagreed on shadings of policy, Bostonians against the Spanish War were moving to give more substance to their opposition as a result of Bradford's appeal, the latter noting how it happened: "In reference to the letter 'A Cry for Help' . . . Mr. Erving Winslow called upon me and we got up the meeting at Faneuil Hall, he making the arrangements and I paying the expense." (Bradford added with what could have been proper pride, "That led to the formation of the Anti-Imperialist League.") When Winslow made application to the Board of Alderman to use Faneuil Hall on June 15 "for the purpose of holding a public meeting to protest against the so-called imperial policy of the United States government," besides his own name and that of Bradford, he signed for Moorfield

Storey, Chairman of the Massachusetts Reform Club, Charles Gordon Ames, the Unitarian minister, and labor leaders Henry Lloyd and George E. McNeill. With Winslow's help Bradford had gained the support he wanted.[24]

Moorfield Storey thought the prospects "very dark" and was uncertain whether Faneuil Hall would bring a hostile audience or empty benches, but press estimates of the attendance on June 15 ranged from two to four hundred people. The papers noted that "Boston protest . . . apparently comes from the older element in the community for . . . there was but a handful of young men," that nearly half the audience were women, and that the city's reformers were well represented, "on all sides could be seen the well-known faces of leaders of good causes."[25]

Bradford, Storey, Rev. C. G. Ames and McNeill gave passing support to the government in the prosecution of the war, but the main thrust of their remarks lay in a denunciation of the imperialist policies McKinley was coming openly to espouse. Advance publicity had said that the meeting would give special attention to the Philippines, and Gamaliel Bradford gave it this timely direction. The United States must not annex either Cuba or Puerto Rico. "But," he warned, "that is a trifle compared to the Philippines. We are despatching a considerable army to take possession; which will need to be multiplied many times before we complete it." The meeting echoed his resistance. Resolutions drawn up by Storey and passed by the gathering declared that it would be appropriate "to invite distant populations of alien race . . . to become our subjects and accept our rule, or our fellow citizens, and take part in governing us," only when the United States had set its own house in order, by reforming corrupt domestic politics and a disordered currency, by protecting the rights of blacks and Indians within its borders; meanwhile, "a war begun as an unselfish endeavor to fulfill a duty to humanity must not be perverted into a war of conquest."

The meeting elected a body (including Bradford and Winslow, the latter as secretary) to get in touch with other persons and organizations and to take suitable action. Calling itself the "Committee of Correspondence" in obvious reference to earlier Boston anti-imperialism, this group soon published the speeches made at Fanueuil Hall in a brochure that appealed for cooperation from anti-imperialists in all parts of the country.

Besides Bradford's emphasis on the Philippines another note was sounded at the Faneuil Hall meeting that would later reverberate in the anti-imperialist movement. George McNeill linked burgeoning monopoly and imperialism, saying that "annexation means the strengthening of the speculative industrial monstrosities that are today devouring enterprise."[26]

Since McNeill was the outstanding trade union leader in city and state, his presence at the meeting had practical significance that was immediate. A few days later the Boston Central Labor Union passed resolutions protesting "imperial policy" and the annexation of Hawaii, Puerto Rico and the Philippines. Boston labor, with its large constituency of those sympathetic to Irish independence, also took unfavorable notice of the friendly attitude the pro-war press was beginning to display toward Great Britain, as a result of her support for the United States against Spain, and declared opposition to any alliance with Great Britain.[27]

The Faneuil Hall meeting was not the first time Gamaliel Bradford had cooperated with George E. McNeill. For Bradford was one of the more radical Boston Mugwumps, as his less hidebound attitude toward organized labor made clear.* In 1896 when Lodge and other wealthy Republicans had sought to have the state legislature meet every two years instead of annually, Bradford had worked with McNeill and other trade unionists to preserve annual sessions. His energy and funds helped the cause to victory. The campaign for the annual session, Bradford's first success in a life devoted to reform, seems to have been the model for what he later sought in the anti-imperialist movement: an alliance of labor and middle class reform for democratic ends.[28]

Descendant of the first governor of Plymouth colony, Bradford, after graduating from Harvard in 1849, had gone into a relative's Boston banking house where he became a partner before long. Taken as a boy by his abolitionist father to hear Garrison and Phillips, Bradford was an ardent anti-slavery man; many of his friends volunteered for the Union Army. Consequently his decision not to leave his business responsibilities to enlist weighed on his conscience. "I resolved," he later wrote, "that if I lived I would do more for my

---

* Indeed Lodge lumped Bradford with Altgeld, the Illinois governor whose sympathy for labor made him anathema to conservatives. (*Boston Evening Transcript*, September 10, 1900.)

country than by throwing away my life on the battlefield." Accordingly, a few years after the Civil War, having made enough money in banking to provide an independent income, he retired from business and devoted himself to the study of public affairs and the promotion of political reform. He became a publicist, a maker of speeches, a writer of magazine articles and innumerable letters to the press.[29]

That corporate wealth exercised undue influence upon the government of the United States was a conclusion he had drawn from his years of observation and study. In *The Lesson of Popular Government,* a two volume work published in 1899, Bradford wrote: "The great trusts and monopolies which have sprung up through the country are learning more and more that they have only to bring together sufficient money power to work their will with Congress."[30] Moreover, Bradford believed that Congress, thus dominated by selfish private interests, in turn dominated the Executive branch of the federal government.

Typically Anglophile was his solution to these problems: cabinet government on the English model, the participation of the President and the members of his Cabinet in debate on the floor of Congress, in order to reassert executive authority over that body. Bradford devoted much time to this reform, without practical result, and his efforts only won him reputation as a crank. Especially after he initiated the anti-imperialist movement did the pro-war press ridicule him as a futile bore, although, of course, it was precisely at this moment that he transcended the role of ineffectual reformer to become a figure of influence.

Bradford had joined other Boston Mugwumps in giving active support to the candidates of the Gold Democratic Party in the national elections of 1896 and the state elections of 1897. But in the early summer of 1898 Bradford shifted his interest to the traditional Democrats. McKinley's adoption of a more open imperialist position, as expressed by his dispatch of troops to the Philippines, had its effect on the regular Democratic Party and its leaders, and this Bradford took into account, as did others of like opinion.

On the same day that the Boston anti-imperialists held their first public meeting at Faneuil Hall, William Jennings Bryan, who had volunteered for service in the Spanish War (in line with the support the Democratic Party had given to Cuban intervention), addressed a throng in Omaha, Nebraska. Wearing an army uniform, Bryan spoke out against colonization in the Orient and a war of conquest. Again on the same day Massachusetts Congressman John F. Fitzgerald rose on the floor of the House to charge that Great Britain wanted the United States to annex Hawaii and the Philippines so that she would have an ally in China against Russia and other powers. Another voice of the city's Irish Democracy, the *Boston Post,* which had supported the war against Spain to free Cuba, then warned against the British alliance and the threat of cheap labor from the annexation of Hawaii, the Philippines and Puerto Rico. To complete the picture, Grover Cleveland stepped away from the alignment with the most aggressive imperialists he had established in the Venezuelan episode and declared against the present annexationist program, to Mugwump gratification.[31]

The *Boston Evening Transcript* had opposed Bryan in the election of 1896, but after his Omaha speech the paper hailed him for uniting the "great central West" with the "extreme East" in "opening . . . a backfire against the new American imperialism." Gamaliel Bradford, having initiated the anti-imperialist movement and directed it toward organized labor, also attempted to align this embryonic organization with the anti-annexationist elements in the Democratic Party and to stimulate and guide the latter. In an "Appeal to the Democrats . . . of Massachusetts" he warned that the Philippines and Hawaii would constitute "lightning rods thrust out into the Pacific" entailing "an army and navy equal to those in Europe." Citing the positions taken by Bryan and Cleveland, Bradford declared the Democratic Party "the sole hope" of escape from these evils. He urged that the currency question be dropped in the interests of anti-imperialist unity, "Can we not sink our differences and unite our efforts in a cause as noble as ever appealed to the people of our state."[32]

As the forces that were to give political challenge to McKinley's imperialism on the home front took more definite shape, so did those that were to offer the Administration military resistance at the opposite ends of the earth. On June 12, three days before the Faneuil Hall meeting, Aguinaldo issued a Philippine Declaration of Independence, and a national flag was unfurled. After his return to the Philippines, Aguinaldo had set up a military dictatorship, but on June 23 a revolutionary government was established with Aguinaldo as President; a Cabinet was provided for and a Congress composed of representatives from the provinces. Local government was organized on democratic lines.[33]

Bolstering this revolutionary government was the success Aguinaldo had in fighting the Spanish. By the end of June, the insurgents had won control of the whole of Luzon, the main island, with the exception of Manila and a few scattered Spanish garrisons. Manila, the chief city of the islands, was surrounded on the land by the Philippine rebels; Dewey's fleet blockaded the city by sea. To the authorities in Washington, Dewey reported that Aguinaldo's military progress was "wonderful," his treatment of Spanish prisoners most humane.[34]

Not all Americans, however, looked on these events with favor. Writing Roosevelt, Lodge made slighting reference to Bradford's anti-imperialist meeting, but the *New York Sun* came down with full force on what it called "Treachery in Boston." Citing the news report about the Boston merchant who remarked "that he believed it would be best for us, though he should hate to have it occur, to suffer defeat in the battle in Cuba," the *Sun* exclaimed, "Opposition to so-called 'imperialism' is usually only a cover for . . . disloyalty."[35]

In the case of Aguinaldo and his declaration of Philippine independence, General Merritt's attitude was altogether negative. On June 10 the Mayor and prominent citizens of San Francisco feted Merritt before he sailed with his troops for the Philippines. Responding to a toast in his honor, Merritt said that the success of American soldiers in the Philippines could not be doubted and that territory acquired by the United States should not be relinquished. What the Navy had won, the Army would hold. Fresh from his White House conferences, the General revealed himself as an adherent of what Senator Lodge called "the whole policy." To hearty applause he proclaimed, "I believe in the new national policy of the United States which looks to the acquisition of additional territory, represented in outlying islands that are requisite for the development of national strength and growth."[36]

Early in June the circuit from industrial establishment to civil government to military machine and back again was made complete when Senator Lodge received a letter from a friend in Massachusetts who wrote, "The big mill-owners see pecuniary advantage to themselves in empire. That settles the question for them."[37]

At the end of the month the *American Wool and Cotton Reporter* spelled it out. Emphasizing the fact, so crucial to Massachusetts industry, that cotton cloth was the largest item of United States export to China, the editor pointed out that this trade had increased from $3,854,146 in 1896 to $7,438,703 in 1897. (Showing like increase was the second largest export to China, mineral oils, product of the Standard Oil trust.) * A policy of friendship with imperial Britain was important in relation to the Chinese market because "England understands the commercial value of a policy of equal rights to everybody. But it remains to be demonstrated that the same can be said of Russia, Germany, and France." Annexation of the Philippines was important because "the contingencies of our China trade bid fair to be such as to make the Philippines exceedingly valuable to us as a basis for operations against the continent of China." In effect the Boston industrial journal proposed the seizure of the Philippine Islands as the power base from which the United States could best carry out what became known as the Open Door policy toward China, in league with her new ally, Great Britain.[38]

The war with Spain thus promised to bring a new issue before the people of Massachusetts and the country as a whole: the conquest of the Philippines. This was something of a popular surprise, since the Administration had declared the purpose of the war to be the liberation of Cuba. Although this other goal does not appear to have figured in the Administration's first reckonings about a war with Spain, it evidently became a matter of policy before the conflict began.

In a history of the Philippine question he later prepared for the Anti-Imperialist League, Erving Winslow wrote,

> The . . . conclusion must be that the Administration had entertained the design of a permanent conquest of the Philippines as early as the late winter of 1897-1898, when the situation in China and the situation in Cuba combined to direct the thoughts of statesmen to the possibilities of a war with Spain.[39]

Then the powerful economic, political and military forces that fostered the Spanish War came to see it not only as a means of strength-

---

* The *Springfield Republican* of March 22, 1899, pointed to this monopoly as a source of imperialist policy, writing, "It is a rare day when 'Standard oil interests,' are not deep in some mid-asian scheme which is to revivify and enrich some drooping speculation."

ening United States hegemony in the Western Hemisphere, but also as a way to better America's imperial position in Asia, especially in relation to the Chinese market. It was the Caribbean and Pacific colonies of the decrepit Spanish rival that furnished the stimulating opportunities.

But even as the McKinley Administration prepared to take advantage of these possibilities, elements of opposition in the United States and the Philippines began to muster to block the growth of American empire. American anti-imperialism and the movement for Philippine liberation began to run their parallel and inter-related courses.

6

Aging Abolitionists, Rejuvenated Racism

McKinley declared the Spanish War to be a humanitarian crusade, but many Bostonians who led the fight against it had participated in the anti-slavery struggle, and for them the nation's high pretensions abroad tended to throw a harsh light on the worsening conditions of the black people at home. Their anti-slavery training also heightened their antagonism toward the new foreign policy, which showed unmistakable features of white supremacy. The imperialist posture, in attitude and ideology as well as in practice, stimulated white racism. All this was soon to become evident under the impact of the war.

The war with Spain in the Caribbean was over almost as quickly as it was in the Pacific. An American expeditionary force arrived in Cuba on June 20 and ten days later began its march on Santiago, for the Spanish fleet lay in the harbor of this city, and its destruction was the main objective of the American effort. July 1 the United States army scored victories over the Spanish at San Juan Hill and El Caney, the heights commanding Santiago. July 3 the American naval force blockading Santiago destroyed the Spanish fleet, and the Cuban war was over.

In its very first days some black soldiers of the United States Army were put in charge of Spanish prisoners being sent by train from Tampa, Florida to Atlanta, Georgia. In Macon, Georgia, the evening paper protested against black soldiers being used to guard white prisoners, and some white ladies of the city sympathized so keenly with the Spanish prisoners because they were in the charge of black Americans that they went to the train and distributed flowers among them.

When the editor of the *Boston Evening Transcript* heard of this episode he wrote that what happened at Macon was "colorphobia amounting to disloyalty." Pointing to the illiteracy of Southern blacks and to recent legislation denying them the vote, he warned lest a crusade against ignorance and oppression abroad lead to their neglect at home.[1] The editor's indignation came naturally, for of all the white anti-imperialists in Boston the *Transcript*'s Edward H. Clement was one of those most concerned as the plight of the American black reached its nadir in the days of William McKinley. Born in Chelsea just outside of Boston, Clement grew up in the heady atmosphere of the anti-slavery struggle before the Civil War. Influenced by the ideas of Wendell Phillips and his fellow abolitionists, Clement had gone South, after graduating from Tufts College in 1864, to aid in the cause of the freedmen (his parents, with two sons already in the service, having forbidden him to volunteer as he had wished). Entering Savannah, Georgia, in the wake of Sherman's army, he became editor of that city's daily paper, using his editorial columns to further black equality. When Reconstruction collapsed, white supremacists forced Clement out of the paper and he returned North, eventually to become editor of the *Transcript*, where he again used his pen in defense of black rights.[2]

In the middle of July, the *Transcript* carried the story of a Southern officer, "not a negro lover," as he would have it, who went so far as to say that at Las Guasimas near Santiago, "If it had not been for the negro cavalry, the Rough Riders would have been exterminated, the negroes saved that fight."* According to most accounts the black soldiers performed creditably on the field of battle in the Spanish War, despite mounting discriminations at home. A contrary opinion was registered by the Colonel of the Rough Riders, Theodore Roosevelt. Although this zealous imperialist had spoken favorably of the black troops on more than one occasion, in print he took another tack. Several months after the war's conclusion Roosevelt wrote in a magazine article (later a chapter of his book on the Rough Riders) that in the fighting at San Juan Hill "none of the white regulars or Rough Riders showed signs of weakening; but under the strain the

---

* The *Transcript* did not capitalize the word Negro until 1900, when it was the first paper in the country to do so. (Rayford W. Logan, *The Betrayal of the Negro*, Collier Books, New York, 1967, p. 220.)

colored infantrymen . . . began to get a little uneasy and drift to the rear." Whereupon, wrote Roosevelt, he had drawn his pistol and threatened to shoot them if they did not return to the front; then the black soldiers "had flashed their white teeth at one another, as they broke into broad grins, and I had no more trouble with them." According to another participant, when this incident took place it had been explained to Roosevelt that the black soldiers had been returning to the rear under orders to bring up rations and entrenching tools, and the next day he had expressed regret for his harsh language. But his recollections on paper were more satisfying to the racists.[3]

Integral to Roosevelt's imperialist point of view was his sense of white, Anglo-Saxon superiority. He gave this further vent in the same article, when he wrote that black soldiers were "of course peculiarly dependent upon their white officers." Here Roosevelt collided sharply with Boston's militant black minister, Rev. W. H. Scott. Before Roosevelt's article appeared Scott had used the letter columns of the *Transcript* to condemn "Anglo-Saxon race prejudice" in the United States Army, which, he charged, prevented the appointment of black officers. Scott said that black soldiers wanted black officers, from colonel to second lieutenant. He called on whites to remember the blood shed by black troops around Santiago and to do them justice.* While many white papers cast doubt on the ability of the blacks to make good officers, the *Transcript*'s Clement supported Scott editorially, expressing confidence that "the time will come when the courage and devotion of the colored soldier will open to him the same chances that his white brother possesses."[4]

The role and treatment of black soldiers evoked debate over white supremacy, but the issue of white racism came most sharply to the fore as a result of Washington's goals in the Spanish-American War. In both the Philippines and Hawaii there were blacks, and the overwhelming bulk of the population was composed of darker peoples. In Puerto Rico and Cuba a large proportion of the population was black. It was just these islands that the imperialists wanted to annex (or in the case of Cuba, at least to bring under American influence). The United States was, in fact, in the process of building an empire

---

* Scott did not give up on this fight, denouncing army discrimination against black officers in the Philippine War as well. (*Boston Globe*, August 16, 1900.)

of black subjects.⁵ The effort to achieve this goal gave new impetus to white supremacy in the United States and further convinced Boston anti-imperialists that the country was headed in the wrong direction.

Early in May, as the President moved to send troops to the Philippines, he displayed a related initiative on the Hawaiian question. On May 5 the *Transcript* reported that McKinley felt Hawaiian annexation to be necessary as a war measure, and had begun to call in Senators and Congressmen to persuade them of this. Since Spain's military resistance in the Pacific had been rendered hopeless by Dewey's destruction of her fleet, the Hawaiian islands now seemed to have military necessity only "as part of future colonizing schemes, and as a base for carrying out imperial policy." The *Transcript*'s Washington correspondent was quick to point this out.⁶

Administration pressure for Hawaiian annexation put Massachusetts senior Senator, the Republican George Frisbie Hoar, in a dilemma. Hoar was caught between his conscience which had been formed in the anti-slavery struggle and his Republican partisanship which had hardened in the post-Civil War decades. He solved this problem in characteristic fashion. He declared that if Hawaii was to be the first step toward "the acquisition of dominion over barbarous archipelagoes in distant seas" or "competition with the powers of Europe in the plundering of China" it should be resisted "to the death." Having offered this bold defiance, he immediately declared himself "satisfied, after hearing and weighing all the arguments and much meditating this thing that all this is needless alarm"; he would support the Administration request.

Hoar also grasped at racist reinforcement. Hawaii, the Senator decided, came to the United States as the result of years of work by Yankee missionaries; as for the island's population and their wishes, "It would be as reasonable to take the vote of children in an orphan asylum or an idiot school." The Hawaiian government and "dusky Queen" were "things of the past," like Cleveland, Blount and their Mugwump followers.⁷

On July 7 the McKinley Administration annexed Hawaii. Despite the pressure it was able to engender in the war atmosphere, the Administration feared to risk a two-thirds vote in the Senate that a treaty of annexation would entail. Instead Hawaii was annexed by joint resolution requiring a simple majority in both houses.

Puerto Rico fell to the United States shortly after Hawaii's annexation. With Spanish resistance in Cuba smashed early in July, the Administration turned its attention to this neighboring colony. On July 25 the United States army occupied Puerto Rico, meeting with only token opposition. For all practical purposes the war with Spain was over, and the next day the Spanish government sued for peace. On July 30 the McKinley Cabinet decided on preliminary peace terms which included the surrender of Puerto Rico to the United States, and Madrid agreed.

Meanwhile in Puerto Rico, "American investors followed swiftly after American soldiers, and it was estimated by one on the ground that at least three hundred of this class were in the province of Ponce alone before the details of evacuation had been completed." Annexation may have pleased investors, but it angered Massachusetts anti-imperialists. Moorfield Storey spoke for them in a letter to the *Herald*. Calling to mind the Congressional pledge of independence to Cuba, he asked: "Do these words, these solemn promises, mean nothing? To say that we mean only Cuba, and no other territory of Spain, is to construe a great public document as if it were a criminal indictment." He concluded that if we were to take Puerto Rico "not by will of its citizens, by grant from Spain . . . one oppressor succeeds another, and the people whose liberties we interfered to defend are not consulted by either."[8]

The argument was unanswerable in the light of the traditional democratic principles of majority rule and self-determination of nations. The imperialists did not attempt to answer it on these grounds. They retreated to white racism, the legacy of the defeated slave-owners.

The July issue of the *Textile Record* gave voice to the new rationale in rough outline when it explained that the real basis for building an American empire lay in these premises:

> Supremacy in the world appears to be the destiny of the race to which we belong . . . the most competent governor of inferior races . . . the clear path of duty for us appears to be to bring to the people of the Spanish islands in the Pacific and the Atlantic an opportunity to rise from misery and hopelessness to a promise of just government and commercial success.[9]

Slave-holding doctrine was thus renewed, freshened up with Puritan cant about duty, and extended to the world at large. Apparently conservative newspapers were accurate in attributing to the Spanish War and foreign expansion the final reconciliation of the former Confederate states with those that had supported the Union.

If imperialism abroad bolstered white supremacy at home, Edward H. Clement believed the reverse to be equally true: white supremacy at home was an aid to imperial expansion abroad. On July 15 the *Transcript*'s editor complained bitterly about a United States Supreme Court decision denying a black challenge to the new Mississippi constitution, which was framed expressly to bar blacks from voting. Clement charged that the Supreme Court made the decision "as if to provide for the very contingency of the annexation of masses of population unfit to participate in the ancient rights and duties of citizenship."[10] (Clement appeared to question the fitness of the Philippine people to participate in the government of the United States, even while he insisted on their right and ability to govern themselves. This contradiction was typical of much white anti-imperialist thinking. It indicated a lack of consistency, even though many who thought thus were among the most thorough-going opponents of racism at the time.)

The close relationship of white chauvinist ideology to imperialist practice was underscored in the next expansionist move of the Administration, involving the Philippine Islands. From Madrid's diplomatic correspondence with Washington just after Dewey's victory at Manila Bay, the McKinley Administration had understood that the Spaniards were anxious to have the Americans complete the conquest of Luzon. "It was the only hope the beleaguered whites had of salvation from the bloodthirst and rapacity of Aguinaldo's barbarian hordes," as a member of the Admnistration explained it.[11] Accordingly Washington rushed troops to Manila, while Madrid put the Spanish command in that city under orders to surrender only to the United States.

Since the Philippine revolt against Spanish rule took the form of a struggle against white domination, the sympathy of the United States imperialists with Spain's desire to maintain white supremacy in those islands quickly brought the former belligerents together in a common front against what both saw as a threat to white imperialist rule from a colored people.* The surrender and occupation of Manila, the Philippine capital, was the issue immediately at stake.

Military pressure of the Philippine insurgents against the Spanish in Manila at the end of June made their challenge even sharper than in May. On June 21 a dispatch to the *Transcript* described the Administration's reaction: Washington was confident that Augustin (the Spanish commander at Manila) would hold out till a sufficient force of United States troops arrived, so that he could surrender to the Americans instead of the insurgents. "We should then take possession of Manila, and constructively of the whole Philippine group, establish a military government and await further events, the insurgents being given their choice between submitting to our authority peacefully or by compulsion." To achieve these ends the authorities were doing everything possible to bolster Merritt's expedition, even to the extent of drawing upon men and material needed for operations against Cuba and Puerto Rico.[12]

By the middle of July it had become clear to the Spanish at Manila that they could expect no reinforcements from the mother country. Dewey knew that Merritt's arrival with a strong force was only some ten days away and initiated discussions with Augustin through the Belgian Consul at Manila, André. Augustin soon notified Madrid that the situation was hopeless and was fired. But Augustin's successor, Jaudenes, continued to negotiate with Dewey.[13]

It was evident at once that the Spanish and American negotiators both wanted to keep the Filipinos out of Manila, and they discussed this objective in unmistakably racist terms. Dewey had taken over from the Spanish their contemptuous manner of referring to the dark-skinned Filipinos as "Indians," and early in the negotiations he told André that the Americans "would enter the city and keep the Indians out." Using, like Dewey, a derogatory tone toward the Filipinos, General Merritt (who arrived at Manila on July 25) made plain that Dewey's position reflected the attitude of United States policy makers. He told André that he had come with orders not to treat with the "Indians," not to recognize them, and not to promise them anything. "Aguinaldo is just the same to me," he said, "as a boy in the street." Similarly André got from Jaudenes the vehement as-

---

* Madrid was specially influenced, perhaps, by concern for the security of the land holdings of the Spanish clergy under possible insurgent government.

surance that "For himself, he was willing to surrender to white people, but never to niggers."[14]

In return for the American promise to keep Aguinaldo and his followers out of Manila, the Spanish agreed to surrender the city to the United States armed forces. Profiting from Augustin's experience, however, Jaudenes insisted upon making a show of resistance to appease the fire-eaters in Madrid. Once agreement had been reached, the main concern of both parties became how to keep Aguinaldo and his troops out of Manila in the process of its occupation by the Americans. The Spaniards weakened their forces on the Malate front facing the American troops in order to reinforce the fronts to the north and east against the insurgents, and the United States command plainly warned Aguinaldo that its troops would fire on the Filipinos should the latter attempt to enter the city.[15]

The United States thus turned from cooperation with the insurgents to destroy Spanish rule to cooperation with the Spanish against the insurgents to reassert white supremacy under American hegemony. The exclusion of the Filipino insurgents from the occupation of Manila was the first step toward this end.

The use of force against the Philippine insurgents at Manila was endorsed by President McKinley. A few days after the Spanish surrender Merritt and Dewey reported to Washington that the insurgent demanded joint occupation of the city, and asked how far to "proceed in forcing obedience of the insurgents in this matter and others that may arise." The President immediately replied: "Use any means in your judgement necessary to this end." A week earlier, the *Boston Herald* had reported from Washington that McKinley had become "an enthusiastic imperialist." The President's reluctance over the prospect of war had vanished; perhaps the fact that "Aguinaldo's barbarian hordes," rather than the army and navy of a white rival, loomed as the antagonist was a factor.[16]

The occupation of Manila by the United States inaugurated a new stage in American relations with the insurgents, making it possible for the McKinley Administration to "establish a military government and await further events." To the United States command it appeared that the insurgents understood the change in American attitude and reacted sharply to it. On August 16 General Anderson, who had been negotiating for some time with the Filipinos, noted their "astonishing" change from what he termed "reasonable" to "aggressive" demands and felt that the change could "only be accounted for on the theory that Aguinaldo and his councellors [sic] plainly perceived . . . that we intended to hold the Philippines under our military rule."[17] United States-insurgent relations entered a period of latent hostility on both sides.

On August 12 General Merritt sent Aguinaldo the ultimatum denying the Philippine insurgents access to their principal city, and on the same day in Honolulu, another capital, American representatives lowered the Hawaiian flag that flew over the government buildings and raised that of the United States, in a ceremony marking the end of Hawaiian independence. While occupying Manila and moving a step nearer the annexation of the Philippines, the United States completed the annexation of Hawaii.

The Spanish-American agreement to arrange the surrender of Manila at the expense of the Philippine insurgents did not become public knowledge till some time after the event, but the heavy racist thrust of United States imperialism in Hawaii was immediately apparent, and drew corresponding response from Massachusetts anti-imperialists. The *Springfield Republican* ran a story on the ceremony of the flags at Honolulu based on an account published in the *New York Sun,* which, the *Republican* asserted, could not be suspected of "prejudice in favor of the natives." The *Sun* related that on this day Hawaiians remained in their homes behind closed doors and shuttered windows, so that at the ceremony there were Americans, Portuguese, Japanese and Chinese, but hardly any Hawaiians. There were only six on the platform; one was a lawyer who came for business reasons; another was his wife who came "because he required her to." The latter bore up very well until the band played the Hawaiian national anthem; then she broke down in tears. The other Hawaiians "who were forced to be there" covered their eyes when their country's flag was pulled down, and many wept. The Hawaiian members of the band, when it came to playing the national anthem, "threw away their instruments and fled," and only ten men, none of them Hawaiians, were left to provide the music, with poor results. The imperialist-minded *Sun* summed up the affair: "It was but another roll of the Juggernaut car in which the lordly Anglo-Saxon rides to his dream of universal empire." And the *Springfield Republican* added bitterly, " . . . what matter the victims whose consent was lacking? Are they not poor, feeble, dark-skinned child-like persons, unworthy of lordly

Anglo-Saxon recognition?" Of the Hawaiians' grief at the loss of their national independence Clement wrote at Boston, " . . . they will soon get over it, as the slave-traders used to say of the black mothers when they sold their children away from them."[18]

Although the country's best known black, Booker T. Washington, generally made it a policy to avoid anything that could be construed as a political challenge to the *status quo,* late in August, at the invitation of Charles Eliot Norton, he addressed a public gathering in Ashfield, Massachusetts, the latter's summer place of residence. There Washington came forward to condemn the annexation of Hawaii. His remarks took on an unusually sharp tone as he punctured the pious pretensions of defenders of the Administration like Senator Hoar. "We went," said he, "to the Sandwich Islands with the Bible and prayerbook in our hands to win the souls of the natives; we ended by taking their country without giving them the privilege of saying yea or nay," and he reminded Americans that Spain, in building empire, had left her own subjects in misery and ignorance.[19]

Applauding Washington's speech in the editorial columns of the *Transcript,* Clement drew attention to the exploitation of dark-skinned peoples which provided the economic backdrop for the ideas of white supremacy then gaining ground and he promised retribution:

> For all the heaped up millions of dollars to be coined by American syndicates out of the blood and sweat of underpaid toil of subject races in tropical islands, an accounting will be exacted in some such harvest of evil as Spain has reaped after centuries of wrong.[20]

7

The New England Anti-Imperialist League

Two events led up to the organization of the New England Anti-Imperialist League: the adoption by the Massachusetts Reform Club of an anti-imperialist position and the public avowal by the McKinley Administration of its intent to annex the Philippines.

Before summer adjournment the Executive Committee of the Massachusetts Reform Club split over whether or not to hold a meeting against imperialism. It was decided to poll the members, and the result was that the first meeting of the fall was given over to opposition to current foreign policy, with Patrick A. Collins making the main address. Since Collins was an outstanding leader of the Democratic Party, his appearance at the Reform Club meant that a step had been taken toward the establishment of the unity between anti-imperialists and Democrats that Bradford urged. After hearing Collins, the club set up a committee to further anti-imperialist organization and appropriated funds for printing literature "pointing to the fallacy of acquiring the Philippines."[1]

If the opposition to anti-imperialism by a minority in the Massachusetts Reform Club indicated the need for a new organization, the Club's adoption of an anti-imperialist position put a solid and established base under the efforts of those who had gathered at Faneuil Hall. Now the anti-imperialist come-outers could proceed to organize with a secure footing among Boston middle class reformers.

The second event did not come about in such a straightforward manner. The McKinley Administration led up to its declaration of intent to annex the Philippine archipelago as a whole by suggesting that it did not intend to annex the Philippine archipelago as a whole. The public was misled as to the government's purposes.

Toward the summer's end McKinley laid the political groundwork for annexation at Washington, just as Merritt and Dewey, under the President's direction, had made military preparations to this end at Manila. After her defeat, Spain, on August 12, agreed to the terms proposed by the McKinley Administration: independence for Cuba, United States annexation of Puerto Rico and an island in the Ladrones, the American military occupation of Manila pending the disposition of the Philippines by peace treaty negotiations. This left the question of the Philippine Islands, chief prize of the Spanish War, the outstanding matter before the treaty meeting to be held in Paris in the fall. For these negotiations McKinley selected a commission of five members, three of whom were known to be expansionists favorable to annexation, Senators Davis and Frye, and Whitelaw Reid, owner of the New York *Tribune*. William N. Day, McKinley's retiring Secretary of State, would speak for the Administration as chairman of the commission, and Senator Gray, the Delaware Democrat, was an anti-expansionist.[2]

At mid-September McKinley called the commissioners to the White House before they left for Paris to take up their duties. In conference the President presented the surface of indecision and pliability that had become the hallmark of his tactical style. He told the commissioners that he thought the United States could not possibly give up Manila, and doubted the wisdom of attempting to hold it without the entire island of Luzon to which it belonged; beyond this he did not seem inclined to go. He did suggest that, after the commissioners had heard from General Merritt and Admiral Dewey, they might find it necessary for the safety of Luzon to acquire some of the smaller islands near it.[3]

But Robert Lincoln O'Brien, Washington correspondent of the *Boston Evening Transcript,* put no faith in McKinley's declarations at this point, and O'Brien was well placed to know. Before joining the *Transcript*'s staff O'Brien had been one of President Cleveland's personal secretaries; he was favorably regarded by President McKinley and his standing in the White House gave him advantages possessed by few Washington correspondents.[4] On September 17, the day after McKinley's conference with his peace commissioners, O'Brien wrote his paper that, contrary to the effort of the Administration to make it appear that the instructions to the Peace Commissioners were to claim only Luzon, "your correspondent is in a position to assert with assurance that this Government has its eye fixed at the present moment on the whole Philippine group . . . That . . . was determined upon a good while ago."

According to O'Brien the reason for this decision was plain: if the United States took only Luzon, Germany would take Palawan, the next most desirable island from the standpoint of trade, and that "would seriously embarrass us." There was basis for this belief. After Dewey's defeat of the Spanish fleet, Germany had sent, from her base at Kiaochow Bay, a naval aquadron into Manila harbor. The provocative behavior of this strong naval force toward Dewey's lesser one had made imperial Germany's Philippine cravings very clear.[5]

Perhaps the explanation of the discrepancy between the Administration's public declaration and O'Brien's claims lay in the fact that November was to see a Congressional elections take place. For McKinley to minimize his annexationist demands at the moment, therefore, would tend to minimize the anti-imperialist criticism of his administration that the elections were bound to bring out. In the meantime the President left the final decision for the acquisition of the whole archipelago quite securely in the hands of Day and the three expansionists on the commission, even directing them to give special consideration to the testimony of General Merritt, whose annexationist views were a matter of public record.

It remained for McKinley to put a gloss of popular approval on a decision already taken at a higher level. About a month after his conference with the peace commissioners the President made a Western tour. When in his speeches he broadly suggested the annexation of the Philippines, the crowds that turned out to hear him applauded. The decision to annex the Philippines was promoted as a result of popular demand rather than imperialist calculation. Charles Emory Smith, the President's close advisor at the time, would have none of this. He wrote of the President's Western tour, "What is much nearer the truth is that he led public sentiment quite as much as public sentiment led him, and the popular manifestations on that journey were in response to the keynotes he struck."[6]

The peace commissioners, after their arrival in Paris, followed the President's instructions and held hearings on the moot question before them. Of the two men whose testimony the President had specially recommended only Merritt appeared; Dewey sent a message, but remained in the Philippines. The General showed concern for

Americans with capital to invest and goods to sell, remarking that "our interests in the East would be helped by the cheap labor in the Philippines, costing only 20 to 80 cents a day according to skill," and that "if we took Luzon alone and powerful European countries got other islands the trade would be deflected from Manila." It was on these grounds that he told the commissioners that he favored taking the Philippine archipelago as a whole. (On this key issue, Dewey's message was disappointingly evasive, and Merritt confided his belief that Dewey did not commit himself because of presidential ambitions.)[7]

The General denied that the United States had made any binding commitments to the Philippine insurgents; in fact both Dewey and he had "kept clear of any compromising communications." Contradicting Dewey's tribute to the insurgents' humane treatment of Spanish prisoners, Merritt said that "insurgents would murder Spaniards and priests and destroy their property if the United States withdrew." In effect he urged upon the commissioners the racial and social preferences he had expressed during the negotiations for the surrender of Manila.

When Senator Davis brought up the question of insurgent opposition to a United States takeover, Merritt answered that "Aguinaldo and his immediate followers would resist it, but his forces are divided and his opposition would not amount to anything." The same problem worried Day, and Merritt gave the same reply, " . . . natives could not resist 5,000 troops."[8] (In the first week of August Merritt had requested that his command be increased from 20,000 to 50,000 men to meet the insurgent threat.[9] But when it came time to bolster the commissioners, 5,000 troops would do the job.) Thus the press reported that "in an official manner, the United States commissioners . . . satisfied themselves that the difficulties in the way of annexation, so far as they might be expected to depend upon the will of the natives, [had] been very much exaggerated," and "one of the most disturbing elements" was "removed as a factor in the calculations."[10]

Especially reinforced by what Merritt had told them, the commission majority wired Washington October 25 asking that their instructions be broadened to include a demand upon Spain for all the Philippine Islands. The next day Secretary of State Hay wired back that, as a result of "information which has come to the President since your departure," the latter agreed to the demand for the whole archipelago, and on October 31 the papers carried the news.[11]

According to Postmaster General Smith the information that the President received "came to him from the officers in command," in other words, the very testimony that Merritt brought to Paris. But McKinley declared that the decision to annex the Philippines came to him from "God Almighty," after he had spent several sleepless nights on his knees praying for guidance. Upon receiving this revelation (which included, according to the President, points about Philippine unfitness for self-government, the United States civilizing mission and the danger of German commercial rivalry) he had gone to bed and slept soundly.* Then the next morning the Chief Executive had sent for the government map-maker and told him "to put the Philippines on the map of the United States."[12]

So, eight days before the voting, the Administration revealed its Philippine decision. Meantime the election campaign had all but run its course. The Massachusetts Democrats in their state convention on October 4 took a stand of "uncompromising opposition to imperialism," and Henry Lloyd, of the Boston Central Labor Union, who was nominated for Secretary of State on the Democratic ticket, spoke out vigorously against the annexation of the Philippines and the threat of cheap colonial labor to Massachusetts workers.[13]

The Republicans, on the other hand, took advantage of the stance of delay and deferment assumed by the McKinley Administration to parry the Democrats' thrust and avoid confrontation on the Philippine issue. Lodge told delegates to the Republican state convention on October 6 that while former Spanish colonies must not be turned back to Spain, future policy in the East would have to be decided in the future, and the convention "seemed perfectly content to do as the speaker advised and leave the matter to be decided by the commissioners now sitting in Paris." But Congressman W. H. Moody expressed considerations that lay below the surface at the convention. He declared that Massachusetts wage and hour legislation put

---

* More recently President Johnson sought divine aid in carrying out the Vietnam War. Fearful that United States bombing raids on North Vietnam might accidentally trigger off World War III, late one night in June 1966 he spent half an hour on his knees in prayer. President Johnson woke the next morning "feeling refreshed and renewed"; the bombing raid had been successful; World War III had not started. (*Boston Globe*, May 13, 1967.)

the industries of the state in an unprofitable competitive position in relation to other sections of the country, especially the South, where labor was cheap and hours long. He urged Massachusetts industrialists to make up for their losses on the home market "by seizing new markets abroad." Even while saying this, however, Moody was "inclined to be diplomatic in his treatment of the Philippine problem." In this evasive Republican atmosphere, Senator Hoar called for self-government for the Philippines under the auspices of the United States, and did this in such a way that the *Springfield Republican* claimed Hoar and his speech for the anti-imperialists, while McKinley's cabinet member Smith did the same for the imperialist side.[14]

The announcement of McKinley's Philippine decision caused agitation among Boston anti-imperialists and they belatedly injected themselves into the campaign. On November 7, election day, the *Transcript* carried an advertisement signed by eighteen of them (including Adams, Atkinson, McNeill and Winslow) who called upon the voters to reject all candidates supporting Philippine annexation in favor of those opposed to "this new and dangerous policy."[15]

Anti-imperialists took what comfort they could from the election results in Massachusetts. All Republican Congressional candidates won save three. In Boston the Democratic John F. Fitzgerald, who had expressed anti-imperialist sentiments, was returned to Congress. The Republicans lost the seats of two incumbents, Walker of Worcester and Barrows of Boston. The defeat of Barrows by Henry F. Naphen of South Boston was particularly pleasing to the anti-imperialists, since Naphen had made Barrows' support of McKinley's foreign policy the brunt of attack. The *Springfield Republican* noted that the combined majority of all the state's Republican congressional candidates ran behind that amassed by Wolcott, the successful Republican gubernatorial candidate, by some 30,000 votes. In this discrepancy the paper saw disenchantment with the national policies of the McKinley Administration.[16]

The publication of the United States demand upon Spain for the Philippine Islands engendered more than momentary electioneering on the part of the Boston anti-imperialists. It crystallized their determination to set up a separate and distinct organization that would carry on a sustained, nation-wide campaign against the imperialist program now made explicit. The committee formed in September by the Massachusetts Reform Club had joined with the committee established in June by the Faneuil Hall meeting, and together they decided to initiate an anti-imperialist society. Meetings for this purpose took place November 18 and two days following in the offices of Edward Atkinson. A "score of gentlemen" attended.[17]

Charles Francis Adams found the proceedings "pretty dreary and discouraging." Indeed, those present were faced with the heavy task of overturning national policies that had the support of powerful business interests and considerable popular endorsement. Despite the difficulties of the prospect, they went to work and established what turned out to be a simple but effective body. They chose the Lincoln appointee and former Massachusetts Governor, George S. Boutwell to be president, the Union Army general, Francis A. Osborn, treasurer, and Erving Winslow, secretary. A long list of vice presidents was named, including the steel magnate, Andrew Carnegie, who sent in a check for $1,000, and labor leader, Samuel Gompers, who had spoken against the Spanish War before its outbreak.* All those who sent in their names to Boston headquarters were to be enrolled as members, and membership meetings were to be held at least once a year. However, the key to the organization, from the very first, was an executive committee of some ten members who met twice a week and were responsible for the work.

As the first activity of the New England Anti-Imperialist League, its organizers proposed a petition against annexation to be circulated nationally and presented to authorities in Washington. In addition, the group decided to canvass the nation's newspapers with an anti-imperialist information letter modeled on the Civil War broadsides that Edward Atkinson, Charles Eliot Norton and others of the New England Loyal Publication League had issued in the previous crisis.[18]

A few days after these meetings took place Atkinson wrote Lyman Gage, the Midwestern Gold Democrat McKinley had appointed Sec-

---

* Association with the anti-imperialist movement placed very few in a more contradictory position than Andrew Carnegie, as Secretary of State Hay later noted. Remarking that Carnegie predicted the ruin of the United States government as a result of its shooting down insurgent Filipinos, Hay said, "He does not seem to reflect that the Government is in a somewhat robust condition even after shooting down several American citizens in his interest at Homestead." (W. R. Thayer, *Life of John Hay*, Houghton Mifflin Company, Boston and New York, 1915, II, 199.)

retary of the Treasury, that the "leading Labor Reformers, Gompers, McNeill and others are with us . . . Leading Irishman have written . . . The grangers are with us under the lead of Herbert Myrick." The Boston man was quick to tell Gage, who had the ear of the President, that the anti-imperialists planned to set on foot a movement of coalition character, which, if realized, would have significant political impact.[19]

Atkinson added, "We . . . are proceeding very rapidly to organize the whole country," and correspondence was reported, even at the first meetings, with New York, Philadelphia, Baltimore and Chicago, where similar organization was getting under way. From all over the country men who had seen press accounts of the Boston organization wrote in to ask for suggestions for forming branch leagues.[20]

The sentiment of the city's mercantile community provided some encouragement to Boston anti-imperialists as they started to organize. On November 10 the Boston Merchants Association held a largely attended meeting which unanimously resolved "that . . . acquisition of any part of the Philippine Islands, except that which is needed for a naval station, would be detrimental to the interests of the United States."[21]

But the merchants' qualified opposition to McKinley's imperialist policies was set off against wholehearted industrial support, and the accustomed split in the upper-class opinion of Massachusetts was revealed. At the semi-annual meeting of the New England Cotton Manufacturers Association late in September, the president, a Rhode Island industrialist, repeated the support for annexation that textile interests had expressed more than once before.[22]

Two other meetings reflected this division. When the Home Market Club met in November the secretary's report favored independence for the Philippines, but vigorous opposition to this was expressed by Eben and George Draper of the textile machinery firm, by a member from the textile town of Fall River and others. At the Massachusetts Board of Trade on November 23, Atkinson offered a resolution opposing annexation, and a Boston man spoke in defense, but representatives from Fall River and Lynn, the shoe town, opposed, so that the resolution failed to pass.[23]

Senator Lodge expressed the support of Massachusetts shoe manufacturers for Philippine annexation. At their association's banquet, November 16, Lodge "pleased everybody . . . with his sound business views," according to the *Boot and Shoe Recorder*. He told these industrialists that Spain's defeat in the Western Hemisphere would bring the United States vastly increased trade in the Caribbean and South America, while annexation of the Philippines would supply the key to the great China market.

In addition to his customary economic emphasis, Lodge gave voice to that other important theme in the imperialist refrain, the idea of white Anglo-Saxon supremacy, as he paid tribute to "the success of the English-speaking race." It was this "victorious spirit of the race" which, if provided with military support abroad, would soon bring the United States dominion of the world's trade and commerce. Lodge's speech therefore carried with it a process of sublimation whereby the very substantial industrial superiority of the United States among the nations of the world was transformed into "the victorious spirit of the race," something more dubious and shadowy, and the requirements of imperial ideology were fulfilled.[24]

Racism took violent form in the United States around election time. The South experienced one of the worst outbreaks of repression and brutality against the blacks since Civil War days. In Wilmington, North Carolina, following an attempt by some of the black population to run candidates for office, the "best elements" of the local white population organized an armed mob and resorted to violence, murdering a dozen blacks, burning a building housing a black newspaper and driving elected black officials and their white allies out of town in terror for their lives.[25] Then white supremacists followed suit in Greenwood County, South Carolina, where the few blacks not disenfranchised by the new state constitution tried to vote on election day. Before nightfall ten blacks were killed; five lay dead all day long by the roadside, four others were lynched in adjoining woods. The *Springfield Republican* gave account of the tenth to die, a black named Harrison:

> Down the road came a squad of 15 mounted men, with Harrison marching ahead with guns and rifles drawn on him. The 15 men lined up on the roadside. The negro was stationed in the road and told to go forward to the pile of four dead negroes. As he moved there was a ring of rifles and Harrison pitched forward, to pillow his bleeding head on the bosom of those who died ahead of him.[26]

To the *Boston Evening Transcript* these events and the annexationist policy abroad proved that "the lesson of the sacrifices of our civil war has become a vague memory in danger of sinking into utter oblivion." The anti-imperialist *Boston Advertiser* was direct and to the point: "The white man's government of the North Carolina pattern is precisely the government which so-called expansionists hope to put in operation . . . in the Philippines." A Southern paper of imperialist sympathies, the *Memphis Commercial Appeal,* agreed with the contention of its Northern anti-imperialist counterpart, declaring, "How are we going to govern the Philippines, Hawaii, and other new possessions? Peaceably if we can; or like the white men are doing in the Carolinas, if we must, but govern them we will." Quoting this from the Memphis paper, the *Springfield Republican* added, "Ah, No tabbycat platitudes about the blessings of democracy in that!" Scorning annexationist claims to democracy and benevolence, Massachusetts anti-imperialists cautioned their fellow-citizens that the violent oppression of the blacks in the South was a foretaste of what United States imperialists had in store for the Philippine people.[27]

What happened at the Paris treaty negotiations in the first week of December seemed to corroborate this. After the Spanish had submitted to the United States demand for the Philippines, the American commissioners turned to lesser matters, including the disposition of Spanish war materiel in the islands. Major Strother, the staff officer to whom General Merritt referred the commissioners for opinion on this question, was opposed to giving over to the Spaniards both the heavy artillery emplaced in fortifications at Manila and other important places and the heavy Spanish field artillery. The latter, he said, "would be especially necessary in the Philippines, and necessary at once, provided the insurgents became troublesome."[28]

The Spanish, however, complained of harsh treatment and did not want to give up either type of artillery. Judge Day wished to avoid a breach at this point and suggested that they accede in the matter of heavy field artillery, and they agreed. Then, speaking of the artillery in fortified places, Senator Frye remarked, "We have some disquieting late subjects largely belonging to Spain called Tagalogs. Would the Spanish Commissioners consent that these guns should remain in their present position for six months?" The leader of the Spanish delegation replied that "he did not think this remark in place here. We were engaged in making a treaty, not conducting a campaign."[29]

Nevertheless, the treaty contained the provision that "pieces of heavy ordnance, exclusive of field artillery, in the fortifications and coast defenses shall remain in the emplacements for the term of six months," and gave the United States the right of purchase.[30] The United States, with the help of its defeated rival, prepared to rule the Philippines as white men ruled the Carolinas.

The anti-imperialists of Massachusetts organized and gave warning.

8

Opposition to the Treaty

A week after the November elections Senator Hoar wrote his Republican colleague from Maine, Senator Hale. Anxious to know what Democratic support there would be in the Senate for men like Hale and himself who opposed holding the Philippines, Hoar suggested that Hale ask Gorman, the Democratic leader in the Senate, with whom he was on intimate terms. At the end of November Hale wrote back that Gorman thought that not more than four Democratic Senators would vote for the treaty. This information gave Hoar great hopes for the defeat of the treaty, if only the Democratic party would stand fast.[1]

Hale urged his Massachusetts friend's early return to Washington so that he could see the President before the latter got up his annual message to Congress. Back in Washington Hoar did meet McKinley, who, upon greeting the Senator, took him affectionately by the hand and said, "How are you feeling this winter, Mr. Senator?" Determined that there be no misunderstanding, Hoar replied, "Pretty pugnacious, I confess, Mr. President." The tears came into McKinley's eyes, and he said, grasping Hoar's hand again, "I shall always love you, whatever you do."[2]

George Frisbie Hoar, whose suggested disagreement so affected McKinley, was one of the Republican Party's most prestigious figures. Of Puritan and Revolutionary stock, born and raised in the Concord of Emerson and Thoreau, he was exceedingly conscious of these attributes. Nor was he unmindful that his lawyer father, Samuel Hoar, had won national prominence in the 1840's when he went to Charleston, South Carolina, to initiate a constitutional challenge to the slave-holders on their own ground. The threat of a lynch mob had driven Samuel Hoar out of the courts of Charleston and back home, where, some ten years later, he had helped found the Republican Party of Massachusetts as an anti-slavery organization.

Following his father's example, young George Frisbie Hoar had taken part in Free Soil and Republican politics after graduation from Harvard Law School, and he had been elected to the United States Congress in 1868, some years later to the Senate, where he had served ever since. Worcester, where he made his home, was an industrial city and Hoar had gone along with the Republican national leadership in supporting protective tariff legislation to benefit his manufacturing constituency. Among the latter were the Drapers of Hopedale, and the senior partner in the family textile machinery firm, William F. Draper, who had been a Union General, was Hoar's special friend and associate, much as the younger brother Eben was Lodge's.[3] In 1884 Hoar had broken with his Boston anti-slavery friends and supported Blaine. Thereafter, and especially during his recent support for Hawaiian annexation, Boston Mugwumps had been critical of him for putting political expediency above moral rectitude.

Hoar had shown his partisan preoccupation during the November elections when he had written a foreign policy plank for his party's state election platform that had papered over the conflict of opinion in Republican ranks between the supporters and opponents of McKinley's imperial policies. Hoar had desired to avoid a party split, in order to secure the unanimous re-election to the Senate of his fellow Republican from Massachusetts, Henry Cabot Lodge, the arch-imperialist.[4]

But after the elections, as the conflict over the disposition of the Philippines loomed, his Massachusetts associates on both sides of the fence worried about the Senator, whose increasingly frequent declarations against Philippine annexation made the imperialist-minded fear that he would desert party for principle, while the memory of his Hawaiian shuffle made anti-imperialists fear that he would not. Between them they began a struggle for the soul of George Frisbie Hoar.

Early in December William D. Sohier, chairman of the Republican Club of Massachusetts and president of the *Boston Journal,* corresponded with Hoar in an attempt to win Hoar's support for the treaty, and he set forth privately what was later to be the Administration's public answer to those with misgivings: Philippine annexation was to be only a short-term, not a permanent policy. In reply, Hoar affirmed his party loyalty and took a wide swing at Mugwumps "of the Gam Bradford . . . stripe" for having "about as much sense as a chicken partridge who has been hatched five minutes and has the shell on his head." Nonetheless he told the *Journal* president in plain terms that he was opposed to annexation either permanent or temporary.[5]

For their part the editors of the *Boston Evening Transcript* and *Springfield Republican* used their columns to offer Hoar a cautious encouragement in his stand, but Gamaliel Bradford wrote Hoar bluntly what the editors implied. Bradford congratulated Hoar on his anti-annexationist declarations but added that many of the Senator's friends were anxious lest he allow these to be outweighed by what might be urged upon him at Washington. The anti-imperialist leader again spoke for others when he fervently besought Hoar to use his influence in the right direction with his fellow Senators, "We ask you only to vote and act with regard to the Spanish treaty as you think William Bradford and George Washington and Samuel Hoar would have done . . . " This prodding Hoar answered with marked irritation: he didn't require Gamaliel Bradford to remind him whose son he was.[6]

The uneasiness and strain of the Bradford-Hoar exchange proved typical of the Senator's relations with the Mugwump leadership of the anti-imperialist movement, since each wanted what the other could not give: Hoar wanted all anti-imperialists to be thoroughgoing Republicans, and the anti-imperialists wanted Hoar to be a thorough-going supporter of their cause. In contrast to his stand on Hawaii, however, Hoar, after his own fashion, maintained opposition to Philippine annexation throughout the treaty debate and after. He told the *Boston Globe* early in December, "If we take the Philippines under the treaty of peace, the downfall of the American Republic will date from the Administration of William McKinley," and his belief that the Philippine acquisition represented the ultimate commitment of the United States to a policy of imperialism may help explain the change in his behavior. (Of importance to Hoar, as well, perhaps, was the fact that other regular Republicans of the Civil War generation, notably his close associate, William F. Draper, could not support Philippine annexation.)[7]

If President McKinley and his supporters in Massachusetts were disappointed at Hoar's new found obduracy, the Boston anti-imperialists were soon dismayed by a collapse in their line of battle. When their recently acquired ally, William Jennings Bryan, was released from the army on December 13, he took the occasion to reassert his opposition to imperialism, but at the same time, and in the most unexpected manner, to declare for the passage of the Paris treaty, as he spoke to a meeting at Savannah, Georgia. In the South there was considerable support for imperialist policy and this was reflected in the Democratic party of the region. Bryan's Savannah speech tended to conciliate Southern imperialists, and he did not leave the matter at this point, but went at once to Washington to lobby for treaty votes among Democratic and Populist senators.[8]

Massachusetts anti-imperialists had no confidence in Bryan's judgement on this score. The editor of the *Transcript* found Bryan "either insincere or incapable of leading," and noted the endorsement of Bryan's position by the *Memphis Commercial Appeal.* Even more telling than the support Bryan received from this racist and annexationist organ of Southern Democracy was the word from Washington that President McKinley was pleased with Bryan's attitude and now believed ratification assured. Imperialists in both parties were satisfied. "Who wouldn't be," complained the *Springfield Republican,* "at seeing an opponent fall on his own sword."[9]

The New England oppositionists did what they could to offset Bryan's influence and close up the ranks. When the Democratic leader argued that the Philippines could be granted their freedom later, once the treaty was passed, the Boston league mailed out a statement to every member of the Senate and the House of Representatives pointing out that the treaty could be defeated by one-third of the Senate, but that subsequent legislation to free the Philippines would require a majority vote of both houses and the approval of the president; it would be best by far to reject the treaty now.[10]

Senator Hoar heard that Bryan put forward private arguments for ratification that differed from those he offered publicly. Democratic Senators whom Bryan approached and who refused to follow his advice told Hoar that Bryan urged his position on them for partisan reasons: he thought the Democratic Party would gain votes in the elections of 1900 if the Republicans were saddled with the annexation of the Philippines. While Bryan publicly declared treaty ratification would restore peace, privately he told the Silver Republican

"*The downfall of the American Republic will date from the Administration of William McKinley.*" Senator George Frisbie Hoar, leading Republican ally of the anti-imperialist movement.

Senator Pettigrew that the treaty should be passed, then, if the Republicans made war to conquer the Philippines, they would be driven from power.[11]

In this light, Bryan treated the destiny of the Philippine people like a political football in order to woo Southern Democrats and gain political advantage; the President of the United States soon followed his example and made a special effort to solicit the strong imperialist sentiment existing in the former slave-holding states. In the latter part of December McKinley made a tour of the South that antagonized liberal opinion in the Northeast, where it was charged that he took this trip to win votes for the treaty.[12] In Atlanta McKinley proclaimed that "where the American flag has gone up it should never be hauled down," and the *Springfield Republican* denounced this as a "piratical doctrine."[13]

Arriving in Atlanta the President was welcomed by a civic parade from which those in charge had excluded black quarrymen and stonemasons. The white members of the Atlanta Federation of Trades had withdrawn from the parade in protest against this discrimination, and the *Republican* thought that McKinley and Booker T. Washington (who rode in the President's carriage) should have done likewise.[14] Clement of the *Transcript* was dissatisfied that "not in Atlanta, any more than in Washington, has the President ought to say on the race question," but the paper's Washington correspondent explained that those who were closest to him said that McKinley "is as fully convinced of the necessity of white supremacy as are those who have received and entertained him in Montgomery and Savannah during the last fortnight."[15]

The anti-imperialists' criticism of McKinley and Bryan in the month of December was complementary to their effort to mount a popular campaign to defeat the treaty. The Boston League made their petition to the Senate the base of this attempt, and their petition campaign in turn provided a stimulus for Senator Hoar's fight against the treaty on the Senate floor. In the middle of the month Hoar presented the Senate the League's petition with some two thousand signatures attached, ten days later with another three thousand names.[16]

Of the first two thousand names, over two-thirds came from Massachusetts; but the movement started at Boston continued to spread over the country. Bostonians made efforts to reach out — Atkinson, for example, wrote the New York Reform Club, and Dana Estes visited Johns Hopkins at Baltimore. The like-minded elsewhere got in touch with Boston — from Chicago and Detroit came letters asking help in organizing meetings. By the middle of the month the Executive Committee reported league offshoots established in over 30 states. The New England Anti-Imperialist League had won a national reputation; "the kicking Bostonese," a Los Angeles paper called them.[17]

In their effort to diversify and broaden the movement, the anti-imperialists found powerful allies at hand: those agricultural interests fearing potential competition from colonial acquisition. Herbert Myrick, through the columns of his agricultural journals, appealed to these interests with such effect that Senate supporters of the treaty made him the object of personal attack. Well they might, for the domestic producers of sugar beets and sugar cane, tobacco and rice, were a powerful lobby against the treaty.[18] The strongest bloc in opposition was made up of senators from agrarian states in the South and West.*

Following a mailing from the League to all labor bodies in the country, central labor bodies in Boston, Springfield, New York, Philadelphia and the President's own state of Ohio adopted anti-annexation resolutions, and Samuel Gompers put the national convention of the American Federation of Labor on record for the defeat of the treaty.[19]

In Boston Patrick A. Collins spoke against Anglo-Saxon racial supremacy at the Young Men's Democratic Club. Shortly afterwards the Massachusetts Democratic State Committee, largely Irish-American in membership, voted against annexation. An increasing number of Protestant ministers in the city spoke out against expansion, although they remained a minority in their calling. When the black clergy of Boston sponsored a gathering to protest Southern violence, the meeting's chairman declared that the United States could not

---

* Among them Southern Democrats whose racial antipathy to the Filipinos was a feature of their opposition to annexation. Of such Southern Democrats League Secretary Winslow said, " . . . it is interesting to note how frankly Anti-Imperialists in the North, even those who look with disfavor upon the present attitude of some southern Democrats toward their colored fellow-citizens, may cooperate with them in the cause we have at heart." (5th Annual Meeting of the New England Anti-Imperialist League, Boston, 1903, Secretary's Report, p. 9.)

afford to go crusading for democracy in the Philippines eight thousand miles from home, "while the blood of citizens, who came here . . . before the Mayflower, is crying out to God against her from the gutters of Wilmington."[20]

The blacks called for Federal legislation enabling the President to protect the rights of their Southern brothers, but on coming back from the South McKinley set off on quite a different tack. At the end of December the Philippine insurgents had besieged the Spanish forces at Iloilo, the second city of importance in the archipelago. It was understood at Washington that the Spaniards wanted the United States to take possession of the city in order to prevent its occupation by Aguinaldo's troops. Hence McKinley directed the old Indian fighter, General E. S. Otis, who had supplanted General Merritt in command, to send troops to Iloilo to relieve the Spanish. But the troops, led by General Marcus P. Miller, arrived too late. The Spanish had already evacuated Iloilo, and the insurgents occupied the city.[21]

The argument for American occupation of Iloilo was the same as that used at Manila: it was necessary to prevent lawlessness. But the press reported that after the occupation of Iloilo, the insurgents "immediately established a municipal government and placed guard over foreign property." There was some looting at night, but five of those guilty were shot, "which had an exemplary effect on the rest."[22]

The insurgents refused to give permission to the American troops to land in force. So the United States soldiers remained on board ship in the harbor of Iloilo, even after it was clear that they were not needed to "prevent lawlessness." This gave credence to the anti-imperialist charge that the real reason the Administration had sent troops to Iloilo was to check the insurgents and overawe their desire for independence.[23]

As if to make this point perfectly clear the President then cabled General Otis to publish both at Manila and Iloilo a proclamation the Chief Executive had prepared with the assistance of General Merritt, in order that there might be "no further misunderstanding among the natives about the intentions of the United States."[24] In this proclamation the President asserted that with her signature to the treaty Spain had ceded the sovereignty of the Philippine Islands to the United States and that accordingly the United States intended to extend to the whole archipelago the military government now maintained at Manila. The United States would replace "arbitrary rule" with "the mild sway of justice and right"; her mission to the Philippines was one of "benevolent assimilation."[25]

The fact was that although Spain had signed the treaty, the United States Senate had not yet ratified it, so that from the constitutional standpoint alone McKinley's assertion of sovereignty was arbitrary and without foundation, and speakers at a meeting of the Boston Merchants Association expressed alarm at the way that the Philippine issue "was being driven along without due consideration by the representatives of the people." Similarly Moorfield Storey wrote Senator Hoar that the threat of American military force at Iloilo was without constitutional authority since Congress had declared war against Spain, not the Filipinos. But Bowles' *Republican* put the Massachusetts criticism of the President's actions in the strongest terms when it warned that imperialism endangered popular liberties with a growing concentration of power in the hands of the Executive "backed by the large standing army and the enormous financial power of the trusts and monopolies bent on 'capturing the markets of the world.'"[26]

Whatever strains the President's deeds had, in the eyes of the anti-imperialists, put upon constitutional democracy at home, the Filipinos saw the proclamation and the Iloilo expedition of the American President as placing the independence of their country under open and unmistakable threat of military violation. They answered with defiance. Aguinaldo issued proclamations promising to fight if Miller attempted to take Iloilo, denouncing American assumption of Philippine sovereignty and calling on his fellow-countrymen to stand united in defense of their liberty and independence. A new insurgent cabinet was formed that was united on resistance to American military occupation of the Philippines. Throughout Manila houses displayed flaming posters bearing the inscription "Independence or death."[27]

Faced with the imminent outbreak of hostilities at Iloilo, the McKinley Cabinet came together to canvass the situation. After this meeting a leading member of the Cabinet told O'Brien of the *Transcript* that the Administration favored avoiding any conflict at Iloilo; the feeling was that "the menace of insubordination on the part of the Filipinos is a double-edged affair." On the one hand it might impel the Senate to a more speedy ratification of treaty;

on the other hand, by bringing to the attention of the nation at large the future which we are opening for ourselves in the Far East by taking possession of the Philippines, it may start a popular agitation against the treaty which will prove too strong for the Senate to withstand.

The Administration believed in "going slow at Iloilo."[28]

A few days later McKinley spelled this out for Otis and Dewey, cabling them that conflict in the Philippines would be "most unfortunate considering the present and might have results unfavorable affecting the future." The President advised, "Tact and kindness [are] most essential just now." But McKinley ended his message to his military chiefs with this reminder: "You are the masters of the situation there and must not relax your power or vigilance," suggesting that the needs of policy might change. (The President's instructions could not have been difficult for Otis to assimilate. At the end of November he had wired Washington: "Policy now to preserve quiet and to act vigorous when the time for action comes." It was the same thing in fewer words.) [29]

As he decided to avoid hostilities at Iloilo, McKinley submitted the treaty of Paris to the Senate for ratification, and the very next day Erving Winslow, secretary of the New England Anti-Imperialist League, arrived in Washington to stiffen the backbone of the opposition. The policy of the League in the Senate treaty fight had been outlined by its president, George S. Boutwell, in a letter to Senator Hoar at the end of December: it was to postpone the vote on the treaty till the next session of the Senate, in order to build up a decisive public opposition.[30] Winslow's activities in Washington were in line with these goals. He first met with President Gompers of the A.F. of L., and other trade union leaders, who assured him that the Federation would use its influence against the treaty. Winslow then spoke at length with anti-imperialist Senators like Hoar and Pettigrew and sought conferences with Gorman and other Democratic leaders. He told the Senators that sentiment against the treaty was rising in the country, particularly in the West, and that the longer the vote was put off the more the opposition would crystalize and the less the chance of ratification.

Returning to Boston Winslow told the Executive Committee of the League that he brought back the impression that the Senatorial opposition was so well organized and determined that a vote would not be permitted in the coming session if it appeared that two-thirds of the Senate were in favor of the treaty; the Senatorial opposition seemed to accept the League strategy of delaying the vote as long as possible; a filibuster was plainly indicated.[31]

At the same meeting of the executive Winslow noted that since they last met the Boston office had received protests against expansion from the paper-makers' union of Holyoke, Massachusetts, a cigar makers' local in Boston and the trades and labor congress of Dubuque, Iowa, from farmers in Georgia, Iowa and Michigan and businessmen in Los Angeles, from the Nebraska State Council of Catholic Knights of America. Here was verification of the League's recommendations to the Senate: popular opposition to the treaty was on the rise throughout the country.[32]

"Crowning the efforts of a national constituency, the Anti-Imperialist League," so did Boston's weekly review, *Time and the Hour*, describe Hoar's speech against the treaty on January 9.* The Senate galleries were filled with those coming to hear him, and the legislators themselves listened with an attention they had not given anyone else on the issue. Hoar's speech was not only the high point of Senatorial opposition to the treaty, it was the high point of his anti-imperialist activity, and probably of his career, when he showed maximum courage, independence and concern for what he saw as the popular welfare, rather than personal or partisan advancement. Its reflection of these features made the speech outstanding; otherwise it was an extended and scholarly rehearsal of constitutional arguments against annexation, loaded with judicial and classical citations.

The public at large may well have looked upon this Massachusetts man as the spokesman for the anti-imperialist movement, but in his own mind he preferred to think of himself as a good Republican. The first moments of his address made this plain. Proud of the part he had played in the birth of the Republican Party, he would not now walk at its hearse, said the Senator, rather, he would, if he could, save it from its own mistakes. It was the Republican Party of the anti-slavery days that he had in mind, as he warned Americans that their nation, having just risen to abolish slavery,

---

* Although he took pre-eminence because of his Senatorial prestige, Hoar was not the only member of Congress from Massachusetts who then opposed imperialist policy. Besides Representative Fitzgerald, the Republican Congressmen, McCall, Gillett and Lawrence spoke out.

was now asked to accept the principle "that it is right to conquer, buy and subject a whole nation if we happen to deem it for their good." Invoking Abraham Lincoln's words that "No man was ever created good enough to own another," Hoar declared, "No nation was ever created good enough to own another."

What was the man to do when the party to which he professed allegiance was no longer the party of Lincoln, but instead the party of McKinley? That was Senator Hoar's dilemma, which he tended to solve by closing his eyes, denying its existence, and so going along with the Republican leadership. But on this occasion he acknowledged that reality differed from the ideal and he challenged his party and its leadershp.

By all means the most popular form of attack on President McKinley was to contrast his past condemnation of "forcible annexation" as "criminal aggression" with his present policies, thus exposing what the anti-imperialists saw as his duplicity. This is just what Hoar did, quoting the President's brave earlier words, and then, in sly paraphrase of McKinley's current slogans, crying out, "Who shall haul him down . . . Who shall haul down the President?" In his moment at the center of the national stage Senator Hoar took aim, fired and hit his dear friend, the President of the United States, right between the eyes.

Hoar also ventured to bring to the fore what the Administration wished most to keep out of sight: the spectre of a colonial war in the East. In another compelling passage he reminded his audience of the great picture of the signing of the Declaration of Independence that hung in the Capitol building and suggested that this painting be turned with its face to the wall. In its place, Hoar said, should be hung "a representation of some great battle where the guns of our army and navy are turned on the men struggling for their liberty at Iloilo."[33]

The Administration lost no time in answering Hoar. The next day Senator Foraker, from McKinley's own state of Ohio and generally considered a Presidential spokesman, rose on the floor of the Senate to say that McKinley did not contemplate a permanent annexation of the Philippines and that "no one, so far as I am able to learn, is preparing by force and violence to hold them . . . " Upon hearing Foraker's statement, Senator Hoar murmured, "reverently" but loud enough for all his colleagues to hear, "Thank God for that!"[34]

But Foraker's response to the Massachusetts man's speech created confusion in the ranks of the imperialists, with some claiming that he did not speak for the President, others, that indeed he did.[35] Indicating that the Administration was not averse to the impression Foraker created, there now appeared publicity in the press about a civilian commission the President had appointed to visit the Philippines and advise him on policy. In this way additional emphasis was given to the possibility of peaceful and non-military solutions to the questions under debate.[36]

Hoar's speech brought jubilation to Massachusetts anti-imperialists. Many of his severest Mugwump critics rushed to congratulate him. Boston's *Time and the Hour* had been most harsh about the Senator's stand on Hawaii; now this anti-imperialist weekly hailed him for having "caused the Administration to . . . mend its wild scheme of occupation of the Philippines by substituting the word 'temporary' for 'permanent.' " The *Springfield Republican* was equally appreciative, exclaiming, "against the memories evoked by Mr. Hoar even the federal executive trembles. A proud week for Massachusetts, truly, in her national annals." Gamaliel Bradford agreed that the speech was magnificent, but he added, "The President — not for the first time — appears disposed to hedge till he can get past the hitch in the ratification of the treaty, then he will be ready to start out again." Bradford's penetrating observation cast a cold light on the exuberance of his fellow anti-imperialists and the "reverent" murmur of Senator Hoar.[37]

In his comment Bradford referred to the "painful sacrifices . . . involved in relation to his party" Hoar's speech carried with it. But even as the anti-imperialist Hoar made a break with the Republican leadership, the partisan Hoar's past services to that same leadership came to fruition. In mid-January the votes were delivered that had been secured in the fall at party caucuses and conventions under the cover of Hoar's compromise platform. The Republicans dominant in the Massachusetts legislature, with only one dissenting vote, reelected Henry Cabot Lodge.

Before his re-election Lodge had been quiet in the debate; ten days afterward he rose to tell the Senate that passage of the treaty would not commit the country to permanent annexation, but would bring peace. In effect Lodge repeated Foraker's disavowals and went unchallenged as spokesman for President McKinley. Senator Hoar was the first to congratulate him on his speech.[38]

By the third week of January the fate of the treaty was uncertain. The energy of the anti-imperialist campaign had shocked the Administration out of its first assumption of an easy victory, and treaty supporters in the Senate had turned their efforts to what they saw as a hard fight. As a result, for some time the treaty had hung in a wavering and indecisive balance. Now the opposition to the treaty would claim that it had the votes and that the defeat of the treaty was assured; then supporters of the treaty would do likewise, and so it had gone. Senator Hoar confessed that his hopes rose and fell from day to day.[39]

At this point, only a few weeks remained of the current session of Congress which was to adjourn March 4. On January 18 the *Transcript* reported from Washington that it could hardly be remembered when there was such a congestion of work toward the end of a session. Many pressing matters of legislation still remained to be considered, including the most important appropriations bills, and, more urgent still, the bill to increase the standing army to 100,000 men in order to provide fresh troops for the Philippines. "There never was a better time for filibustering," the *Transcript* reporter wrote. "Compared with the historic fights of the past, it would not take much to 'hang up' the treaty now."[40]

The next day it was reported that President McKinley was very disturbed by the continued backing and filling in the Senate with reference to the ratification of the Treaty of Paris and was so expressing himself to Senators. In deference to the President's wishes Chairman Davis of the Senate Committee on Foreign Relations (the expansionist who had helped negotiate the treaty) gave notice of his intention to hurry things along. Administration senators began throwing out feelers to leading anti-expansion senators.[41]

The next day after that Senator Gorman, the leader on the Democratic side, who had done more than any other one senator in organizing opposition to the treaty, made an announcement. He told the press that he had no intention of filibustering against the treaty, that he was quite willing to allow advocates to set a date for a vote to be taken and that he believed that the treaty would be ratified before March 4.[42]

This was not all. President McKinley did not like another feature of the debate in that it had become weighted down with amendments more or less in line with the assurances Foraker and Lodge had given, as spokesmen for McKinley, that annexation would be temporary. Senator Hoar proposed, for example, an amendment declaring the United States intention to free the Philippines after treaty ratification. But now the President said that he wanted the treaty passed with no amendments. Senator Gorman then made an effort to line up the Democrats against amendments, placing himself, in the eyes of the *Transcript*'s O'Brien, "in the strict Administration column."[43]

In sum, Gorman submitted to the desire of the McKinley Administration for a quick vote with no amendments and threw over the policy recommended by the Boston anti-imperialists: to delay the vote and rouse popular opposition. Shortly after the Presidential assertion of authority and Gorman's surrender thereto the friends of the treaty and the Democrats agreed to bring the treaty to a vote in ten days, or on February 6. Senator Hoar gave his agreement as well, writing an anxious Boston anti-imperialist that this was all for the best.[44]

Both Hoar and Gorman, respectively the Republican and Democratic leaders of the Senatorial opposition, closed the struggle against the treaty when the Administration cracked the whip. With Hoar this submission, in all likelihood, resulted from his partisanship. Gorman's case was more questionable.

Before entering the treaty fight Gorman had established a reputation as an imperialist. He was one of the few Democrats who had broken party lines to support McKinley and vote for Hawaiian annexation. Then the Maryland man had opposed the treaty, saying, like other Southern Democrats, that he did so because the assimilation of the Filipinos, a colored people, would "degrade" white Americans. Besides this it was generally understood in Washington that Gorman opposed the treaty in an attempt to wrest the national leadership of the Democratic Party from Bryan with an eye to the presidential nomination in 1900.[45]

The sudden collapse of Gorman's opposition to the treaty reminded the *Transcript*'s Washington correspondent of the Senator's behavior in the Wilson-Gorman tariff episode of Cleveland's second term, which O'Brien had observed at close hand as the President's personal secretary. Then Gorman had thwarted the desire of the Boston Mugwumps for the tariff reform the President proposed, using his vantage point within the Democratic Party to further the program of big industry in a tariff that immortalized his name and caused Cleveland to cry "Treason!"

Noting that the Democratic leader, though a protectionist and an expansionist, did not hesitate to ride the free trade and anti-expansion horse when it would help him cover the ground, O'Brien put Gorman's tariff reform sell-out alongside his surrender on the treaty and concluded, "With his habit of mind and methods, it pays better for him to be in the enemy's uniform and inside the enemy's camp than to be exploiting frankly the policies in which he believes." The implication was that Gorman's misleadership was both deliberate and venal.[46]

The day after Senator Gorman announced his abandonment of a filibuster the members of the Massachusetts Reform Club held a meeting. John Jay Chapman of New York City, the speaker of the day, made bitter comment on the state of American politics, and the approval with which the audience greeted his talk indicated that he voiced the mood of many of Boston's liberal anti-imperialists at this particular juncture. Chapman, whose student years at Harvard had left him an ardent Mugwump, said that he knew nothing of political corruption in Massachusetts save that Henry Cabot Lodge had been returned to the Senate; instead he dwelt on his experiences in New York, where, as he saw it, the trouble was that all reform movements had been gobbled up by machine politics. "The difference in name," he said,

> as far as parties are concerned, is merely external . . . In New York we have had it demonstrated time after time that there was only one machine in town; that it worked at one end, and put money into the pockets of both Democrats and Republicans . . . In other words all the things we hate, all the corruption in American politics is a unity . . . As politics now are, there is not one word in any political platform of either party which has any meaning . . . There is not an issue today in American politics. You cannot throw an issue in them, because it turns to money when it strikes.

Winning much laughter and applause, Chapman closed with the injunction, "Put up your independent candidate."[47]

9

The Treaty Passes

Not since the impeachment proceedings of President Johnson had there been such a hard fought contest in the Senate as that on the Paris treaty. The galleries were filled to overflowing, and more members were present than at any session since the Senate assembled in December. At three o'clock when the Senators went into executive session some fifty newspaper correspondents stood in the corridor outside the Senate chamber. All felt the excitement and suspense, but the representatives of the stock exchange papers were especially anxious, lest a defeat for the treaty bring a slump in the price of stocks. Shortly after it became evident that the voting was over Mark Hanna, the millionaire Midwestern industrialist who was McKinley's special friend and advisor, burst through the Senate doors at a lively trot toward the circle of waiting correspondents. Hanna's message was laconic: the treaty had been ratified.[1]

It was, as Senator Lodge expected, a close vote. The treaty carried with only one vote to spare, but enough to end the struggle that had started two months before. With considerable help from the Massachusetts anti-imperialists an aggressive fight had been waged; wide popular opposition had been expressed, and the Senate had felt the impact. In spite of this the treaty passed, if only by a one vote margin. How did it happen?

Senator Hoar, of course, had his own ideas about this. He held Bryan at fault, asserting that the treaty would have failed had it not been for his intervention. Whatever Bryan's influence, Democratic votes helped pass the treaty: 24 of the 29 votes opposing were Democratic, but 11 Democrats voted for the treaty, saving the day for the imperialists.

Hoar seemed to forget that he had acquiesced in the President's desire for an early vote; instead he pointed his finger in Gorman's direction. He called to witness the successful Democratic filibuster Gorman had led several years before against a measure guaranteeing blacks the vote, and said, "The same spirit that defeated the Election Bill in spite of the majority in its favor, would have easily accomplished the same result. The Democratic Party, as a party, never meant business in this matter."[2]

Senator Gorman agreed with Hoar about Bryan's role, but he emphasized the primary responsibility of the Republican Party.[3] During the debate he told a journalist that if an honest vote could be taken he doubted the treaty would muster even a bare majority, "but all the railroad interests . . . all the commercial interests are bringing pressure to bear on the Senate in the most shameful manner." It was "an outrage" the way Hanna and his friends were working the treaty through the Senate.[4]

Hoar, the outstanding Republican Senator against the treaty, exerted next to no influence on the rest of his party. With the exception of his friend Hale, not one of the regular Republicans in the Senate voted to oppose. Almost to a man, the Republican Senators voted for the treaty.

Claiming much credit for himself and his party associate Aldrich of Rhode Island, Senator Lodge plainly identified the success of the treaty with the Republicans. He wrote Roosevelt: "Aldrich and I . . . were down in the engine room and we do not get the flowers, but we did make the ship move."[5]

Among the levers that moved the political machine was the Administration's disposition of appropriations. Securing funds for local improvements meant political survival for some members of the minority. Here the McKinley regime held the whip hand. A few days before treaty passage an Administration supporter told one of the minority, in a "waggish" tone, "I am perfectly willing to give you $200,000 to shovel out that harbor of yours, but while I'm doing it, I do not see why you need to be so mean about the treaty."[6]

Political preference and patronage were also in the hands of the Administration. Democratic Senator Gray of Delaware, who had opposed annexation as a Peace Commissioner in Paris, on his return to Washington spoke and voted for the treaty. McKinley awarded him a federal judgeship.[7] Senator McEnery, the Louisiana Democrat, spoke against the treaty but voted for it. Three days later several

Sentries on Philippine lines at Santa Ana outside Manila, before the outbreak of the fighting.

Presidential appointments in Louisiana, over which there had been a protracted struggle, were distributed among men friendly to McEnery.[8]

Senator R. F. Pettigrew, the anti-imperialist Silver Republican from South Dakota, noted the part played by Lodge's friend Aldrich in the debate. The day before the treaty was passed the South Dakotan went to Cushman Davis, chairman of the Senate Foreign Relations Committee, and said to him, "You are going to ratify this treaty, but it is the most terrible thing that I have seen in my twelve years service in this body."

"What do you mean?" Davis asked.

"I mean," Pettigrew replied, "the open purchase of votes to ratify this treaty right on the floor of the Senate and before the eyes of the Senators and all the world."

Davis became very serious, looked at Pettigrew, and said in a steady voice, "They came into my office and tried to tell me about it and I said, 'Gentlemen, get out of here. You cannot open your stinkpot in my presence.'"

"Well," Pettigrew answered, "I can guess who came into your room and whom you ordered out. It was Aldrich of Rhode Island."

To this Davis made no reply.[9]

Pettigrew charged and Gorman hinted that business pressure took the form of outright purchase of votes, and this was widely rumored in Washington at the time of the treaty's passage. But whatever the facts about this, the influence of business and finance upon the Senate for the passage of the treaty was undeniable and acknowledged on all sides. Administration supporters made no secret of their belief that strong pressure from the business world would be forthcoming to help them put the treaty through.[10] They were not disappointed.

The culmination of such support came in the last week of January when the convention of the National Association of Manufacturers adopted a resolution "most earnestly petitioning the Senate promptly to ratify the treaty." The New York Chamber of Commerce did likewise, and the stock market interest actively made itself heard.[11] In Boston business pressure for the treaty also gathered strength. Early in December the millionaire owner of the *Herald* overruled the paper's anti-imperialist editor. A month later E. H. Clement wrote Atkinson about the *Transcript*'s owners, "The temperature is rising so downstairs — I may not be able to give you even the space of a letter." The imperialist-minded noted with satisfaction a change in the slant of the paper's headlines. To League president Boutwell it seemed that support for the treaty was growing "among business men who anticipate an increase of trade by an increase of dominion."[12] Late in January Massachusetts industrial wealth made a dramatic show of solidarity with the embattled Administration when President Plunkett of the Home Market Club journeyed to Washington to invite McKinley to address a great public gathering in Boston. Just before the vote Senator Hoar told the press that he was being "bombarded" with pro-treaty letters and telegrams from his state's business community.[13]

As business and industry put pressure on the Senate for the passage of the treaty, so did the military. (Militarism, injected into the national life by imperialist policy, appeared in turn to foster that policy.) Early in December the Washington correspondent of the *Transcript* wrote that the army was always for expansion and war, the navy even more so. "For these two great arms of the Federal Government our entry into the complexities of European politics means business, and they would be dull indeed if they did not realize it." Thus "the attitude of the national capital itself" was a "factor in the imperialistic campaign."[14]

But the military in the field generated even more pressure for the treaty than the army and navy at home. Both Otis and Dewey, according to the *Boston Journal,* informed Washington that capital would not feel safe to invest in the Philippines unless the United States annexed the islands.[15] They put these views into practice with great effect: two days before the Senate voted on the treaty, the high command at Manila made war on the Philippine independence movement.

The war came as the climax to the deterioration of United States-insurgent relations that had begun in August when Merritt excluded the Filipinos from the occupation of their capital city. Then Aguinaldo had withdrawn his troops to lines outside Manila and tension had mounted during the summer and the fall. In October General Otis occupied Pandacan, a town both the Spanish authorities and General Merritt had considered outside the city limits of Manila. Since the peace parley with Spain had given the United States the right to occupy Manila alone, Aguinaldo made protest, giving way only under the threat of force, and Pandacan was established as a source of United States-Filipino conflict.[16]

In December the United States expedition to Iloilo brought a new threat of war, but McKinley, in view of the looming treaty debate, had given Otis instructions "to preserve the peace," and the American forces had held their fire in the face of Philippine defiance. In fact Otis went to extraordinary lengths to prevent hostilities. Before he published the President's proclamation at Manila, he took it upon himself to delete from it all references to United States assumption of Philippine sovereignty.[17] Since General Miller issued the proclamation in its original form at Iloilo, the result of Otis' action was the opposite intended. The insurgents' resentment at the President's threat to their independence was intensified by the General's attempt to hide it.

After the President's proclamation in late December, Aguinaldo had begun active preparation for armed resistance, using the month of January to entrench his lines and place artillery in position.[18] At the same time the Filipino leader made an attempt to avert hostilities by negotiations, asking Otis for conference to relieve the sharpening tensions. Again in line with the President's instructions to preserve the peace, Otis agreed and appointed a commission of American officers that met with a similar Philippine commission six times in January. The insurgent delegates presented a compromise proposal for Philippine independence within an American protectorate and brought forward grievances, chiefly their exclusion from the occupation of Manila and American encroachment on territory outside the city limits, i.e., Pandacan. Disregarding their grievances, Otis forwarded the insurgents' offer to accept protectorate status to Washington, but got no reply.[19]

Finally, during this period, Otis made statements to the press minimizing the war danger, and these offset the warnings of Hoar and others that McKinley's policies would lead to war.[20] When the prospect of hostilities appeared to lessen in the first weeks of January, popular anxiety was quieted and Administration difficulties eased in the Senate debate.

Then, on January 19, with a success that was almost immediate, President McKinley intervened so as to get Senate agreement to cut off discussion by an early vote, and treaty debate entered its final phase. Having successfully shifted from the defensive to the offensive on the political front, the Administration made a corresponding turn in military affairs. On January 21 Secretary of War Alger wired Otis to "give copy to Dewey of all official dispatches to you relating to joint operations."[21]

On January 24 the War Department alerted the public to this change of emphasis. It announced that "General Otis reports an expectation on his part that the insurgents are about to force an issue," adding the significant information that "if this should be so, the result cannot be foreseen. For it must be understood that there is nothing in General Otis's instructions to prevent him [from] most vigorously defending himself and the interests confided to his charge."[22]

When the insurgents had forced the issue at Iloilo, McKinley had ordered Otis and Dewey to avoid conflict. Now, however, the War Department ordered Otis to show Dewey the plans for joint operations, then announced that the General had permission to do battle. With the Democrats' agreement to curtail opposition at hand and the end of treaty debate plainly in view, the Administration seemed no longer so anxious to avoid conflict.

On January 25, as the Senate set the treaty vote for February 6, Senator Teller of Colorado drew attention to the domestic advantage that might result from the policy just revealed by the War Department, saying that as soon as one American soldier fell in an attack by the Filipinos, sentiment would vanish, and the American people would stand behind the Army as they had always done. O'Brien of the *Transcript* recalled "what an effective argument the firing upon Fort Sumter was with persons who had hesitated to agree to a policy of coercion," and thought that Teller had made "a striking point of considerable present pertinency." In his next dispatch O'Brien reported that all branches of the Executive Government believed that the question of war and peace with the insurgents was hanging in the balance.[23]

On January 14 General Otis had declared that the Americans were in absolute control of the situation at Manila, that the insurgent leaders had issued strict orders to their troops to act only on the defensive and that the idea of a Filipino attack on the city was ridiculous and suicidal.[24] On January 24 the War Department declared his opinion to be quite the contrary. But the activities of Otis and his command at this time reflected the Administration's change of emphasis in more important ways than the altered tone of his dispatches.

In line with his orders from the War Department of January 21, General Otis requested Admiral Dewey to place his ships so as to give American troops supportive fire, and Dewey obliged. Then Otis ordered back to Manila some of the troops at Iloilo. At the same time General Arthur McArthur, in charge of lines around Manila, ordered artillery to be put in place near the troops stationed at Pandacan.[25]

Aguinaldo got an inkling United States military policy was entering a new phase when he received an intelligence report on January 21 that the American members of the joint commission had said that they had held their last meeting with their Philippine counterparts and were now able "to complete the execution of their plans." (Later the insurgent leader heard that on February 2 and 3 the United States Navy had dismissed all Filipinos employed on its ships in Manila harbor, for no apparent reason.) [26]

On February 2 Colonel Frederick Funston gave secret orders to Lieutenant John F. Hall of the 20th Kansas Volunteer Infantry to bring about a conflict with the insurgents if possible, and several regimental commanders gave such orders to their officers and men, according to the lieutenant's testimony.[27] On that same day Colonel John M. Stotsenberg of the 54th Nebraska Regiment entered into a violent altercation with a Filipino officer in charge of insurgent troops at Santol, a town lying ahead of a Nebraskan outpost in the disputed Pandacan area and hitherto unoccupied by the Americans. Since the Americans at this time were still under orders to withhold fire, the American command negotiated with the Filipino command at this point in the line, demanding insurgent withdrawal from Santol. The Filipino command ordered their troops to withdraw, which they did, under protest, and the Nebraskans moved into the town.[28]

The day after the encounter at Santol, Howard Bray, an English associate of the insurgent junta at Hong Kong, cabled Senator Hoar to caution him against "news of hostilities." Bray told Hoar that the Filipinos thought the incident of the day before "a political move influence vote in Senate . . . in any case insignificant skirmish due intentional provocation."[29] Hoar, however, made no appreciable use of the Philippine message before the treaty vote, so that General Otis proceeded on his course without question from the United States Senate.

On February 4, the day after Bray sent the cable, Otis acted so as to give its warning the utmost significance. The General took the decisive step: he ordered the Nebraskans to open fire on further insurgent "intruders." Charged with this order, Colonel Stotsenberg put the finishing touches on American preparations, arranging for a system of signals.[30]

During the afternoon of February 4 a report reached foreign residents of Manila that American troops had been put under arms.[31] That evening Private Willie Grayson and a friend named Miller drew sentry duty at Santol; they were ordered to patrol ahead of the village to a distance of 100 yards, in a still further advance on the unoccupied territory the insurgents regarded as their own. After proceeding as ordered, they "waited to see if there were any insurgents in the vicinity."[32] Then Private Grayson told what happened:

> About eight o'clock . . . something rose slowly up not twenty feet in front of us. It was a Filipino. I yelled "Halt!" . . . he immediately shouted "Halto" at me. Well, I thought the best thing to do was to shoot him. He dropped . . . Then two Filipinos sprang out of a gateway about fifteen feet from us. I called "Halt," and Miller fired and dropped one. I saw that another was left. Well, I think I got my second Filipino that time. We retreated to where our six other fellows were, and I said, "Line up, fellows, the niggers are in here all through these yards."[33]

The insurgents in the immediate area returned the fire, and General MacArthur related the result:

> We had a pre-arranged plan. Our tactical arrangements there were very perfect, indeed. Everything was connected by wire . . . and within an instant after the firing at the outpost I received a message from Stotsenberg . . . "The pipe line outpost has been fired on; I am moving out with my entire regiment." . . . When I got Colonel Stotsenberg's report I simply wired all commanders to carry out pre-arranged plans, and the whole division was placed on the firing line.[34]

Private Grayson's account of the incident had the air of casual spontaneity (with a racist overtone) — General MacArthur's, that of deliberate premeditation. This contrast reflected the difference in rank and role, but what made the spontaneity on Grayson's part more seeming than real was the order he had been given an hour before to shoot if need arose. (Later on, perhaps, Willie Grayson began to feel that he had been used. On a ship going home, his tour of duty ended, he said "the damn bull-headedness" of the officers in invading insurgent territory was responsible for the firing of his shot.)[35]

Through the winter months there had been several border incidents of this type before, as a result of which General Otis had issued orders to outpost guards not to bring on a conflict with the Filipinos.[36] On February 4 Otis countermanded these instructions with his order to the Nebraskan outpost to open fire on the Filipinos, and then the General backed up this order with the full force of his striking power. Without any question Otis and his command thought it time "to act vigorous" and start a war. So it began, as was likely in the circumstances, with the effort of the United States military to extend its control beyond the confines of Manila.

The Philippine lines gave way before the offensive of the United States Army (supported by fire from Dewey's ships) and the carnage was great among the insurgents. On the afternoon of February 5 Aguinaldo sent a representative to General Otis to say that the fighting had begun accidentally, without his authorization, and to call for the cessation of hostilities and the establishment of a neutral area between the troops. To Aguinaldo's requests General Otis gave the reply that the fighting once begun, must be carried on to the grim end.[37]

Just before midnight February 4 President McKinley received a report, as it was told the press, "that the insurgents had attacked Manila." The next evening McKinley held a Cabinet meeting where it was decided to send instructions to Otis "to follow up his victory over the insurgents and crush the power of Aguinaldo in the Philippines." Thus when Otis refused Aguinaldo's offer of ceasefire, he was carrying out the Administration's intentions exactly.[38]

The *San Francisco Call* of February 5 reported that after the news of the conflict with the insurgents reached Washington "President McKinley said to an intimate friend . . . that the Manila engagement would, in his opinion, insure the ratification of the treaty tomorrow," and, in an interview with the *Call*'s representative, Senator Lodge said the same thing.[39] On the day of the voting the *Springfield Republican* reported that the general opinion in Washington was that the news from Manila guaranteed the ratification of the treaty. League secretary Winslow thought it decisive.[40]

The suspicion was whispered in Washington that the clash at Manila was timed for the treaty vote, and the next day "Pitchfork Ben" Tillman of South Carolina, agrarian rebel, white supremacist and opponent of the treaty, put this charge on record when he rose on the Senate floor to say, "Time alone will tell whether this battle was provoked by the Filipinos for purposes of their own, or by the Americans . . . to sway men in this Senate to ratify the treaty and change the status."[41]

It is possible that the Administration opened the way to conflict with more than one eventuality in mind. On February 4 a "prominent Republican Senator" told O'Brien of the *Transcript* that should the treaty be defeated, "We shall then have to go ahead and . . . take actual possession of the Philippine Islands, and if Aguinaldo gets in the

At Santa Ana after the war's outbreak. Filipino dead where they fell.

way to push him out of it."[42] If this, indeed, represented the opinion of the Administration, then it may be that the decision to unleash Otis was taken with an eye to the possibility of treaty defeat as well as treaty victory.

In any case hostilities could not have been better timed from the Administration standpoint — coming too late to arouse effective popular opposition to the treaty, but just in time to put effective pressure on the Senate for its passage. If as the Cabinet member thought, conflict with the insurgents was a "double-edged affair," the Administration handled it adroitly, holding off the edge that cut against itself and pressing home the edge against the Filipinos. First the Administration had lulled domestic anxiety at the prospect of a war for Philippine annexation, then it launched the war under more favorable circumstances. Going slow at Iloilo had been a useful prelude to full speed ahead at Manila.

In his version of these events General Otis indicated that the insurgent command had not expected a conflict at the time, as many of the general officers of the insurgent army were spending the evening at a ball when the fighting occurred. Moreover the General affirmed, very definitely, that the United States forces moved on the offensive, the Filipinos on the defensive.[43]

But the Administration stuck to the story that the Filipinos had attacked the United States forces at Manila: the insurgents had "fired on the flag," brought the conflict on, and were responsible for it.

Before long, however, some of the circumstances of the war's outbreak became known in the United States through official military reports and otherwise. The information that the Americans fired the first shot while on territory to which their rights were dubious, that Otis refused to parley once the fighting had begun, was put to use by McKinley's opponents.[44] In their argumentation, the charge that the United States Army instigated the war against the insurgents took a place beside the accusation that Dewey betrayed Aguinaldo.

Just before the vote was taken the Senate was given one last display of Massachusetts initiative in the fight against imperialism. It received a memorial in opposition to ratification signed by an imposing list of public figures, including ex-President Cleveland, former Secretary of the Treasury John G. Carlisle, Andrew Carnegie, President Charles W. Eliot of Harvard University, Samuel Gompers, Moorfield Storey and eighteen other men of prominence. This was the work of Charles Francis Adams, assisted by Carl Schurz. It was, like the protests of labor and farmers, like of the rest of the anti-imperialist campaign against the treaty, to no avail.[45]

The pressure generated by industry, the military, by partisan and personal interests proved too great, the atmosphere of racism and chauvinism too pervasive. The Massachusetts men who fought the treaty believed that, given time, they could muster an overwhelming popular opposition, and the success of their efforts gave support to this belief. Whether such a movement could have been built or not was not tested; the collapse of the fight against the treaty at its weak political center removed that possibility.

In the treaty crisis, if the views of the leading participants are taken into account, both parties must be held responsible for its passage, with the Republicans carrying the major burden. Both Republicans and Democrats proved incapable of expressing popular opposition to the treaty, because both were incapable of resisting the pressure of big business and its allied military interests. The national legislature, which had brought into being the union of industry and the military, was in turn dominated by its creature; the child devoured the parent in the reverse of the legend. Not to be discounted, either, was the influence of William McKinley. In the midst of this decisive series of events, the President came forward to offer sinuous leadership to the political and military machines, and the ends desired by his supporters in industry and finance were achieved. The treaty was passed, the war with the Philippines begun, and the United States set on an imperial course.

Without question the passage of the treaty brought about a speedy reconciliation between President McKinley and Senator Hoar. McKinley's Secretary of State, John Hay, told his friend Henry Adams about it, and Adams put it down with an acid pen:

> Last Tuesday morning, just the morning after the Senate vote, Hay, walking into the President's room, stood agog to see sitting by the President's side, with arms around his neck as it were, unctuous, affectionate, beaming, the virtuous Hoar! Cabot Lodge, entering at the same time, was struck dumb by the same spectacle. Only a few hours before, in the full belief that his single vote was going to defeat and ruin the administration, Hoar had voted against the Treaty, and there he was, slobbering the President with assurances of his admiration, pressing on him a visit to Massachusetts, and distilling over him the oil of his sanctimony.[46]

10

Against the Philippine War

It was now a new situation. The Senate had passed the treaty and the United States government was warring on the Filipinos. Indeed the war was nothing but the military measures needed to carry out the annexation. When the anti-imperialists failed in the Senate fight against the treaty, they were left with the war. Having lost their first battle, they proceeded without delay to the second, the fight against the Philippine war.

The *Springfield Republican* quickly stated what became the anti-imperialist position in the new situation. On the day following the Senate action the paper maintained that treaty ratification had settled nothing; the question of annexation was still open and could be reversed by public discussion. Meantime the United States should stop fighting and open negotiations with the Filipino insurgents. "Go to them; disclaim any purpose of acquisition not based on their consent; proclaim the policy of the United States to be to establish them into a self-governing state and then withdraw."[1]

On February 10, three days after the *Republican* editorial, the New England Anti-Imperialist League held a general meeting in Boston to discuss resolutions embodying demands for an immediate suspension of hostilities in the Philippines, and for a Congressional pledge of self-government and independence to those islands (i.e., the position taken by the *Republican*). These resolutions were "unanimously passed with great enthusiasm."[2]

These two resolutions were again brought to public attention at a meeting of the League executive committee in March, at a large rally in April, and at other times besides. They became in fact the charter of the League, on the basis of which that organization in the late winter and early spring of 1899 promoted mass meetings, helped establish local branches and issued printed material in great bulk.[3]

The passage of the treaty, a major defeat for the anti-imperialists, was a major victory for their opponents. When the Boston *Boot and Shoe Recorder* appeared after the Senate vote, it reflected the jubilant, aggressive mood of the imperial-minded, calling on shoe-manufacturers to give "three times three for Old Glory, and bend all efforts toward expanding our business." The "obstructionists" who had opposed the treaty would have "shut off one of the richest, natural portions of the earth from legitimate industrial development . . . impossible without a stable responsible form of government."* Worse still, once fighting had broken out, they were guilty of "treason," of "favoring the open enemy."[4]

While the anti-imperialists took the ground of opposition to the war (and were charged with "treason" as a result), the imperialists pressed the advantage of their recent success. They held what amounted to a victory celebration in Boston, the home of their defeated opponents.

In January W. B. Plunkett, the wealthy Massachusetts textile manufacturer, had invited his friend in the White House to address a banquet of the Home Market Club. The President accepted and the event took place in Boston on February 16. It was the largest banquet in the country's history, with 1914 diners, 400 waiters, 12,000 plates, half a ton of fish, and other food in gigantic quantities that took an hour and a half to consume.[5] For days in advance the Boston press was full of it.

Since this was the President's first public declaration after treaty passage, there was nation-wide interest in the affair. Those who expected some solid exposition of presidential intent, however, reckoned without their man. In the South McKinley had declaimed against hauling down the flag, but he was in Boston now. Accordingly he asserted that "no imperial designs lurk in the American mind." Destiny had recently brought the United States to the Philippines, and Congress would decide upon their future treatment, so that, in the President's view, his own responsibility neared the vanishing point. Similarly the war against the Philippines could scarce be seen, and then only in the gentlest light. The President declared his main

---

* The Manila correspondent of *Leslie's Weekly* concurred, "When Uncle Sam shall have made terms with Aguinaldo . . . the entire country will be a safe place for investment." (Quoted in the *Boston Evening Transcript*, February 16, 1899.)

concern to be the happiness and welfare of the Philippine people, but "neither their aspirations nor ours can be realized until our authority is acknowledged and unquestioned." Meanwhile, "the blood-stained trenches around Manila" caused him "anguish."[6]

Postmaster General Charles Emory Smith, the President's close advisor, followed and told the manufacturers of Massachusetts, "what we want is a market for our surplus." Smith then compared McKinley to Lincoln, to the latter's disadvantage: he had only emancipated 4,000,000 human beings, while McKinley had "lifted 10,000,000 into light and freedom."[7]

Above the speakers hung huge portraits of Washington, Lincoln and McKinley, inscribed "Liberators."[8] To these, and all other features of the imperial review, the four thousand Club members and invited guests responded with enthusiasm.

The next day the President addressed a much smaller reception given for him by prominent businessmen in the rooms of a Boston club. In this more confidential atmosphere McKinley dispensed with the references to fate and loving kindness of the night before and came to the point about certain decisive contemporary matters of fact:

> Our enormous export trade has made American balances satisfactory, and almost for the first time the money of the country has been so abundant and and the wealth of the country so great that our capitalists have sought foreign investments. We are fast going from a debtor to a creditor nation.[9]

On the whole the President's visit was "in the nature of a triumphal procession."[10] His followers throughout the country looked upon it as a resounding success. "The home of the Anti-Imperialist League has unequivocally declared for the President," boasted the *New York Journal and Commercial Bulletin*.[11] Certainly the Home Market Club affair was an emphatic demonstration of support for McKinley's policies by Massachusetts leading industrialists and their hangers-on.

Long before the program of speakers was arranged the octogenarian president of the Anti-Imperialist League, George S. Boutwell, had requested an opportunity to speak at the Home Market Club banquet so as to counter its effect. Those in charge refused his request, however, so that the anti-imperialists were forced to use other means of rebuttal.[12] This they did with vigor.

On the day of the banquet the *Springfield Republican* called it

"Belshazzar's Feast" and wrote, "Back of the suave and comfortable faces of the Home Market Club lower the visages of the slain, the bereft, the homeless, the martyrs of liberty."[13] The anti-imperialists saw the President's festive reception against the background of the Philippine war, and his visit served to intensify and provide an early focus for their opposition to that war.

The night after the banquet Edward Atkinson answered McKinley at a meeting of the Workingman's Political League and the night following that William Lloyd Garrison did so at the Free Trade League.[14] Other speakers followed, and agitation filled the press.

William James wrote a letter to the *Transcript* that was much discussed. James condemned "the cold pot grease of McKinley's cant at the recent Boston banquet — surely as shamefully evasive a speech, considering the right of the public to know definite facts, as can have fallen from a professional politician's lips." As for the Philippine operation, it "reeked of the infernal adroitness of the great department store, which has reached perfect expertness in the art of killing silently and with no public squalling or commotion the neighboring small concern." It was "bold, brutal piracy . . . horrible, simply horrible."[15]

The leaders of the Anti-Imperialist League sought and won allies for the fight against McKinley's war, as they had previously against the treaty. The Massachusetts Reform Club, the American Peace Society, the Massachusetts Sons of the American Revolution, all held meetings at which anti-war declarations were made. The women of Cambridge circulated a petition among their sex throughout the country for signatures to end the war. At a meeting of Boston's black citizens to commemorate the 129th anniversary of the death of Crispus Attucks, speakers attacked Anglo-Saxon colonization and opposed killing Filipinos because they were "fighting for just what our forefathers sought thirty-five years ago."[16] In March the *Boston Post* called for a negotiated peace. In April the Young Men's Democratic Club of Massachusetts voted against the United States attempt to force its sovereignty on the Philippines. Irish-born citizens of Boston formed a "Committee of Safety" to inaugurate state-wide agitation among Americans of similar descent for peace, withdrawal of troops and Philippine independence.[17]

On the occasion of the President's visit, here and there in the streets of Boston jeering cries of "Beef! Beef! Beef!" and "Hurrah for General Miles!" had been directed at Secretary of War Alger's carriage in the McKinley entourage.[18] At their March meeting the Boston Merchants Association gave the platform to Miles, whose criticism of Secretary of War Alger for buying rotten beef from army contractors had inspired the one note of public disapproval during McKinley's visit. The general recalled his early employment by a Boston merchant and eulogized the city's mercantile ideals, linking them, by implication, with his exposure of the "beef trust." It was the "honesty of purpose" of Boston's merchants that had taught him to oppose "grasping avarice, sharp practice, the taking of merciless advantage, forming unscrupulous combinations for the aggrandizement of the few to the injury of all others."[19] While Miles, in his speech, censured McKinley for the maladministration of the Spanish War, he didn't mention the Philippine. Judging from their choice of speaker and the content of his remarks, at this point the Boston Merchants Association was maintaining a distance from the Republican Administration without endorsing the position taken by the anti-imperialists.

After defeat in the treaty fight, the leaders of the Anti-Imperialist League decided that "especially every effort should be made to strengthen the anti-imperialist position of labor and agricultural unions and organizations."[20] As a consequence, a public meeting was held in Boston on March 21 at which Samuel Gompers was the main speaker, seconded by George E. McNeill and Henry Lloyd. Gompers denounced the United States war "against the only Asiatic country that has ever made an attempt to establish a republican form of government," and warned that "if peace cannot be secured in any other way, the time is coming when federated labor will refuse to make implements that are intended to strike down their fellow-men."[21]

Despite the Gompers meeting, the participation of trade unionists in the New England Anti-Imperialist League seemed confined to a few leaders like McNeill and Lloyd. Lloyd thought that the predominant character of the League leadership made a difficulty in this regard. Late in March he wrote Atkinson that it was hard to get labor men to join a club with rich men; McNeill was willing, but who else?[22]

Lloyd asked Atkinson what plans the League had for a large public meeting in the near future. Other members of the Anti-Imperialist League shared Lloyd's desire to see their organization speak out after McKinley's visit. When F. B. Sanborn, the special Boston correspondent of the *Springfield Republican,* reported that an anti-imperialist rally was to be held on April 4 under the sponsorship of a number of Massachusetts Republicans, he complained that the meeting had not been called soon enough and was too narrow in character: opposition to the Philippine war was not limited to Republicans.[23]

There was a broader participation in the April 4 rally than Sanborn expected. Edward O'Donnell, corresponding secretary of the Boston Central Labor Union, joined several prominent Mugwumps in sending messages of support, and George E. McNeill sat on the platform together with a number of Republican state legislators. As the speakers condemned the war and called for an end to the fighting, a "hot audience" filled the hall with constant applause and cries of indignation.[24]

While the meeting was an earnest reply to McKinley's visit, it appears that the anti-imperialist leadership had a more influential Republican in mind for this purpose than Massachusetts former Attorney General A. E. Pillsbury, who made the main address on April 4. On February 24, a week after the Home Market Club banquet, over 450 prominent Bostonians signed a letter to Senator Hoar asking him to attend a meeting at which the people of their city might express gratitude for his "courageous and patriotic defense in the Senate . . . of the principles on which our government was founded." Among those who signed were such leaders of the Anti-Imperialist League as Boutwell, Winslow, Bradford and Atkinson.

Hoar took his time about this rather impressive invitation, not answering till over a month later. The Senator's response reflected the careful balance he was accustomed to hold between anti-imperialism and partisan consideration, and his tendency to place more weight on the side of partisanship in matters of practical (as distinguished from oratorical) effect. He declined. It must be remembered that Hoar had barely made up with the President after his showdown with the latter on the Senate floor in the treaty fight. Accordingly he did not lend himself to the Massachusetts anti-imperialists for another such confrontation, this time in the native bailiwick he shared so gingerly with Senator Lodge, and for the purpose of countering the effect of the very visit to Massachusetts that Hoar himself had urged upon the President at the time of their reconciliation. In declining Hoar said he did not think the time ripe for a meeting to protest the war.[25]

Hoar was not, however, averse to speaking in Boston before a gathering of state legislators (not an anti-war affair) where he both defended his own anti-imperialist principles and praised the bravery of American troops in battle. His refusal to speak at the peace meeting and his speech before the legislators led to Boston comment that the Senator was blocking the development of the anti-war movement and "pulling his punches on the home front."[26]

But Hoar, in his public letter of refusal, defended the struggle Aguinaldo was waging for his country's independence and answered those publicists who said that the Philippine resistance was due to the agitation of American anti-imperialists in general, and of the Senator in particular. "There never was a more unfounded or a more foolish calumny," wrote Hoar. A strict military censorship had been exercised over the cable to the Philippine Islands during the whole period, and to prove it the Senator had one of the original circulars of the cable company, warning that no dispatch would be transmitted having the least relation to politics without the assent of the military authority of the United States. Moreover "a gentleman of high standing in Hong Kong" had tried to send an abstract of the Senator's January 9 speech against the treaty, "and its transmission was refused."

The accusation that the anti-imperialists were responsible for the Philippine nationalist struggle, like the charge of treason, was put into circulation immediately after the fighting broke out in the Philippines and had currency as long as that lasted. Rebutting this with the counter-charge of military censorship, all the while refusing to stand up and answer McKinley in Boston, Hoar gave with one hand what he took away with the other.

The Senator pointed out that military censorship affected news coming from the Philippines to the United States as well as the other way around. "The information which we get as to the events in the Philippine Islands comes almost wholly from sources interested in the promulgation of the war." He hoped that "every effort will be made to give the people full and accurate knowledge of the facts . . . so carefully withheld or perverted by the organs of imperialistic policy."

The Anti-Imperialist League, after its own fashion, proceeded to fulfill the Senator's hope. It began to publish pamphlets dealing with the origin, purpose and character fo the Philippine conflict. One of these, especially, lent substance to the anti-imperialists' belief that the United States was waging a racist war. It came to be in this way:

When Otis had driven the insurgents from their trenches around Manila with the aid of Dewey's guns he had reported heavy Philippine losses of some 4,000 killed, wounded and prisoners to 250 American casualties.[27] In the weeks following, as the United States troops continued to drive the Filipinos back, reports persisted of terrible insurgent losses. It was the view of the *Boston Evening Transcript,* however, that official dispatches cast little light on the situation, "but thousands of private soldiers are every week sending home letters which tell the horrible truth."[28] Relatives and friends were turning these letters over to the press and so they reached the public.

Toward the end of May the Anti-Imperialist League published *Soldiers' Letters,* a collection of the same. It was, in large part, a record of racism and slaughter. Some letters told of the action at Caloocan, a town outside Manila. Wrote Captain Elliott of the Kansas Regiment: "Caloocan was supposed to contain seventeen thousand inhabitants. The Twentieth Kansas swept through it, and now Caloocan contains not one living native. Of the buildings, the battered walls of the great church and dismal prison alone remain." A Kansas private: " . . . with my own hand set fire to over fifty houses of Filipinos after the victory at Caloocan. Women and children were wounded by our fire." Still another Kansan told that his company took four prisoners at Caloocan and asked an officer what to do. "He said, 'You know the orders,' and four natives fell dead." Other letters described the war in like terms. Calling it a "goo-goo hunt," a private in the Utah Battery wrote, "With an enemy like this to fight, it is not surprising that the boys should soon adopt 'no quarter' as a motto, and fill the blacks full of lead before finding out whether they are friends or enemies." A volunteer from the state of Washington wrote: "Our fighting blood was up, and we all wanted to kill 'niggers' . . . This shooting human beings beats rabbit hunting all to pieces."[29]

The *Republican* thought these stories "only what was to be expected . . . when dealing with an enemy whose colored skin invites for them about as much consideration from the proud whites as an animal."[30] Moreover, the anti-imperialists soon published the account of a witness at first hand, A. L. Mumper of the First Idaho Regiment, who claimed that racist feeling among the rank and file was stimulated by the white supremacist attitude of officers over them. Mumper wrote, "It kept leaking down from sources above that the Filipinos were 'niggers,' no better than Indians, and were to be treated as such." Mumper's observation was borne out by the views of one of the most notable officers, Colonel (later Brigadier-General) Funston, who commanded the Kansans at Caloocan. He said, "The boys go for the enemy as if they were chasing jack rabbits . . . I, for one, hope that Uncle Sam will apply the chastening rod, good, hard, and plenty . . . until they come into the reservation and promise to be good 'Injuns,' "[31]

On April 8, the first warm day of spring, F. B. Sanborn reported that the most crowded sidewalk in Boston was in front of the Old Corner Bookstore where the illustrated papers in the windows had photographs of the trenches beyond Manila packed to the full with bodies of a dead Filipinos, "the heathens we are converting by this new missionary method."[32]

The anti-imperialists thought that there was altogether too much indifference to the killing and tried to rouse the public. Just at this time the mayor of Boston was attempting to rid the city of the English sparrow. City employees were busily destroying nests and eggs. Polite opinion was in an uproar. Edwin D. Mead found the campaign to save the sparrow remarkable: "Pages of letters to newspapers, petitions with thousands of names, every dinner table mortgaged to them, anger and anguish running over," while, "in the Pacific, out of sight, but within our ken, in our name and with hourly reports, hundreds and thousands of our fellow-men are being ruthlessly slain . . . and there is infinitely less outcry over it all than over the sparrows on Boston Common."[33]

On March 22, "Listener," the Transcript's columnist, wrote that one night the war became for him quite literally a nightmare:

Overleaf: *"Now Caloocan contains not one living native."* Funston's troops marching through. (Drawn by an American artist on the spot for the Harper's Weekly *of April 22, 1899*).

> I dreamed that I was out there and was overlooking a big tropical jungle . . . To smoke the rebels out of it, our people had brought up, not artillery, but steam fire engines, which proceeded to spray the whole jungle with far-thrown streams of petroleum. . . . When the trees and bushes were well sprinkled on this way they were set on fire, and in a moment there were vast columns of black smoke rising to the sky, with very red flames at their base . . . I was horrified to see that there were villages in the jungle, filled with women and children, and that these villages and all the people in them were being overwhelmed by flames. I heard the people's shrieks and saw their torments.

As April closed, their nerves already jarred by reports of racist brutality in a war of conquest, the anti-imperialists felt a further shock of horror. On Sunday, April 23, a white mob at Newnan, Georgia, burned a black farm-hand named Sam Hose at the stake. Hose had been accused of killing his white employer in a dispute over wages, and of raping his employer's wife (this last Hose denied to the end). Recently the papers had carried accounts of another Georgia lynching and an assault on black troops in Tennessee, but the Hose killing was extraordinary in its barbarity, and the Boston press reported it in full. The black man had been chained to a tree and horribly mutilated before oil had been poured over him and the torch applied. Over a thousand whites were at the scene and after it was over the remains of Hose were cut up and sold; "small pieces of bone went for 25 cents and a bit of liver crisply cooked for 10." When the news of the lynching spread to nearby Atlanta the railroad put on special excursion trains to take nearly 4,000 whites to the affair. Arriving too late for the burning, they returned home with souvenirs.[34]

Massachusetts citizens received the story of the Hose lynching with indignation, and the anti-imperialists were very vocal. Black Bostonians held a meeting of their own (at which *Transcript* editor E. H. Clement was a platform guest), and the main speaker, W. H. Lewis, a member of the Cambridge City Council, gave an emphasis to his remarks with which the anti-imperialist leaders were in accord. The young black attorney found shame for America both at home and abroad: "What a spectacle America is exhibiting today. Columbia stands offering liberty to the Cubans with one hand, ramming liberty down the throat of the Filipinos with the other, but with both feet planted upon the neck of the negro."[35] The *Springfield Repub-*

lican queried:

> Is the contempt we have shown for the rights and protests of the natives of the Philippines . . . the killing of them by the thousands and the looting of their homes . . . calculated to increase the southern white's regard for the negro as a fellow-being of like feelings and claims to life and liberty as himself?[36]

George Frisbie Hoar agreed. He said he could see no difference beween lynching a Negro and lynching a people — but at the same time, the Senator, as he left for a summer abroad, took pains to remind his constituents that he had an undying affection for President McKinley.[37]

Hoar's diplomacy, however, found no echo in the leadership of the New England Anti-Imperialist League. Without mincing words, they called for the suppression of racist violence at home and abroad. League vice president Thomas Wentworth Higginson presided at a protest rally where A. E. Pillsbury linked public anger at the Georgia atrocity to the demand for an end to the Asian war in the most concrete way. Speaking as "one of that despised class, the anti-imperialists," Pillsbury insisted that American troops be brought home from the Philippines and sent into the South to "repress this rebellion against humanity."[38]

11

Atkinson and the Volunteers

In the winter months of 1899, after treaty passage and the outbreak of the war, the imperialists seemed to carry all before them, while the anti-imperialists struggled to rally their forces on new ground. Then in the spring, with that sudden irony normal to history, there was a shift in roles. The transforming agent was popular opposition to the Philippine War. The agitation of the Anti-Imperialist League was gaining a most active support. Now it was the turn of the McKinley Administration to feel rebuff.

There were 12,000 volunteer soldiers out of some 30,000 troops in the Philippines. They had volunteered for the war with Spain, and with that war's end they were eligible for discharge, or they could re-enlist. It was the demand to bring these troops home that shocked the administration, telling, as plainly as it did, of the Philippine War's unpopularity.

Since the volunteers came mainly from the South and West, it was in these areas that the question arose. The Anti-Imperialist League had made efforts of its own to reach the public in these regions. It had run anti-war advertisements in newspapers with the largest circulation in the Northwest and one or two Southern states, receiving a large number of letters in response.[1] Such League activity was of course only parallel and complementary to the opposition to McKinley's foreign policy that was native to the areas concerned, coming from the West's most prominent politician, William Jennings Bryan (who renewed his opposition to the administration after treaty passage), from South Dakota's R. F. Pettigrew, from numerous Southern Democratic Congressmen, and others.[2] Another source of anti-war feeling here were the letters home from the volunteers themselves.

For this correspondence revealed not only the inhumanity of some American soldiers, but also the distaste for the war felt by others, as League Secretary Winslow pointed out.[3] Finally the Anti-Imperialist League could claim for itself another influence upon rural opinion in the South and West in the person of its Springfield, Massachusetts, Vice President, Herbert Myrick, whose farm papers had thousands of readers in these areas, and whose editorial comment was consistently anti-expansionist.[4]

Reporting on public opinion outside New England early in April, Myrick claimed "an utter absence of imperialist spirit among the rank and file of the people throughout the West and South . . . the unpopularity of the war increases with each Western boy who is killed or wounded." "Each mail from Manila" intensified this feeling, "especially in the Pacific states."[5]

Myrick's observations were confirmed on all sides, as the anti-imperialist press of Massachusetts took care to report. Early in February the California Senate requested that the First California Regiment be sent home as soon as troops could be spared from the Philippines.[6] In March relatives and friends of the men in the Tenth Pennsylvania got letters from Manila that information on death and casualties among the volunteers was being suppressed and that mortality exceeded all published reports. Soon afterward influential efforts were being made to secure the return of these troops.[7]

But in April the movement in the South and West to bring home the troops mushroomed. A public meeting was held in Nashville asking for the return of the Tennessee regiment.[8] Relatives and friends of the Oregon volunteers, supported by newspapers of that state, called for the return of the Oregon troops, "who never enlisted for such a war."[9] While Oregon's Governor Geer refused to heed their requests, Governor Lind of Minnesota, in a message to the legislature, urged the immediate mustering out of the men from that state, and newspapers of all shades of opinion approved.[10] In South Dakota Governor Lee joined the popular demand for the return of the volunteers, writing President McKinley that the Philippine war was "repugnant to the fundamental principles of government," and that the South Dakota men were being held in the army against their will. Senator Pettigrew backed up the Governor.[11] Perhaps the President could discount the protests of these last two, for Lee was a Populist and Pettigrew an avowed anti-imperialist, but it was more difficult to disregard another message from the parents of several hundred members of the First Nebraska Regiment who demanded that "the government send back home those who have not contributed their precious fever-stricken or bullet-torn bodies to enrich the soil of Luzon."[12]

More worrisome to the Administration, perhaps, than the domestic protest were signs of disaffection among the soldiers themselves. On March 30 the *Boston Evening Transcript* carried an uncensored dispatch from Manila, via Hong Kong, to the effect that "a majority of the United States volunteers are eager to return home . . . 'we did not enlist to fight niggers' is a remark that is constantly heard." (The dispatch also reported the view of an outstanding general in the Philippines that it would take 100,000 United States troops to subdue the islands.)[13] The *Philadelphia Times* printed a letter telling of the unanimous vote of the Tenth Pennsylvania volunteers against serving after their original enlistment expired.[14] Governor Lind made public a telegram from the Thirteenth Minnesota volunteers demanding that "the regiment must be ordered home and mustered out of the service at once."[15]

All this was very embarrassing to the party in power. Since the start of the war, General Otis had repeatedly claimed that it was nearly over, which assurance the Administration had passed on to the public. The General had told Washington that he would need no more troops and that the volunteers would re-enlist.[16] Now the war was still on, more troops would probably be needed and the volunteers would not re-enlist. (In the second week of April Washington admitted that only about 7% of the volunteers would re-enlist, even when offered a bounty of $500 per man.)[17] Clearly the General needed a scapegoat, and the Administration shared his need. McKinley was singularly anxious to avoid calling up more troops for obvious reasons.

Toward the end of April the government was caught between the popular opposition to the war, registered most acutely in the demands for volunteer withdrawal, and its own intention to continue the war until military victory had been won over the Philippine insurgents. The McKinley Administration responded with both concessions and threats.

On April 16 the War Department announced that it expected to be able soon to make public the names of volunteer regiments that would be brought home, and that probably three of these would be the Thirteenth Minnesota, the First South Dakota and the Tenth Pennsylvania, since powerful efforts had been made to secure their dismissal.[18] Three days later a Washington dispatch to the *New York Tribune* asserted that the government would send 14,000 regulars to take the place of the 12,000 volunteers. (Perhaps this decision was reached none too soon. In June a Manila newspaper correspondent wrote a London friend, "The volunteers, or at least a portion of them, were one time on the verge of mutiny, and unless Gen. Otis had begun sending them homeward there would have been sensational developments.") [19]

On April 21 the story was leaked from Washington to a few select pro-war papers (of which the *Boston Herald* was one) stating that the cabinet meeting that day had "discovered that anti-expansionists in this country, believed to be connected with the Anti-Imperialist League, or influenced by it, have been sending letters or telegrams to the volunteers in the Philippines stirring them up to discontent, and that this is at the bottom of the pessimistic reports from Manila by way of Hong Kong, and the appeal for the recall of the volunteer regiments." General Otis had brought the matter to Washington's attention, reporting "seditious" telegrams addressed to volunteer regiments. The Administration believed that this could be "considered constructive treason" and had decided to "expose the men who have thus been hampering the government."[20]

The Executive Committee of the Anti-Imperialist League reacted promptly, if somewhat defensively, to this news, demanding that the government produce any names other than those of relatives and friends of the volunteers who had written to them urging their return from "an unpopular and unrighteous war."[21]

The *Springfield Republican* agreed with the Anti-Imperialist Executive Committee on the need to "let in the light — all of it." Then it added in a bolder vein, "It may as well be recognized that the right of opinion and freedom of speech is going to be preserved in this republic. If martyrs are called for in this cause, they will be forthcoming."[22]

Before this prediction appeared in print a candidate stepped forward to fulfill it. The day after the *Herald* ran its story of the cabinet meeting, Edward Atkinson wrote his friend Secretary of the Treasury Gage saying that he believed the government mistaken in its belief that the Anti-Imperialist League was stirring up trouble among the troops in the Philippines, but the suggestion was a "valuable one," worth trying. Then he sent off a letter to Secretary of War Alger asking for lists of names of officers and privates in the Philippines so that he could send them large numbers of anti-war pamphlets of his own writing. When the War Department failed to answer, he sent copies of his pamphlets (entitled "The Hell of War," "The Cost of a National Crime," "Criminal Aggression") to General Otis, Admiral Dewey, two other generals and a couple of civilian worthies in Manila, "as a test."[23]

Atkinson told the Boston papers of his efforts and was asked whether giving the troops information about domestic opposition to the war might not lead to insubordination. His answer was straightforward:

> Yes, the kind of insubordination which, I hope . . . will ere long pervade all armies, to the end that criminal aggression may be made impossible by the refusal of soldiers who think for themselves to carry out orders which are as abhorrent to them as they are inconsistent with any moral, economic or political principle.[24]

The cabinet met without delay. Postmaster General Smith announced that he would remove Atkinson's pamphlets from the mails at San Francisco. The Attorney General declared the Boston businessman to be, without doubt, guilty of treason and subject to heavy prison sentence and fine. The pamphlets were indeed seized, but since neither party to the dispute did anything more to further it, the confrontation between Atkinson and the federal government ended quickly, though a national debate about it lasted for several days. Many, if not most, of the papers supported the government, but such a storm was raised, with such a surge of interest in Atkinson and his pamphlets, that before long the government wished it had never taken notice of the man.[25]

The *Springfield Republican* expressed the attitude of most of those who supported Atkinson. It doubted the "propriety" of the Bostonian's attempt, but declared that the action of the cabinet against him, "was at bottom an attempt to intimidate the opposition generally and attack free speech."[26] This was the position the Executive Committee of the Anti-Imperialist League eventually took, although their initial reaction was more one-sided and cautious.

Learning of Atkinson's project (he was not a member of the Executive Committee), they speedily and publicly disassociated themselves from it, saying that they did not think it the business of the League to propagandize the troops. Stung by their action, Atkinson offered to resign from the League, but Secretary Winslow refused even to consider this suggestion.[27]

The disagreement between Atkinson and the Executive Committee represented the re-emergence, in very sharp terms, of a question that had previously divided the anti-imperialists: whether to oppose an unjust war and still give the government some measure of support, or to adopt a more thorough-going policy. The *Springfield Republican* put the first position clearly when it wrote on March 30, "As opponents of a war of this kind we may agitate for its cessation and for the repudiation of those responsible for it, but while it continues the government deserves the support of its citizens." Some two months later Erving Winslow wrote the *Republican* expressing the other view, "Let it be distinctly and solemnly asserted that to defeat this active conspiracy against the constitution" (i.e., imperialism) "the only way appears to hinder, and if possible to paralyze, the president's war."[28] At bottom the point of division among anti-imperialists seems to have been recognition of United States military defeat as a logical corollary of their anti-war position, an implication many found hard to face. It also appears that the majority of the Executive Committee of the Anti-Imperialist League leaned toward the ambiguity of the *Republican* editorial, while Erving Winslow, who served them as secretary, in his individual capacity sympathized with Atkinson's more militant consistency.

But there is more to be recorded of the Executive Committee of the Anti-Imperialist League in this moment of crisis. They not only refused to move with Atkinson to a more advanced position when the government opened fire, they also retreated from ground they had previously held. Just after the cabinet made known its discovery of "treason," Winslow, in the name of the Executive Committee, sent McKinley a telegram that urged Philippine independence only after a United States military occupation of five years, and at the price of Philippine surrender of a small island for a United States naval station and Philippine assumption of the $20,000,000 the United States paid Spain. Administration spokesmen were quick to take advantage of this, claiming that it was not far from the McKinley program. (To make matters worse, the press had misprinted the statement so that the League Executive appeared to call for United States retention of "small islands," in the plural.) [29]

Anti-imperialists immediately rebuked their elected leadership for this backward step. A few days after the Executive Committee telegram the *Transcript* printed a letter from one who signed himself an "ante anti-imperialist" and asked some pointed questions. Was it possible that "just as the fire of freedom begins to burn bravely elsewhere the beacon lighted here is smoking and smouldering?" Was "the apparent success of practical politics and war measures . . . threatening its vital spark?" The writer called upon the next meeting of the Anti-Imperialist League to void the Executive Committee telegram. League Vice President Rev. Charles F. Dole associated himself with this criticism: any thought that the United States must assume responsibility for Philippine sovereignty (as the committee telegram implied) was, in Dole's opinion, nothing more than a concession to the "notion of being a superior race" in relation to the Filipinos because their skin was colored.[30]

The Executive Committee quickly responded to such pressures from the ranks. At the next meeting of the League, held May 16, those present passed resolutions that restated the position the organization had taken shortly after the war's oubreak: immediate cessation of hostilities, unhesitating recognition of Philippine independence and abandonment of any claim to American sovereignty. The meeting condemned "unjustifiable censorship of the press" and "high-handed violation of the mails." The five year occupation and the naval station were forgotten.[31] After flinching as the government shook a fist, the Executive Committee of the Anti-Imperialist League recovered their composure, stood their ground, and supported Edward Atkinson in his challenge, even if they did not join him.

Though he was quite alone, Atkinson carried his defiance with engaging candor and insouciance. Perhaps this was because he had become accustomed to standing out in the 72 years of his life. Of old Boston family, his father a merchant, his own youth spent as a mercantile apprentice, Atkinson had espoused anti-slavery in its early days, raising funds in Boston to buy rifles for John Brown in Kansas. Entering the manufacture of textiles after the Civil War, he so zealously championed free trade that he made enemies among protectionists who dominated the industry, losing his position with one company as a result. Eventually he left the textile industry to become the executive of a fire insurance company, and it was as such that he carried on his anti-imperialist activity. A largely self-taught man of giant energies and ego, his interests were very varied and very intense. As union labor took shape in the post-Civil War years, Atkinson quarreled with it most vigorously, from the standpoint of conservative individualism. To hold up his end of the argument he invented something he called the Aladdin stove, whereby working people could improve their diet without increase in wages, using cheaper cuts of meat, soup-bones, and so forth. He promoted this stew-pot with such enthusiasm that union leaders called him "Shinbone" Atkinson.[32] Then his turn-about (as he urged a policy of "combining" with organized labor against imperialism) set him beyond the pale of his conservative admirers.[33] Now his latest stand put him out ahead of many of his liberal friends, but he fell into it easily, as if by nature trained. Let the leading body of the Anti-Imperialist League disagree; he was an organization in his own right and capacity. Before the hullaballoo with the cabinet he had by himself secured subscriptions for over 20,000 copies of his pamphlets, although he had only "put $100 capital into the business." He was delighted to see the government become his own best salesman. After Postmaster Smith seized his harsh tracts from the mails, their sales increased "enormously," and Atkinson rejoiced in the belief that some then reached the soldiers in the Philippines, though not by his own hand.[34]

"The 'treason' cry arose in government circles as soon as it became known that the volunteers in the Philippines would not re-enlist. So the government jumps on Edward Atkinson, whose pamphlets have no circulation at all among the soldiers," wrote the *Republican* at the time.[35] What his contemporaries understood about the Atkinson episode those who have written about it since have most often lost sight of.[36] Perhaps the bravura of Atkinson's gesture has tended to obscure its real significance as a symbol of the popular opposition to the war, above which it glittered in display; like a lightning rod it caught the governmental wrath really aimed at what lay below.

The opposition to the Philippine War won the demand to bring home the volunteer troops. Since this demand came mainly from the Western states, Atkinson's intervention stressed anew the informal unity of action that had come about between the Populist anti-imperialism of the West and the Mugwump anti-imperialism of the

East, first against the treaty, then against the war.

If the government sought to silence the opposition to the war with its talk of treason, it failed, by and large, to accomplish its purpose. After a momentary hesitation, the Anti-Imperialist League resumed its agitation for negotiations to end hostilities on the basis of Philippine independence. For the most part the government's threatening attitude, press censorship and interference with the mails served only to remind the anti-imperialists of the slaveholders' attempts to suppress abolitionist agitation and to-convince them that they were right in the belief that an imperial policy abroad would undermine democracy at home.[37]

On the other hand, those who called for an end to the war failed to win their objective. Four times during the months of April and May Aguinaldo sent emissaries behind the American lines with offers to stop the fighting and begin negotiations for a peaceful settlement. Each time General Otis rebuffed the insurgent overtures, with Washington's full support.[38]

In this light the McKinley Administration's concession on the question of volunteer withdrawal falls into a subordinate place beside its relentless prosecution of the war. Even more, this concession removed from the anti-imperialist leadership what was, at the moment, their most effective support in the thousands of American families who wanted their sons back home, and so dampened an opposition that was becoming troublesome.

If the policy of concession benefited the Administration, it is likely that the policy of threats helped secure an advantage other than the temporary disorientation of the League leadership. This more serious effect resulted, perhaps, from the fact that the government's menacing attitude lent additional weight to a pressure already heavy. For the treason charges were not by themselves alone, but came on top of treaty defeat, the outbreak of the war and its unbending pursuit; they were yet another in a series of blows to the anti-imperialist movement that had a cumulative effect, causing difficulties.

This was most noticeable in the quickened shrinkage of upper-class support for anti-imperialism, a process begun the December before with the defection of the *Boston Herald* at the bidding of its wealthy owner. Toward the end of April the *Boston Evening Transcript* began to abandon its editorial anti-imperialism and edge toward support of the government, as was particularly striking at the time of the Administration's action against Atkinson. Then editor Clement (feeling once again the restrictive disapproval of his ideas that had forced him to leave the South as a younger man) wrote Atkinson that he was grieved and humiliated at "the positions the *Transcript* has been taking," but that the paper was not his to control as against its owners.[39]

Before the passage of the treaty the Boston Merchants Association had joined the Anti-Imperialist League in rejecting annexation of the Philippine archipelago. After the outbreak of the war, however, the Association did not call for its end, and so appeared to shift away from the anti-imperialist leadership. The Republican District Attorney for Massachusetts (a McKinley man) claimed that there was indeed such a change in Boston merchant opinion, when, on April 1, he told the *Transcript*'s O'Brien, "The merchants have come to look upon expansion as an accomplished fact . . . and so are preparing to meet the new conditions."[40]

On the same day Charles Francis Adams confided a similar mood to his diary. He had "passed an hour" with Carl Schurz in New York City, "grumbling in utter impotence over the situation, — the subjection of the Filipinos and the progress of imperialism, agreed we were powerless." A little later Adams let the public know his change of heart. On May 17 the Cambridge branch of the Anti-Imperialist League held a rally at which Edward Atkinson, fresh from his tussle with the government, demanded the war's end and brought forward a new proposal for the neutralization of the Philippines. Adams, whose support had been asked, instead wrote the meeting a letter (not read at the gathering but afterward released to the press) announcing that he had given up the struggle against imperialism and urging others to do the same; the adoption of an imperial policy was an accomplished fact; it was useless to protest further, better "heartily cooperate" in order to lessen its worse effects.[41]

The check to upper-class support for the Anti-Imperialist League was not confined to Boston. Massachusetts anti-imperialists linked Adams' defection with the recently announced refusal of C. J. Bonaparte, a prominent Mugwump lawyer of Baltimore, to serve as a vice-president of the League. (Bonaparte had before this made anti-imperialist declarations.) [42]

Evidence of well-to-do back-sliding was painful to those who remained staunch. The *Transcript*'s "flip-flop" was condemned on all sides, and the *Springfield Republican* told Adams what, in effect, he had told the *Herald*'s owner in December, "God hates a quitter." The paper asked, "Would Mr. Adams have the slaughter go on to the bitter end?"[43]

Despite these setbacks, the fact remained that in the late winter and the spring of 1899 the Massachusetts anti-imperialist leaders had held to their demand to end the war. They helped organize a nationwide opposition to it that, in the campaign for volunteer withdrawal, shook the McKinley Administration. They had rallied most of their Boston friends and allies to their side; Democrats and dissident Republicans, leaders of labor, Irish-Americans, women and the blacks spoke out against the war.

Massachusetts opposition to the war, moreover, had been brought emphatically to the nation's attention. After McKinley made his Boston triumph and the imperialist press hailed the repudiation of the President's critics on their native ground, the country had learned that Massachusetts anti-imperialists were still very much to be heard from. Hoar may have begged off, and the League not planned it so, but Edward Atkinson had stuck his neck out and done the job. He answered the President, telling him in the plainest way that his war was not worth fighting.

12

The Rise of Monopoly and Finance

As the United States government persisted in its war against the Philippine independence movement, Massachusetts anti-imperialists reached a new understanding of the forces that opposed them. This fresh insight was closely connected with certain economic developments in the United States, — foremost of these, the monopolization of industry and the accumulation of a capital surplus.

In May 1899 the *Protectionist* (newly named magazine of the Home Market Club) drew the attention of Massachusetts industrialists to the growth of trusts and syndicates: in the 12 months of 1898, 200 such concerns were organized with an authorized capital of over three billion dollars, while in January and February of 1899, 353 organizations were affected with a capitalization of over five billion. On March 22 Boston's *Transcript* offered the opinion that this was the "most stupendous revolution ever accomplished in the history of the world's economic growth," placing "nearly our entire industrial system upon the monopolistic basis."

Neither textile or shoe, the two main industries of Massachusetts, lent themselves to monopolization. In contrast to the general condition of the state's industry, however, was the organization in February 1899 of the United Shoe Machinery Company (virtually monopolizing the manufacture of machinery for the shoe industry), and in March 1899, the American Woolen Company, a large textile combine.[1]

Trustification had been present as a strong tendency before this, but when it seemed so suddenly dominant, a great debate began about the effect of this change on American society and government, in which the anti-imperialists took part. The proponents of the trusts saw the development as having a decided influence on our nation's foreign affairs, and the anti-imperialists were critical of it for this very reason. It was obvious that a monopoly like the United Fruit Company, promoted in April 1899 by Boston financiers, would impinge directly on the country's foreign relations since its purpose was to control the banana trade with small nations to the south.[2] But this was a particular case. Late in May, Charles R. Flint, New York banker and organizer of the United States Rubber Company, a great trust, told Bostonians about the more general relationship of monopoly to foreign trade.

William M. Wood, initiator of the new Massachusetts wool combine, invited Flint to Boston to address a gathering of the city's leading bankers at the Union Club.[3] Monopoly, with its centralization of distribution, cut down the business opportunities available to commission merchants, and mercantile Boston had expressed uneasiness at the concentration of economic power that the trust movement was bringing about (a complaint common to Massachusetts labor and farmers as well).[4] Flint addressed his remarks to the city's merchants, as if to soothe them, pointing out that in 1891 the United States had had $200,000,000 excess of imports over exports of manufactured goods, whereas in the past year there had been a $60,000,000 excess of exports over imports, and this great increase in the export of manufactured goods had been "principally owing to the development of economic manufacture through combination." Flint then made a most positive declaration: the one way the United States could extend and hold its position in the world's markets for manufactured goods was "by securing the advantages of highly developed special machinery which is only possible through centralized manufacture and aggregated capital."[5]

Whether or not Flint persuaded Boston's men of commerce, it seemed clear that mercantile influence was at a low ebb. The organization of another Massachusetts trust, a writing paper monopoly (with a special department for promoting foreign trade), in June 1899 testified to this, for its sponsor was Henry Lee Higginson, nephew of Henry Lee.[6] As head of Lee, Higginson and Company and founder of the Boston Symphony Orchestra, Higginson was rapidly assuming his uncle's place as Boston's first banker and citizen. But the uncle had expressed the antagonism of Boston's merchant class to the dominance of industrial capital in its corporate form after the Civil War, whereas now, after the Spanish War, the nephew plunged into the promotion of industrial monopoly, without a thought for mercantile reservations. (This difference had political reflections as well: a few months before his death the older man had urged public protest against the Spanish War, while the younger man urged public support and, during the Philippine War, contented himself with private misgivings.)

With the changing climate of upper class opinion in Boston and the *Transcript*'s switch to imperialism, the city's anti-imperialists had to turn to Samuel Bowles' paper for the expression of their views from day to day. In 1899 and 1900, the years of the movement's most intense and widespread activity, the *Springfield Republican* held a place as the leading anti-imperialist journal in the state, if not the nation — reportedly read by McKinley himself.[7]

The anti-imperialist view of recent economic developments was soon suggested by the *Republican*'s Boston correspondent, F. B. Sanborn, a Concord school teacher, friend of Emerson and Thoreau. As a young reformer Sanborn had been very active on behalf of John Brown, whom he had supplied with funds and arms. One of a half-dozen men privy to Brown's plans, Sanborn became widely known for his anti-slavery activity after Harper's Ferry, when a congressional investigating committee had summoned him to testify before it, and he refused to appear. The committee then sent five marshals to arrest Sanborn and bring him to Washington. When these presented themselves at Sanborn's Concord home early one evening and gained entry under false pretenses, he put up such a fight and his sister raised such an alarm that before the sheriffs could haul him off Sanborn's Irish neighbors arrived in force and sent the unlucky fellows packing.[8]

In his weekly column, which the *New York Sun* described as the anti-imperialists' "bristling front of war," Sanborn treated the imperialists with the same scorn he had shown the slaveholders and their representatives, fortifying militancy with a school master's knowledge of history and the classics. When he saw a connection between the trusts and imperialism he did not hesitate to make it known. In the *Republican* of March 25, 1899, Sanborn discussed the election prospects for 1900 and maintained that popular support for the Republican Party was being shaken by anxiety at the unscrupulous boldness and greed of the trusts, — in whose hands, without possibility of escape, are McKinley and the party leaders. Imperialism and syndication, like Sin and Death in Milton's parable, — syndication the mother and imperialism the child, —

>"That other shape,
>If shape it might be called, that shape had none
>Distinguishable in member, joint or limb, —
>Or substance might be called that shadow seemed,
>For each seemed either; what appeared his head
>The likeness of a kingly crown had on, —"

this precious pair, I say, now dominate the party that began as the party of freedom, but now is the mere slave of dropsical and insolent wealth.[9]

The identification of monopoly and imperialism as cause and effect, made in 1898 by George E. McNeill at Faneuil Hall, now became widespread, especially among anti-imperialists and those close to them. At a big public meeting in May that led to the formation of the Chicago anti-imperialist league, Roman Catholic Bishop Spalding of Peoria told those assembled that the United States was annexing the Philippines because it was "following the lead of our great capitalists and trust lords."[10] In June a widely publicized national conference on social reform was held in Buffalo, sponsored by such notables as Jane Addams, Booker T. Washington and William Dean Howells, attended by many delegates from East and West (editor Edwin D. Mead, labor leader Henry Lloyd and George Fred Williams, Bryan's lieutenant in Massachusetts, were among those who came from Boston). This gathering adopted by overwhelming vote a declaration written by a Western educator that said, in part, "Militarism . . . expressed in our war of conquest in the Philippines . . . is but the offspring and incident of the greater menace of plutocracy which has established monopoly government in the place of government by the people." The *Springfield Republican* reprinted this declaration in full as "a strong and impressive description of the aggressions of syndicated capitalism."[11]

The assertion of monopoly's connection with an aggressive foreign policy, while significant, was not, essentially, something new. From the first days of modern imperial development in the "vigorous" foreign policy of James G. Blaine, both imperialists and anti-imperialists had looked upon the struggle of American industry for foreign markets as the root cause of the government's assumption of an expansionist role, and this, before the dominance of monopoly. Monopoly, by increasing productivity, heightened the drive of American industry for markets abroad. Indeed, Flint gave monopoly most credit, when the United States finally succeeded in exporting more manufactured goods than it imported.

But at the very moment that the export of manufactured goods was becoming more effective than ever, it was being replaced as the chief cause of imperial policy by the export of capital. Such, at least, was the claim of an astute supporter of the McKinley Administration, the economist Charles A. Conant, who wrote in the June 1899 issue of the *Forum*,

> The opponents of colonial expansion often discuss the question of foreign markets as if the only question were the absorption of finished goods. This is in reality the less important side of the problem. The real opportunity afforded by colonial possessions is for the development of the new countries by fixed investment.[12]

At the time of the Venezuelan episode a correspondent of the *Boston Evening Transcript* had seen, first of all, the United States conquest of South American markets for manufactured goods, and then, glimmering in the distance, the investment of American capital. Now, from the imperialist standpoint, the perspective had radically changed, and there, plump in the foreground, was the question of capital export.

As in the case of manufactured goods, it was the development of a relative surplus of investment capital that led to the question of its export. President McKinley called the attention of Boston businessmen to this new phenomenon in the talk he made to them in February 1899. But Conant brought the point home to government and business in a series of articles he wrote from September 1898 to August 1899 for the *North American Review*, the *Forum* and the *Atlantic Monthly*.

Originally a Massachusetts man and a Gold Democrat, Conant turned to the Republicans on the Philippine issue. He was Washington correspondent of the New York *Commercial Bulletin* and wrote on international monetary affairs for the *Banker's Magazine* of that city. The New York financial community regarded him as an authority, and the McKinley Administration showed its confidence in his views when it appointed him to reorganize the Philippine currency in 1901.[13]

Conant's analysis influenced the anti-imperialists as well.* It was not long before the *Springfield Republican* summarized his views on its editorial page, writing,

> There appeared in the *Atlantic Monthly* some time ago an article by Charles A. Conant of Washington, setting forth the economic basis and significance of expansion or imperialism. Mr. Conant pointed to what he would characterize as the undue accumulation of capital in the United States and other commercial nations. There resulted an undue and unfortunate decline in capital earnings or interest, which seriously threatens the livelihood of the classes depending upon income from capital. New outlets for capital in distant and undeveloped countries and in the islands of the sea must or should be provided, but to insure an adequate outflow of capital the strong home government must go along with it to protect it. This calls for the heavy taxation of capital and production to provide the great armaments necessary to establish and maintain the strong home government in these distant fields which have been seized on behalf of profit, but what of that? The problem is a glut of capital. These vast armaments help relieve the glut.

With the painful exigencies of the Philippine conflict undoubtedly in mind the editor of the *Republican* countered with the suggestion that it would be cheaper, more bloodless and humanitarian to blow up an industrial city like Fall River occasionally rather than to dump great quantities of saved capital into warships and armies "for the purpose of holding in subjection distant countries on behalf of a higher interest rate."[14]

This discussion suggested a re-ordering of priorities in the Ameri-

---

* In its issue of February 25, 1899 (just after McKinley's visit) Boston's anti-imperialist weekly, *Time and the Hour*, printed what appeared to be a poetic reflection of Conant's views,

> All Hail to the Big
> *American Pig!*
> He roots and he will not die;
> By his trough he shall stand,
> And each conquered land
> Shall afford him an elegant sty.

The influence of his or like opinions persisted with the anti-imperialist leadership. In 1908 Winslow wrote that the "class of exploiters" who profited from "land grants, concessions and franchises" in foreign lands were the most powerful agents of imperialism, putting in the shade the army and navy, and those who honestly thought it benefited backward peoples.

can economy. Formerly, in the first stage of imperial development, armaments were seen as a means of protecting industrial markets abroad; now they were seen as protection for capital invested in foreign countries. Then war was regarded as a stimulus to industrial production; now it appeared as a means of absorbing a capital glut.

The speaker at the Fourth of July exercises sponsored by the city of Boston in 1899 brought these new aspects of imperialism forcefully to public attention. Mayor Josiah Quincy (whose anti-imperialism was fitful) invited his business associate, Nathan Matthews, Jr., to make the address. Before the affair took place it was rumored that Matthews would use the opportunity to declare support for the foreign policies of the McKinley Administration, and this he did.[15]

After dilating on the advantages of industrial monopoly to the struggle for foreign markets, Matthews explained that capital had accumulated so rapidly in the past few years that the rate of interest upon investments was falling markedly. Therefore "greater opportunities are needed for the investment of this surplus capital in order to prevent the duplication of industries for which there can be no adequate domestic market." From this standpoint Matthews urged the conquest of the Philippines to guarantee openings for American capital in a China threatened by European partition.[16]

The Boston press reported the civic exercises "slimly attended, owing probably to counter-attractions." Drawing large crowds was a July Fourth celebration the Irish-American Clan-na-Gael held in South Boston. Athletic events and dancing during the day were climaxed by an evening rally of 5,000 people, addressed by Senator William E. Mason, a dissident Republican from Illinois.

Introduced by E. J. Slattery, the state chairman of the Ancient Order of Hibernians, Senator Mason gave direct answer to Matthews' speech at the municipal meeting held that morning. He told his audience that although it was their sons who were fighting and dying in the Philippines, the American workingmen stood to gain nothing from these islands. He scoffed at the charge of treason leveled against the anti-imperialists because they interfered with the investment of American capital abroad. There was, he said, plenty of work for American capital to do at home. The Senator challenged Matthews and McKinley, "How many more hearts of American mothers have we to break . . . how many more American boys have we to kill in order to furnish places for the investment of money?"[17]

The meeting also heard the Bryan leader, George Fred Williams, speak against the war and it unanimously resolved opposition to imperialism and the Anglo-American alliance. The Clan-na-Gael rally indicated that while some upper-class Yankees like Matthews were moving to support McKinley on the imperialist question, Boston's Irish working-class Democrats were strengthening an opposition coalition with Yankee Mugwumps and Republicans. The New England Anti-Imperialist League had secured Senator Mason for the rally, and both Boutwell and A. E. Pillsbury sent it messages of support, the latter paying tribute to the Irish for keeping alive "the spirit of liberty among the American people" — as the Boston *Pilot* was pleased to note.[18]

According to Matthews, concern for China as a field for American capital investment was in the forefront of the Administration's foreign policy considerations. Shortly after his speech the news of the day seemed to bear him out. On July 14, W. Barclay Parsons visited the State Department to secure government support for an Anglo-American project to build railroads in southern China (the cooperation of English and American capitalists in this project seemed, in turn, to lend weight to the Clan-na-Gael's protest against an Anglo-American alliance). Those interested were concerned because the Chinese government was dragging its feet in making the necessary concessions. Since the British capitalists had had similar difficulties in northern China as a result of Russian pressure, it was thought that United States intercession with the Peking regime would have a wholesome effect. The Administration promised to use its influence.

W. Barclay Parsons, who presented the matter to Secretary of State Hay, was the engineer of the American syndicate involved, the America-China Development Company. The Rockellers, the Vanderbilts, the Carnegie Steel Company and others were reported to be financially interested in the syndicate. Such, wrote the *Springfield Republican,* are "the administrators of the administration . . . the capitalists who are moving on China."[19]

If Senator Mason drew the line between Boston's Irish population and finance capital, F. B. Sanborn did the same in relation to monopoly, when he reported Boston's Fourth of July celebrations. Referring to the rivalry between Standard Oil and Russian oil interests over the Chinese market, Sanborn maintained that Matthews and McKinley wanted China reserved for "the Anglo-Saxons to the exclusion of owners of Caspian sea petroleum." Now Boston papers would have to choose "between the Standard Oil people and those who shout 'Erin go bragh' on all convenient occasions."[20]

There were Bostonians, however, who were not content to leave matters at this point of contrast. Accordingly Councillor McInerney of Jamaica Plain introduced a resolution at the next meeting of the Boston City Council condemning Matthews for "upholding Imperialism, Expansion and the Trusts," and for outlining a policy "which would make this Republic an empire . . . simply to gratify the greed of American and foreign capitalists." Such sentiments, it was averred, did not represent the people of the city.[21]

While the Council adjourned for the summer before the resolution could be discussed, one thing seemed clear. The Massachusetts anti-imperialists were successfully communicating their new understanding of imperialism and its workings to many of their fellow-citizens.*

---

* The Council passed the resolution on October 14, 1899, over Republican opposition.

13

An Organization Formed, A Republic Smashed

In the summer and early fall of 1899 the anti-imperialists strengthened opposition to the inconclusive Philippine War, forming a national organization to influence the elections of 1900. The popular opposition to the war also secured next year's Democratic presidential nomination for Bryan and had an important effect on the Congressional elections of 1899. In the face of these anti-imperialist gains, the McKinley Administration made its own preparations for 1900: it took military measures that crippled Philippine resistance.

In July members of Boston's black community struck a resounding blow at the President's war policy when the anti-imperialists (deferring to the nation's segregated institutions) attempted to organize a "colored auxiliary." On July 16, after conferring with Winslow and Atkinson, Clifford H. Plummer, a prominent Boston attorney and secretary of the National Colored Protective League, gave an interview to the press about the proposed organization.

Plummer declared that McKinley was the first president since the Civil War who had refused to speak out against Southern lynchings, and that, as a result, the country's 3,000,000 black voters would desert him in 1900. Now the Administration wanted to get hold of another 8,000,000 Negroes in the Philippines for what they would bring: "They would swallow the devil if he had anything in him of financial benefit." Blacks in this country had full sympathy for the "poor blacks of the Philippines," who, like themselves, were fighting for independence. Were it not for the distance, said Plummer, he did not doubt that many American blacks would take up arms for the Filipinos.

On the next day, a Sunday, Plummer's interview was the topic of discussion in Boston's black community and its churches. Monday night a large audience of blacks and whites attended a meeting to form a colored auxiliary of the Anti-Imperialist League. After Plummer and W. L. Garrison spoke, the assembly passed resolutions condemning McKinley for his war in the Philippines and for his silence on lynching. (Later Plummer's Colored Protective League charged that McKinley kept silent "in order to win support of the South to his policy of 'criminal aggression' in the Far East.")[1]

The anti-imperialist meeting of Boston blacks had immediate repercussions in the nation's capital. Registrar of the Treasury Lyons, Recorder of Deeds Cheatham and Stamp Clerk Green, the blacks holding the highest federal offices, promptly called upon the President to tell him not to be alarmed by the reports from Boston; the blacks of the country were perfectly willing to trust the Republican Party to give the Filipinos good government. The President seemed reassured.[2]

The Administration had reason to be concerned with popular unrest in the summer of 1899. Its Philippine War dragged on without success. Despite General Otis' persistent reports of the defeat and disintegration of the Philippine army, the fact remained that by the middle of June American troops had made practically no headway in suppressing the revolution, having advanced only a few miles beyond the walls of Manila.[3] From the very first it had been the Administration's claim that Aguinaldo represented only a small clique of adventurers, without popular support. Now, however, General Arthur MacArthur, second in command, was telling the press that contrary to his original view, he presently believed "that the Filipino masses are loyal to Aguinaldo and the government which he heads."[4] With oppressive regularity the only word from the Philippines was that of the death of American soldiers from tropical sickness and inconsequential battle (reported to kill even more Filipinos). Since the cost to the taxpayer was $300,000 a day, there were those who wondered whether "the game was worth the candle."[5] The returning volunteers did not help matters. They were nearly unanimous in their disgust for the war and for their commanding general, "old lobster Otis."[6]

Dissatisfaction with the war was not confined to anti-imperialists and their sympathizers; it involved Administration supporters, some of them very prominent. Senator Frye of Maine became disgruntled and struck out at a fellow-imperialist. The Senator, who had been a member of the Paris Peace Commission, ardent for annexation, now charged that General Merritt had deceived the Commission when he told them the Philippine nationalists could be easily subdued with 5,000 troops.[7] On a higher government level, Navy Secretary Long (harking back, perhaps, to his days with the Boston peace society) began to worry the Cabinet with reports of "reckless slaughter of the natives by the navy's vessels."[8] On the field of battle, General Funston, the victor of Caloocan, decided that he was an anti-expansionist ("though not a bitter one") and could see no benefit from the Philippines save for a few "big syndicates and capitalists."[9] In Boston, the *Herald* and the *Transcript,* important converts to imperialism, became critical and querulous about the war.[10]

In this atmosphere of discouragement Theodore Roosevelt (now Governor of New York state) stepped forward to rally support. Visiting McKinley at the White House early in July, he took the occasion to call upon all Americans to stand by the President and pay no heed to the anti-imperialists, who, he said, were responsible for the war and its prolongation.[11] At the same time the Administration reached out to mollify Massachusetts, the mainspring of dissent. In the last weeks of June the President came to North Adams in the western part of the state to lay the corner stone of a textile mill, one of the world's largest, owned by his good friend William B. Plunkett, while a great naval fleet under Admiral Sampson paid a visit to the port of Boston.[12]

In the spring, against a similar background of unease and frustration, the refusal of the volunteers to re-enlist dealt the McKinley Administration an unexpected and damaging blow. The summer brought a second shock, arising also from the war effort, a result of its difficulties and unpopularity. On July 9, all the American newspaper correspondents in Manila, representing "the most radical 'expansion' journals in the country as well as the impartial news associations," called upon General Otis and laid before him a round-robin letter of protest against the military censorship of their dispatches to the United States, and on July 17 this document was published in the United States. The journalists charged that Otis would not let them write the whole truth about the Philippine situation because it would "alarm the people at home." Instead official dispatches had "presented an ultra-optimistic view . . . not shared by the general officers in the field." The publication of this document brought consternation to the imperialists, jubilation to their foes. The anti-war press in Massachusetts declared that the journalists' description of the case fully vindicated Senator Hoar, who had made the same charges six months before.[13]

After the publication of the document in the United States the cabinet met and announced that it would do nothing in the matter. President McKinley was reported to be in favor of keeping the censorship, and, as for showing any disapproval of the correspondents, the Administration's fingers had been burnt by its threats to Atkinson.[14] Besides, the journalists who made the protest, by and large, wrote for pro-administration papers, and they claimed, without challenge, to represent the views of the officers in the field.

The McKinley Administration could afford an appearance of calm when this latest storm broke into the headlines; it had already taken action to provide the public a scapegoat. About a week after the journalists presented their statement to Otis, President McKinley got private word to Secretary of War Alger that his resignation would be welcome, and two days after the journalists' protest was made public the Secretary of War stepped down. The *New York Herald* had said that Alger, as Otis' immediate superior, was to blame for official misrepresentation of the war, and should therefore be dismissed.[15] McKinley evidently agreed. (Administration supporters, including Boston's Henry Lee Higginson, had called for Alger's removal before this, because of the canned beef scandal and other acts of mismanagement.[16])

Alger's resignation, however, did not check the growth of anti-war sentiment, stimulated by the anti-imperialists. At public meetings in July and August Boston leaders called for an end to the war, and this was the prevailing theme of anti-imperialist propaganda.[17]

The question of how far to carry their attitude of opposition continued to agitate the anti-imperialists, as shown by letters to the press. But late in August a speech by Gamaliel Bradford at a Connecticut peace conference drew wide attention to this discussion. Bradford virtually called for the defeat of the United States intervention in the Philippines, saying that he "ardently hoped . . . Aguinaldo and his followers would be able to prolong their resistance to the end of McKinley's term; or if beaten down by force, that we shall fail in establishing any stable government over them."[18]

When Atkinson had urged disruption of the war effort, the issue had been all but thrust aside by what was regarded as the government's threat to freedom of speech. This time the question Bradford raised was debated without distraction. A Rhode Island delegate to the peace conference condemned Bradford's words as "treasonable," and that was the tenor of adverse newspaper comment in Rhode Island, Massachusetts and Maine. But a paper in Lewiston, Maine, answered Bradford's critics, writing that it would be much better for the United States if she failed to establish a stable government in the Philippines. "A little success may easily lead our government to more ambitious schemes in China and South America . . . Better a thousand defeats in the Philippines than once the fetters of German militarism." In Boston Bradford's call for a "moral alliance with the Filipinos" met with favorable comment. "Men have been overheard in the cars saying of it: 'That is it; that is just the thing to say,'" reported the *Republican*.[19]

The anti-imperialists' campaign against the Philippine War gave strength to their organization and made it more widespread. In mid-July when the *Boston Post* and the *Boston Globe* carried feature stories about the League, Secretary Winslow claimed 40,000 members and 40 branches of the organization throughout the country. The Boston office was receiving several hundred letters in every day's mail and, in the previous six months, had sent out at least half a million pieces of literature. The pro-Administration *Globe* described the small room in the business district that housed the Boston headquarters as "the storm-center of a discussion sweeping from sea to sea."[20]

But the leading role of Boston in the national movement had been recognized for some time; what was new at the moment was the emergence of anti-imperialist organization and influence in the western part of the country. Returning from the conference on social reform in July, Edwin D. Mead told Boston friends that the Buffalo meeting had convinced him that "instead of being a mere Boston fad, as is charged by the imperialists . . . the strongest sentiment against imperialism is in the West."[21] At about the same time Samuel Gompers and Herbert Myrick, after touring that region, reported strong anti-imperialist sentiment there among workers and farmers. Even more vocal was the anti-imperialism of another segment of the western population, the German-Americans. The West was thickly settled (in states as far apart as Texas and Ohio) with citizens of German descent, many of whom, like Carl Schurz, had come to this country to be rid of the imperialism and militarism of their native land. Their language organizations and newspapers were very responsive to anti-imperialist agitation, and soon the Boston league was printing thousands of leaflets directed to them.[22] Once again a factor in the upsurge of western anti-imperialism was William Jennings Bryan. With his eye on next year's Democratic presidential nomination, Bryan in the summer of 1899, held a series of political rallies throughout the West, and these became anti-imperialist demonstrations because of the position Bryan took.[23]

Western anti-imperialist sentiment had crystallized in organization. The spring had seen a series of league-sponsored rallies, organized with Boston's help, in Chicago, St. Louis and Toledo; July brought another in Cincinnati.[24] Moreover the Chicago branch of the league, formed in May, wanted to take responsibility for anti-imperialist organization and propaganda in the leading cities and towns of the central West. Around the first of August the organization of the Chicago body was complete, and the Midwest was provided with its own anti-imperialist headquarters.[25]

The basis was now laid for the formation of a national anti-imperialist organization through the cooperation of the new center of anti-imperialist activity in the Midwest wth the established center in the East. In August a gathering of leaders was held in Boston. Among the easterners present was Samuel Bowles; from the West came Governor Pingree of Michigan and Edwin Burritt Smith, a lawyer who was the leading spirit of the Chicago organization. The meeting unanimously adopted a proposal, submitted by Winslow, for a national conference to be held in the autumn.[26]

The convention was held in Chicago on October 16 and 17 attended by more than 100 delegates from 29 states, about equally divided between Republicans, Democrats and Mugwumps. These delegates established the anti-imperialist league as a national organization, with headquarters at Chicago and an eastern office in Boston. They chose George S. Boutwell, the Massachusetts leader, as national chairman. High point of the proceedings was a public meeting attended by 10,000 people, chaired by J. Sterling Morton, Cleveland's Secretary of Agriculture and addressed by Carl Schurz. The convention repeated the call for an end to the war, but also moved on to

"Storm-center of a discussion sweeping from sea to sea." Boston headquarters of the New England Anti-Imperialist League, with Secretary Erving Winslow (glasses and beard) at his desk.

project a new issue: the elections of 1900 and the need to defeat any person or party then standing for the forcible subjugation of the Philippines.[27]

The anti-imperialist convention drew sarcastic comment from President McKinley at a cabinet meeting.[28] The President, however, did not confine himself to sarcasm. While the anti-imperialists assembled their forces for the crucial political struggle a year away, the Administration was preparing for decisive battles in the Philippine War at an earlier date.

Responsible for these preparations was Elihu Root of New York City, the man McKinley chose to succeed Alger. The most sought-after corporation lawyer in the country, Root had among his clients "the Union Tobacco Company and the United States Rubber Company; H. F. Havemeyer and the Sugar Trust; the Lead Trust, the Whiskey Trust, the Watch Trust and the Standard Oil Company." Shortly after Root's appointment his friend Theodore Roosevelt wrote Henry Cabot Lodge, summering in Europe, "Root realizes that the first thing to do is to smash the Philippine insurrection, and he has got the President's authority to enlist additional regiments."[29]

Whereas Otis, who had not stirred out of his office in Manila since his arrival in the Philippines, insisted that 30,000 troops were enough to crush Aguinaldo, the officers in the field believed that twice as many were needed, and Root soon announced plans to have an army of 70,000 in the Philippines. Alger might go and Otis remain, but it was clear where the new Secretary of War placed his reliance for future results.[30]

Meanwhile the United States situation in the Philippines did not improve. On October 2 the *Springfield Republican* reprinted a Manila dispatch from John T. McCutcheon, correspondent for the *Chicago Record*. Summarizing the results of the war so far, McCutcheon listed by name 21 Philippine towns the United States troops had first taken and then abandoned. The Americans had gone through this procedure once or twice with most of the towns involved, but one had been taken and abandoned six times, another four . . . all because Otis did not have enough men both to take and to hold the Philippine positions in the face of nationalist resistance. At the end of October, after seven months of campaigning, American forces had established United States rule in 117 square miles of Luzon's total area of 42,000.[31]

The lagging war continued to erode the domestic political position of the imperialists, and this showed in the internal affairs of the Democratic Party and the Congressional elections of 1899. Evidently counting on anti-war discontent to undo McKinley, Bryan hit hard at imperial policy as he mounted his campaign for the presidential nomination. To head him off, Southern and Eastern Democrats of conservative and imperialist persuasion began a quiet boom for Arthur Pue Gorman. In contrast to Bryan's record, Gorman's past services had put him in the good graces of big business, and, at the moment, the Maryland man was treading softly on the question of imperialism, indicating no other policy than that of carrying the Philippine war to the end. But the Gorman boom was laid to rest in short order.[32]

Before he went abroad for a summer at his English country estate, Tammany's millionaire boss, Richard Croker, declared for imperialism and the Philippine War, and his adjutant, New York City's Mayor Van Wyck, was party to the Gorman boom. But rank and file Democrats at a Tammany Hall Fourth of July celebration had given an overwhelming ovation to a speaker who urged Bryan and his candidacy. Accordingly, in August, when Croker returned from Europe, he spoke against the war and imperialism and announced himself for Bryan, dumping Gorman without ado.[33]

The anti-imperialist sentiment of the Massachusetts Democracy also helped to finish off Gorman. Boston Democrats had made their feelings plain at the Hibernian festival on July Fourth and in the subsequent denunciation of Mayor Quincy's protege, Nathan Matthews, Jr. Quincy also got the message. When Gorman came to New England, shortly thereafter, the Mayor told the press that he had no intention of meeting with the Maryland man. In August Judge Willett of Alabama came to Boston in the interests of the anti-Bryan campaign, with meagre results.[34]

At the end of September, as the off-year elections approached, the Massachusetts Democratic state convention chose a Bryan delegation to the national nominating convention of 1900, the first Bryan slate in the country. There was a show of opposition to this move, led by Congressman Fitzgerald, whose ties were with the conservative Boston leadership; but it was quickly overcome by the support of the convention majority for the Bryan forces. Evidently his Massachusetts followers wanted to nail their state down early for Bryan, setting an example for their fellow-Democrats throughout the nation. With the Massachusetts action Bryan's nomination seemed assured. Gorman was through.

For Governor the Democratic convention nominated Robert Treat Paine, Jr., a young liberal of unimpeachable antecedents (his father, a banker and leader of the peace society, his great great grandfather, a signer of the Declaration of Independence). Paine's nomination helped overcome the disaffection of Boston's Yankee Gold Democrats; Storey and others of this leaning soon declared their support for him. In balance, labor got recognition as the Democrats nominated Henry Lloyd, the A. F. of L. leader, for Secretary of State.

The Democrats further appealed to labor in the new terms of anti-imperialist discussion. Earlier in the year there had been a strike in Coeur d'Alene, Idaho, at the Rockefeller mining properties, where federal troops had been sent against the strikers. The Massachusetts Democrats drew the lesson for the state's trade unionists, condemning the ease with which the great industrial monopolies secured the aid of federal and state troops to overawe the workers. Federal troops against striking miners in Coeur d'Alene, federal troops against Filipinos struggling for their independence — it was all the same thing, said the Democrats.

The influence of the anti-imperialists was strong at the convention. Following their lead, the state platform declared: "In imperialism and militarism the great monopolistic corporations whose growth alarms and astounds the people discern twin agencies for their defense."[35] The *New York Times,* a Gold Democratic journal with views like those of Boston's Matthews, had predicted that Bryan Democrats would never dare adopt an anti-imperialist program. The Massachusetts platform proved the opposite.[36]

Behind it all, from the election of the Bryan delegates to the platform adopted, lay the anti-war sentiment of the rank and file. It was when the speakers called for an end to the Philippine War and denounced imperialism and the Anglo-American alliance that they got most attention and applause from the convention of Massachusetts Democrats.[37]

The Massachusetts Republican Party was not immune to the widespread unpopularity of the Philippine War and the influence of the anti-imperialists. In the first week of October the Republicans held their state convention, and their platform, while fulsome in praise of President McKinley, did not endorse either the conquest or the annexation of the Philippine Islands; instead it expressed hope for their "self-government" and an "early termination" of hostilities, implying the use of honorable concession quite as much as overwhelming force. Although the younger men on the resolutions committee opposed this and wanted a platform more in line with the purposes of the national administration, the older men won out, and so it stood.[38]

What made this difference with the Administration glaring was the fact that in the fall of 1899 President McKinley finally stopped public equivocation on the Philippine issue (assuming the offensive politically, as he prepared to do the same militarily, in tactics that recalled his treaty fight). The President called home the Commission he had sent ostensibly to negotiate with the Philippine nationalists, and, while electioneering in the West, emphatically declared himself for the conquest of the islands by force of arms in order to secure their permanent annexation.[39]

There were special reasons why the Massachusetts Republican convention reflected the popular discontent. The candidate the Republicans wanted for Governor, W. Murray Crane, a Western Massachusetts paper manufacturer whose father had been a Free Soiler, was not a Jingoist and approved the state platform as it was. In addition during the convention, the party's boss and outstanding imperialist, Senator Lodge, was still vacationing abroad.[40]

The *Journal,* Boston's prime Administration paper, was just as displeased with the Republican state platform as the *Springfield Republican* was pleased. President Boutwell of the Anti-Imperialist League was delighted, but Senator Lodge, on his return, was highly irritated and lost no time in speaking at a Republican rally in Boston where he was joined by Roosevelt; both made a spirited effort to nullify the effect of the platform and stem the tide of public opinion.[41]

If Lodge lost out on the Republican platform, he won in another test of strength with anti-imperialist sentiment. He secured the defeat of Herbert Parsons, an anti-imperialist state senator from Western Massachusetts, who had cast the sole Republican ballot against Lodge's re-election to the Senate. Denied the Republican nomination by the machine, Parsons had run as an independent with anti-imperialist support, but the vote of the Berkshire hilltowns defeated him.[42]

Other election results were unsatisfactory to Lodge and his friends. Even though Crane ran on a platform that reflected anti-war sentiment and gained votes from Boutwell and other anti-imperialists, the Republican plurality in the gubernatorial race declined by 20,000 votes, and the Democrats carried the city of Boston for the first time in three years.[43]

In this election, the eyes of the nation had been on Ohio, the state of McKinley and Hanna, and there Western anti-imperialist sentiment had dealt the Administration a massive moral defeat. The combined votes of the Democratic and independent candidates for governor, both of whom ran on anti-war platforms, was 50,000 more than the Republican candidate received; only the lack of anti-imperialist unity allowed the Administration to gain office, as Massachusetts leaders were careful to point out. In Maryland and Nebraska the Administration also suffered losses. McKinley, however, pulled through handsomely in Iowa and gained less spectacularly in some of the other states.[44]

Democrats and anti-imperialists were pleased with the election results. Bryan called attention to the Administration debacle in Ohio, and his Massachusetts aide, George Fred Williams, credited "men like Erving Winslow, and those behind him," with bringing the Democrats large numbers of votes.[45] F. B. Sanborn took pleasure in noting that the Republican majority in Senator Lodge's summer home, the town of Nahant, had dropped from 42 to 4, and that Governor Roosevelt's bellicose campaigning in Ohio, Nebraska and Maryland had come to naught. Ex-Governor Boutwell was led to hope that the next Congress could be pressured to vote no more men or supplies for the Philippine War.[46]

Men of all opinions had looked upon the 1899 elections as a "preliminary skirmish" to the upcoming presidential contest, but the news just before the voting indicated that the Administration was about to unleash a force in the Philippines that would help prevent any repetition of 1899 in 1900. All through the fall new recruits had been enlisted (with many from Massachusetts), and the transports had sailed; so that at the moment there were about twice as many officers and men in the Philippines as had been available for service in the spring. As the Boston *Transcript* noted, the American contingent there was now so numerous that it "would be able to hold advantages once gained, and our troops will not be compelled to

Exterior of the New England Anti-Imperialist League headquarters at 44 Kilby Street, Boston, as it appears today. (Photo by Audrey Schirmer.)

184   REPUBLIC OR EMPIRE

fight their battles over and over again."⁴⁷ The time had come for the offensive against the Philippine nationalists that McKinley and Root had been preparing.

While Otis remained in his headquarters, busying himself as usual with clerical detail, a concerted three-pronged campaign of envelopment was begun against the main force of Aguinaldo and the seat of his government, both to the north of Manila. General MacArthur led the central thrust, and Generals Lawton and Wheaton brought up the flanking movements, and it worked.⁴⁸ On November 24 General Otis cabled the War Department:

> Claim to government by insurgents can be made no longer . . . its Treasurer, Secretary of the Interior, and President of Congress are in our hands; its President and remaining cabinet officers are in hiding . . . its generals and troops are in small bands, scattered through these provinces.⁴⁹

On this occasion, the General's dispatch was quite accurate.

There was only one flaw in the campaign; Aguinaldo, the main catch, slipped through the noose of encirclement. As he fled from Americans close behind him, Aguinaldo made his way through a mountain pass. There he left his young friend, General Gregor del Pilar, with a picked body of men to hold up his pursuers. The Americans shot down this rearguard and filed through the pass. The last body they encountered on the trail was that of the young General. As the American soldiers passed Pilar they took his insignia, silver buttons and spurs, the scapular from his neck, then his clothing, leaving his body completely stripped. They also took a diary from the General's pocket, in which they found a final entry, "I am holding this position against great odds and fear the consequences. Still, I glory in the danger, because I am enduring it for the sake of my beloved country."⁵⁰

* * *

If, in the early days of imperial development, Boston's merchant class had been losing leadership to Massachusetts manufacturing capital, later, at the time of the Philippine War, manufacturing capital in its pre-trustified form was losing place to monopoly and finance. The Massachusetts Democratic platform of 1899 said:

Today our trust magnates are our bankers. They hold the bank stock, they sit on the boards of directors . . . and they will apply to their command over the supply of the nation's money the same merciless and extortionate methods which they use in turning to profit their present monopolies.⁵¹

This observation carried the discussion of monopoly and imperialism a step further, pointing, as it did, to a new grouping at the top of our country's social structure, those men who were both monopolists and bankers, like Higginson in Boston, Morgan and Rockefeller in New York, and whose control over both industry and finance brought them power and profit of another order of magnitude altogether. (Capital surplus turned monopolists into bankers, bankers into monopolists, and interested both in foreign investment. The newly ascertained features of imperialism were interlinked.)

It was not long before the shoe manufacturers of Lynn, ardent and early supporters of Senator Lodge in his quest for foreign markets, were crying out against the exactions laid upon them by the United Shoe Machinery Company, at the very moment the latter was successfully crushing competition in foreign fields.*

Similarly the Massachusetts textile manufacturers were pleased to welcome the Philippines and China as markets for their goods, but their magazine, the *Protectionist,* showed absolutely no enthusiasm for American investment abroad. In December 1899 when the representative of an Anglo-American syndicate for the development of Philippine railroads declared that there was plenty of very cheap labor in those islands, the *Protectionist* took note and commented sourly,

> The common belief is that the syndicates of capitalists which are preparing to exploit the Philippines will hire labor as cheaply as they can get it, and will practically control the laborers under a disguised kind of peonage or slavery, unless our government shall intervene to prevent it, for these capitalists are not embarking in colonial enterprise for philanthropic purposes.⁵²

---

* The anti-imperialists thought to take advantage of such antagonisms. Some years later Erving Winslow wrote hopefully about the possibility of winning small manufacturing capital as an ally against imperialism. (Erving Winslow, *The Anti-Imperialist League,* Boston, 1908, p. 15.)

(Obviously cheap labor in foreign lands boosted the rate of profit on American capital invested therein, while, at the same time it threatened small manufacturers at home with costly competition.)

At the close of the century, as the United States moved fully onto the imperial path, there was a shift of the center of gravity in the country's upper class, and a corresponding shift in outlook. From this new vantage point the death of General Gregor del Pilar and the destruction of the Philippine Republic and its army could be seen as costs incidental to the export of American capital.

14

Forging an Anti-Imperialist Coalition

"The real firing line is not in the suburbs of Manila. It is here. The enemy is of our own household." So their Chicago host, Edwin Burritt Smith, addressed the delegates to the convention that founded the anti-imperialist league as a national organization in October 1899. Smith thought that the main reason for establishing such an organization at that moment was to prepare for the elections of 1900, there to come to grips with "the enemy . . . of our own household." Atkinson, Boutwell and other delegates also saw this as the purpose of their meeting.[1]

At the same time, on the other side of the earth, the next year's American elections figured in the thoughts of the Philippine insurgent leader, Emilio Aguinaldo. Facing the defeat and dispersal of his army by the re-inforced American troops, he urged his followers to take up guerrilla warfare and to press the fight till November 1900 when it was possible that Bryan and those who stood for Philippine independence would win office. As Aguinaldo advised, the insurgents turned to guerrilla war after their army broke up.[2]

George Frisbie Hoar also looked toward the coming elections. Shortly after the anti-imperialists' Chicago meeting he predicted that McKinley would be re-elected for a second term. In the Senator's opinion the nation's prosperity would over-ride the growing anti-imperialist sentiment and carry the Administration back to office.[3]

The country had indeed become prosperous, and the Massachusetts textile industry exceptionally so. As the election year opened the *Springfield Republican* sought to determine the causes of this condition and offered the increase in the world's gold supply and the agricultural depression abroad as two of the stimulating factors. The third cause, thought the *Republican,* was of domestic origin: "The gathering and expenditure by the government of large sums on armament, munitions of war, naval increase and transport service, are having the effect of greatly stimulating the ship-building and iron and steel and related trades."[4] War, it seemed, had given a boost to the economy, as Senator Lodge had foretold.

With the approach of the elections the anti-imperialists developed differences about the tactics to pursue. As early as the summer of 1898 Gamaliel Bradford had called upon the Democratic Party to take a strong anti-imperialist position so that a powerful coalition might gather around it. Since that time the Massachusetts Democrats had followed Bradford's advice. However, by his support of the treaty, the party's national leader had gravely compromised himself with Massachusetts anti-imperialists. In an apparent effort to rehabilitate himself in their eyes, Bryan had written the *Springfield Republican*, just after treaty passage, to commend it for renewing the fight against imperialism and to urge all friends of Philippine independence to do likewise. Since then he had come to take so explicitly anti-imperialist a stand that the *Hartford Courant* thought he sounded like the editorial columns of the Springfield paper. Moreover, Bryan seemed to be bringing his party with him, on the whole, throughout the country.[5]

As the year opened, Bradford's orientation had the support of most of the Massachusetts anti-imperialist organization. There was a minority in Boston, however, who favored a third ticket, finding it impossible to consider Bryan because of his stand on the currency.[6]

But the main impulse for an anti-imperialist third party in 1900 came from a group of New York reformers. For years these men had seen the Democrats in New York City controlled by Tammany's boss Croker, the Republicans in the rest of the state controlled by boss Platt, and the domination of both Croker and Platt by New York's powerful business interests. All through the 1890's these reformers had run independent candidates for local office in the attempt to counter-act the Croker-Platt-big business influence. Carl Schurz was the best-known figure associated with this group, but John Jay Chapman was its spokesman and theorist. Chapman had aired his plea for independent political action before the Massachusetts Reform Club at the meeting held after treaty passage, and in January 1900, using the pages of the *Atlantic Monthly*, he brought this viewpoint to a national audience.[7]

In the imperialism of the McKinley Administration Chapman saw the end product of the commercialism that corrupted local politics, and he and his friends leapt at the chance to put their ideas of political reform, hitherto practiced in city and state, to work on a national scale.[8] In December 1899, at the suggestion of Carl Schurz, the Chicago, or national, committee of the anti-imperialist league sent out notices for a conference to be held in January in New York City, inviting Schurz, John Jay Chapman, Andrew Carnegie, Senator Pettigrew, Elwood S. Corser, Herbert Welsh, Winslow Warren, G. S. Boutwell, Erving Winslow and others.* A small group attended and decided to launch an independent political party for the presidential campaign, Carnegie pledging twenty-five thousand dollars to the effort as a start.[9]

But the January attempt at a third party proved disappointing. Samuel Gompers and other labor leaders, whose followers would supply important third party votes, did not attend the conference, although invited. Another crippling difficulty followed. Carnegie was involved, at the time, in negotiations with J. P. Morgan and others preliminary to the formation of the country's first billion dollar trust, the United States Steel Company. When those arranging the deal heard of Carnegie's third party proclivities they notified him that he must drop them or bow out of the proposed merger (that promised him great profit). Carnegie then cut off his financial support for the third party movement and refused to have anything more to do with it (eventually declaring for McKinley), whereupon this initial effort collapsed.[10]

The aborted third party activity lay behind the scenes. In public view in the first months of 1900 was the congressional debate on foreign policy. From this debate Massachusetts anti-imperialists hoped might come some move for peace in the Philippines (as did Aguinaldo). When Congress opened session, the New Englanders sent Erving Winslow to Washington to secure united action to this end, and a conference of Republican and Democratic legislators was held, without result.[11]

---

* Pettigrew's account in *Imperial Washington,* the only one in print, relates that the New England Anti-imperialist League called the conference, but the Schurz Papers and a denial from Erving Winslow make clear that this was not the case. (E. Winslow to W. A. Croffut, January 3, 1900, Croffut Papers, Library of Congress.)

What the friends of Philippine independence did accomplish at this session was a public airing of issues involved in the conquest of the islands. They forced the Administration to release official documents relating to the conduct of the war, and Senator Pettigrew read into the *Congressional Record* a long statement from Aguinaldo that had first fallen into Erving Winslow's hands, then been reprinted in the *Springfield Republican*. Its gist was Aguinaldo's assertion that Dewey had promised him independence. In the furor following its congressional publication Dewey wrote Senator Lodge denying Aguinaldo's claims, and Lodge had this letter, too, spread upon the *Congressional Record*. When cries of "traitor" flew at Pettigrew, Boston anti-imperialists acclaimed the South Dakotan for his deed.[12]

Senator Pettigrew was the foremost Congressional opponent of McKinley's foreign policies from the West, as Senator Hoar was, from the East. Senator Hoar also contributed to the congressional discussion with his second major speech on the Philippines. Even before he spoke, however, like Pettigrew, he was the target of bitter attack. Under the complaisant eye of party boss Lodge, two Republican organizations in Boston invited out-of-state speakers who threw treason charges at Hoar without restraint. Unlike Pettigrew, however, Hoar responded to these attacks by quickly indicating that, despite differences about the Philippines, he would toe the Administration line in the all-important elections about to come.[13]

Against this background Hoar's Senate speech had a somewhat hollow ring. He addressed himself to a Senate proposal for the permanent retention of the Philippines, but in contrast to the tension and excitement that his first speech had caused, on his occasion Hoar's Republican colleagues made a demonstration of their indifference, chatting and writing while he spoke, or absenting themselves from the Senate floor.[14]

The speech differed from his first in one significant respect: the importance it placed upon the economic motive as a cause of imperial policy. Throughout his talk, with a steady and repeated stress, Hoar recalled "the mountains of iron . . . nuggets of gold, and trade with China" from which the imperialists hoped to profit in the Philippines.[15] This emphasis had been almost wholly absent from the Senator's speech in the treaty fight, with its appeal to moral principle, democratic tradition and constitutional precedent. It was as if Hoar's own defeat, and the defeat of the political idealism for which he stood, had forced him, his personal conservatism notwithstanding, to acknowledge the real power that had brought it about.

The underlying drive of his speech reached a climax that thrust Hoar, for one charged moment, into direct confrontation with Mark Hanna, who above all, symbolized the influence of syndicated wealth upon the Republican leadership. The *Springfield Republican* reported that "when Mr. Hoar reached that passage in his peroration, 'I appeal from the millionaire and the boss and the wire-puller and the manager to the statesman of an older time in whose eyes a guinea never glistened,' etc., he looked squarely at Senator Hanna. The latter's face flushed, and for once . . . his smile of indifference or contempt forsook him. He was visibly angry."[16]

Well might Hoar appeal to the past for relief, since his only remedy for the present was trust in the Republican Party, chief agent of the events he so deplored. Massachusetts anti-imperialists were disgusted. Wrote the *Republican*: "Did ever a statesman come to so lame and impotent a conclusion?"[17]

Linking it to the United States conquest of the Philippines, Hoar condemned the war Great Britain had begun in October 1899 against the Boer Republic of South Africa, and Senator Pettigrew set before Congress a resolution of sympathy for the Boers. There was also opposition to this war in New England. The *Springfield Republican* compared the British empire to a swollen industrial monopoly that goes to all lengths to swallow a neighboring rival, while Patrick A. Collins charged the whole thing to British desire to control South African gold mines, and Irish-Americans held innumerable protest meetings in Massachusetts.* The state legislature and the Boston City Council passed resolutions of condemnation.[18]

But McKinley refused to condemn the war or offer sympathy to the Boers, and the Administration-controlled Congress thrust aside Pettigrew's resolution. In fact the Boer War brought United States imperialists a step nearer their goal of international financial supremacy. The banking house of Morgan financed the Boer War for the British government. American investors quickly subscribed to the 25

---

* When the Colored National League of Boston called the Boers "a diabolical slave-holding republic" and supported Britain (as did Charles Eliot Norton), Patrick A. Collins offered the opinion that the British empire was also notoriously racist. (*Boston Evening Transcript,* January 24, 1900.)

million dollar bond issue Morgan offered to float the loan, and the imperialist press rejoiced that New York was replacing London as the financial center of the world.[19]

In this session the anti-imperialists lost the support of four Massachusetts Congressmen hitherto opposing McKinley on the Philippine issue, and in the Senate, Hale of Maine and Mason of Illinois threw in the sponge.* But in spite of its solid majority in Congress (including Democrats as well as Republicans), the McKinley Administration let the session go by without passing many important measures, including a Hanna-sponsored subsidy bill that would have encouraged construction of ships for the China trade and brought millions to a Rockefeller shipbuilding syndicate.[20] Influential senators thought it wise not to push the Administration program before the elections, lest the opposition attack the Republican dominated legislature as "something worse than a billionaire Congress."[21]

As they failed to get a Philippine peace from Congress, the anti-imperialists turned again to the fall elections. Early in February Bryan made a tour of Massachusetts and other New England states, speaking sympathetically of the Boers, taking a strong stand against imperialism and calling for the return of the Gold Democrats on this issue. Bryan's visit strengthened his candidacy among the Massachusetts anti-imperialist leadership. T. W. Higginson, G. S. Boutwell, F. B. Sanborn and P. A. Collins now joined Gamaliel Bradford in openly declaring for him.[22]

At the end of February the anti-imperialists held a national conference in Philadelphia where they agreed to oppose McKinley and any candidate that endorsed his policies. Although Bradford and others expressed strong support for Bryan, the organization decided to wait till both major parties had held their national conventions before deciding upon any positive action.[23]

Postponing their decision about whom to support until after the Democratic convention, the anti-imperialists put maximum pressure upon the Bryan party to adopt their program. This was quickly communicated to the Democratic leadership by Elwood S. Corser, a Midwestern small businessman and Silver Republican, who was a Bryan advisor. After attending the conference Corser sent Chairman Jones

---

* The Congressmen were three Republicans, Gillett, Lawrence and McCall, and one Democrat, Fitzgerald.

of the Democratic National Committee a note which Jones passed on to Bryan. In it Corser wrote that if the Democratic convention declared strongly against the imperial policy while the Republicans reaffirmed it, he was confident, on the basis of his observations at Philadelphia, that the anti-imperialists would declare openly for the Democrats. Throughout the spring of the year Corser kept Bryan informed of the support for him in the anti-imperialist league (arranging a meeting in March between Bryan and E. B. Smith). Corser also made Bryan aware of third party sentiment among the anti-imperialists.[24]

The Republican convention was to meet first, toward the end of June at Philadelphia. But before it assembled, important events took place in Asia that figured prominently in the thinking of the Republicans and their opponents, in Massachusetts and elsewhere. In the winter of 1900 Senator Lodge and his like-minded colleagues hailed the success of the Open Door policy as a notable boost to the expansionist program. A high official in Washington said that as a result of its achievement "China is ripe for the investment of American capital."[25] On the surface it appeared that Secretary of State Hay had, early in 1900, persuaded Great Britain, France, Russia, Germany, Japan and Italy to agree that in the Chinese territories under their control all powers would have equal commercial rights. More particularly the Open Door policy was an Anglo-American project to limit the growing influence of Russia in China. It had its roots in the outcome of the Venezuelan crisis, when Britain's acceptance of United States political hegemony in South America made it possible for her to win the United States as an ally in Asia. (Hence the support the British fleet had given Dewey at Manila Bay in the face of the German squadron's provocative behavior.)[26]

In Massachusetts a February meeting of the Boston Merchants Association heard W. W. Rockhill, a diplomatic agent of the McKinley Administration, praise the Open Door policy as the direct result of the United States annexation of the Philippines. (With their sponsorship of Rockhill the merchants, had, in a year's time, come the full circle, abandoning any differences they once had with McKinley's imperialist program and its corporate sponsors.)[27]

Some weeks afterwards the National Association of Manufacturers held its annual convention in Boston, and the industrialists emphatically endorsed the Open Door policy. To New England and Southern manufacturers of cotton textiles this policy was especially important, since the recent expansion of the Chinese market accounted in good part for their present prosperity.[28]

Massachusetts anti-imperialists entered their dissent. The *Springfield Republican* thought that Hay acted as he did only because the government did not dare grab Chinese territory outright for fear of opposition at home; the United States opposed further partition because it wanted to preserve the Chinese market it now had; moreover, said the editor, the policy itself was a gigantic bluff, for without military support it could not be enforced, should one of the powers choose to throw it down.[29]

However the immediate threat to the Open Door policy did not come from Russia or any other rival for the markets of China, but from the Chinese people themselves, rising up against the rape of their country by foreign powers.* In the spring and early summer of 1900, under the influence of a militant nationalist society known as the Boxers, Chinese attacked French and German missionaries and did an estimated $5,000,000 damage to foreign-built, foreign owned railroads.[30]

China's Empress Dowager showed her sympathy for the Boxers by arresting the Chinese promoter of the Anglo-American railroad syndicate, sentencing him to life imprisonment, then ordering the arrest of three more Chinese who had similarly cooperated with foreign investors.[31] The imperialist program of capital export to China appeared to be in jeopardy. The uprising's disruption of United States export trade with China also threatened bad times for American cotton mills.[32] Finally the Boxers, aided by Chinese imperial troops, soon put under siege the United States Minister and other foreign legations in Peking. The Open Door triumph of Secretary Hay seemed endangered by the Chinese revolt, and the Shanghai-American Association called upon the McKinley government to put it down, in concert with other powers.[33]

The President, the Secretary of State and the cabinet became increasingly absorbed in this crisis; it brought sharply home to them

---

* As with the Spanish at Manila vis-a-vis Aguinaldo, the need for joint action against a colonial people in revolt caused the United States imperialists to subordinate their antagonism to a rival; soon American troops were marching with the Russian against Chinese.

the difficulties connected with the United States' new role as a "world power."³⁴ First the Administration sent a battleship from Manila to Taku, the Chinese port near Peking, and announced the formation of a naval squadron to cruise the Chinese coast. Then it ordered a detachment of marines from the Philippines to relieve the legation at Peking.³⁵ Making their way from Taku with the troops of other powers and burning villages as they went, these marines were stopped by the Chinese 80 miles from Peking at Tien-Tsin. There the United States forces found the American consulate destroyed, but the installations of the Standard Oil company unharmed. An American observer who made the march from Taku to Tien-Tsin wrote home that he saw the bodies of Chinese, slain by Americans, clogging the river en route, "and there were so many of them that they filled it from bank to bank and it was hard for steamboats to get along." But in the United States a prominent banker told President McKinley that his actions in China were applauded in the best New York board rooms by Republicans and Democrats alike.³⁶

The Republican national convention took place in the third week of June against this background of events. As if to give point to the pre-occupations of the Administration, Wu Ting Fang, the Chinese Minister to the United States, attended the convention on the second day; ushered to a seat alongside the delegates, the Minister, in his "rich oriental silks," attracted much attention.³⁷ He came to the Republicans from the meeting of the National Association of Manufacturers, where he had given an address plainly indicating that he did not share the antagonism of his Empress to the import of American capital. In fact, it had been through his efforts that the America-China Development Company had been granted its railway concession.³⁸

Massachusetts junior Senator Henry Cabot Lodge was most prominent at the Republican meeting as its permanent chairman. His opening speech set the tone of the convention as a triumphant affirmation of McKinley's imperialist policies, above all, the annexation and subjugation of the Philippines. Lodge attacked the Democrats: they would withdraw American troops from those islands, leaving the pro-American Filipinos to certain massacre. Lodge brushed aside the humanitarian pretensions voiced by McKinley and others and bluntly told the members of his party that the United States had taken the Philippines to benefit Americans, no one else; the islands were the key to the great Chinese market, the corner stone of Hay's Open Door policy.[39]

If the convention was a vindication of the policies that Lodge had fostered in the Republican Party, it was a still greater personal triumph for his more charismatic friend, Theodore Roosevelt. Roosevelt's popularity showed invidiously in relation to the President, who stayed in Washington. When McKinley was nominated for a second term, party boss Hanna worked hard to get the convention to show enthusiasm for his protege. It was Roosevelt's convention.[40] Coming each day in his Rough Rider hat, always the first to his feet when the band played the national anthem, the New York Governor perfectly expressed the delegates' Jingo spirit.[41] Members of the press understood that New York finance wanted Roosevelt's nomination as vice-president; boss Platt was anxious to ease him out of state politics; he had a special popularity in the West. All in all, his nomination as McKinley's running mate had an air of inevitability.[42]

Shortly after the Republican convention, as the allied forces of Britain, Japan, Germany, France and Russia prepared to march on Peking, McKinley ordered 4,500 troops from the Philippines to join them. (Root's offensive of the year before had destroyed the Philippine government and army, enabling the Republican convention to assume an air of universal triumph, but the fact was that MacArthur could spare only these troops and no more in the face of constant guerrilla attack.)[43]

Speaking before a meeting of Boston Republicans, Senator Lodge discussed the dispatch of troops from the Philippines to China with singular satisfaction. It proved his point: the Philippines were necessary to the defense of United States interests in China. "Where would our consuls, our missionaries, our merchants . . . our ministers have looked for protection if we had never heard of the Philippines? Before we could have got ships and men there, the danger . . . would be over." And, Lodge added, the United States show of strength in China had prevented Russia from taking advantage of disturbed conditions to grab more territory.[44]

Official weight was given Lodge's remarks by another Open Door note Hay addressed to the European powers on July 3. Calling for the preservation of "China's territorial and administrative entity," Hay discouraged further appropriations of Chinese territory.[45]

The note had domestic implications as well. With its issuance the

Administration foreswore any annexation of Chinese territory by the United States. This had the effect of quieting the public anxiety caused by the Administration's participation in a second Asian war. Leading Democrats felt the Chinese question presented difficulties it was best to avoid, since, at the moment, the Administration appeared to be taking a popular stand against the further territorial division of that country. Texas Democrats reportedly refused a request from Bryan to condemn United States intervention, because the interests of Southern industry in the China market were too great.[46] Very little else was heard from Bryan on the subject.*

As with the Boer War, the New England Anti-Imperialist League didn't take a position on the intervention in China, but individual anti-imperialists expressed themselves against it, condemning Presidential usurpation of powers in sending troops to China without Congressional assent and warning of the danger of a larger war. At first the *Springfield Republican* supported intervention to save American lives. Receiving a stiff letter of rebuke from a local reader, the *Republican* thereafter wrote sympathetically of China and the Boxer uprising, to the approval of Boston anti-imperialists.[47]

The United States intervention in China did not become a major issue in the election campaign. The sharp military crisis was soon over. Before the end of August Peking was occupied (and "systematically looted") by the soldiers of the imperialist powers, the Boxers were quelled, and troops bound for China from the United States diverted to reinforce MacArthur. The suppression of the Philippine guerrillas reasserted its priority.[48]

The anti-imperialists quickly disposed of the Republican convention. An enlarged meeting of the National Executive Committee rejected its platform and candidates without equivocation. The committee was divided between Bryan supporters, third party men and those who wanted to neglect the presidential race in order to concentrate on congressional candidates, but it reaffirmed the February decision to wait till after the Democratic convention before acting. This time, however, Chairman Smith was very specific in warning the Democrats if they did not take a strong stand against imperialism, the anti-imperialists would go ahead and form a third party.[49]

---

* The Democratic platform endorsed the chauvinist Chinese Exclusion Act, as did the American Federation of Labor.

All signs, however, indicated that the key Democratic leadership was bent on winning anti-imperialist support. The *Boston Evening Transcript* believed the anti-imperialists would be the only source of strength for Bryan's "tottering cause," and Senator Lodge remarked on the Democrats' bid for anti-imperialist favor with equal scorn.[50] Shortly after Bryan's visit to New England, Chairman Jones wrote Erving Winslow to repeat the assurance that those who had bolted the ticket in 1896 would be welcome back in 1900. In June the Democratic leadership invited the anti-imperialist league to send a delegation to the Democratic convention to help prepare the plank on imperialism, but the anti-imperialists refused, in order to preserve as long as possible a non-partisan stance.[51]

After seeing to it that the Nebraska Democrats took a strong stand against imperialism, Bryan made sure that the national platform was beyond criticism in this regard. Receiving a draft from Senator William K. Stone, Bryan objected to a plank on the navy which he thought might be taken as support of "the imperialistic idea that our navy might be as large as any navy in the world." In addition Bryan wanted the issue of imperialism to come first, the currency question after. He had his way. As it was sent to the convention for adoption the Democratic platform contained a strong denunciation of militarism, made no mention of the navy, and imperialism had the place of first importance.[52]

Before the Democrats met many observers thought they saw a last ditch effort by Gorman and his friends in the business world to head off Bryan. When first back from the Philippines, Admiral Dewey had suggested his availability as a presidential candidate; now he offered himself to the Democrats. He was again ignored.[53]

Bryan's nomination was not contested at the Democratic convention in July. Some California delegates made ineffectual objection to the convention taking a strong stand against imperialism. However the major debate took place in the resolutions committee on the currency question. Here Eastern Democrats put up a stubborn fight to drop specific reference to silver coinage at 16 to 1 (Bryan's battle cry of 1896), but Bryan refused to allow his supporters on the committee to accede; he did not want to break with his Populist allies. At the same time Bryan made a concession to his new friends, agreeing that a declaration should be inserted in the platform that imperialism was the "paramount" issue of the campaign. For further balance, Adlai Stevenson, Cleveland's running mate in 1892, was chosen as Bryan's vice-presidential candidate.[54]

If the Republican convention gave a resounding "aye" to the Philippine conquest and imperial expansion, the Democrats answered with a thunderous "nay," endorsing Bryan and anti-imperialism. As Senator Benjamin Tillman of North Carolina read the Democratic platform to the convention he was interrupted by cheers and applause, but when he reached the declaration that "the burning issue of imperialism" was paramount in the campaign, there came "a deluge of shouting that was as wild as the untamed spirit of the West." It was the convention's great moment.[55]

With the Democratic convention coming near to meeting the demands of the leadership of the anti-imperialist league, Bryan's endorsement by their conference, set for August 14, seemed very likely, but not all their friends and allies encouraged it. Senator Hoar unwound a particularly keen attack on the Democrats, hitting their anti-imperialist protestations at the weakest point: the militant white supremacy of the Southern Democrats, who were conducting, at the very moment, an aggressive campaign to disfranchise the blacks in many states. Senator Tillman, who read the Democratic platform at the convention, enthusiastically urging independence for the Filipinos, had, only the winter before, made a virulent speech on the Senate floor, threatening Southern blacks with violence and death should they dare to vote. Hoar made the most of all this in a speech well-suited to wean Massachusetts independents and Republicans of anti-imperialist sympathy away from Bryan and the Democrats.[56]

The New York reformers who were for independent political action attempted to intervene directly in the course taken by the anti-imperialist league. In June and July John Jay Chapman made trips to Boston to win the Massachusetts support he considered essential to the third party undertaking.* Moorfield Storey indicated interest in his friend's project, particularly if an outstanding Republican could be persuaded to lead it. But other Bostonians became involved in the third party cause, so that, outside of New York, Massachusetts was the center of such activity in 1900.[57]

---

* Chapman visited, but got nowhere with, Henry Lee Higginson, who, he found, "has the same ideas as the next rich man," though "he weeps . . . over the war and his goodness." (John Jay Chapman to his wife, June 17, 1900, John Jay Chapman Papers, Houghton Library.)

Chapman's visits to Boston were preliminary to the main flurry of third party agitation that was to take place around the July meeting of the executive committee of the Gold Democraic Party and the August convention of the anti-imperialists, both to be held in Indianopolis. The plan of Chapman and his fellow enthusiasts was, as he described it, to "lay our ship along side of them and board them," winning both bodies to a third party campaign in a kind of raiding maneuver, as the New Yorkers' small numbers made necessary.[58]

Chapman's cause was weakened by his inability to get a prominent individual to run as president on an independent ticket. Cleveland turned him down; Thomas B. Reed was keeping to the sidelines; finally Senator Caffery of Louisiana agreed, only to renege, and so it went.[59]

Calling their supporters to Indianapolis on both occasions, the third party anti-imperialists were first rebuffed by the members of the Gold Democratic national committee (of whom Boston's Nathan Matthews, Jr., was typical). These gentlemen were for McKinley and wanted nothing to do with a third party or anti-imperialism.[60] Then the New York reformers tried their hand with the anti-imperialists.

About a week before the anti-imperialists met in their Liberty Congress (as they called their gathering), Bryan made his speech accepting the Democratic presidential nomination. At the suggestion of league secretary Erving Winslow, Bryan devoted the speech to an elaboration of the anti-imperialist plank in the Democratic platform. Bryan's effort was widely recognized as masterful, even Senator Hoar giving it grudging praise. If Bryan intended finally to win the anti-imperialists to his side, he did just that. Anti-imperialist leaders the country over agreed that Bryan's speech turned the tide of feeling within their organization, clinching the attitude the convention was to take.[61]

Both the third party men and the anti-imperialists saw their particular constituency as the nation's independent voters, who put issues above party. But only some thirteen men showed up at the third party meeting in Indianapolis, while some three hundred attended the anti-imperialist convention. Winslow was especially pleased at the participation of black citizens and men of Irish-Catholic and German extraction. The anti-imperialists in Indianapolis represented numerous branches of the league and thousands of active sympathizers, East and West; the third party men, a small group in New York City and a scattering elsewhere. Nearly two years of nation-wide agitation and organization had given the anti-imperialists a broader base from which to make their appeal to the country's independents, as Chapman and his friends acknowledged.[62] Even so, the attendance at the anti-imperialist convention was less than expected. Moorfield Storey explained this by noting that "our friends are not among the men of means," thereby offering a clue to the social composition of the organized movement at the height of its strength.[63]

A Western delegate, a Minnesota judge, told reporters two Boston men, George S. Boutwell and Moorfield Storey, were the outstanding figures at the convention.[64] Boutwell, an octogenarian who typefied the many older Lincoln Republicans in attendance, was elected the convention's permanent chairman; Storey headed the important resolutions committee.

In his opening speech Boutwell stressed the importance of Philippine independence, and condemned United States intervention in China. If Lodge and the imperialists saw the Philippine Islands as a convenient jumping off place for intervention in China, then Boutwell threw this line of reasoning into reverse, asserting that the Chinese saw the United States military subjugation of the Philippines as a threat to their own sovereignty, quite justifying the Boxer revolt.

Boutwell spoke proudly of the anti-imperialists: "We have accomplished something. The anti-imperialistic leagues have made the name and characteristics of imperialism known and spoken in every palace, every log cabin and every prairie camp on this continent."[65]

After long deliberation the resolutions committee (composed of ten who voted Republican in 1896, seven who voted for Bryan, seven Gold Democrats, and one non-voter) brought in the unanimous recommendation that the country's anti-imperialist and independent voters subordinate all differences of opinion to the issue of imperialism and support the candidacy of Bryan because of his forthright stand on that question (with Moorfield Storey reserving the right to vote for a third party candidate should one be forthcoming). When Colonel Charles R. Codman finished reading the resolution there was great applause and cheers for Bryan, led by the Boston crowd.

There followed hours of convention debate during which many spoke in favor of the resolution, including a black delegate and a soldier just back from Luzon who declared the Philippine War "the most damnable crime ever committed in the history of the United

States." Chapman and other third party men presented their case at length, but when the vote came Bryan was endorsed by an overwhelming majority, only fifteen being opposed. The delegates clearly agreed with those who warned that a third party in 1900 would only split the anti-imperialist vote and ensure the election of McKinley.[66]

The endorsement of Bryan did not pass without an important qualification, however. The delegates took pains to separate themselves from the white supremacy strong in the councils of the Democratic Party, with which, indeed, Bryan himself was tainted.* After the passage of the majority resolution the convention voted a declaration of special and unequivocal support for the full rights, civil and political, of the country's black citizens, North and South. A black delegate said that without such a statement the anti-imperialist cause would lose many votes in the fall.[67]

In the opinion of the *Springfield Republican*'s correspondent at Indianapolis it was the delegates' consciousness of the Philippine War and its "bloody continuance" as "a thing to be stopped, and stopped at once, employing all legitimate means to that end," that threw the anti-imperialist convention to Bryan.[68]

In any case the anti-imperialists' endorsement of Bryan killed the third party movement in 1900 and began another political process of short but vigorous life. The day after the Liberty Congress ended the anti-imperialist leaders held a private conference. There they decided to cooperate with the Democratic National Committee, which, for its part, would bear the expense of mailing the literature sent out by the league. Such was to be the pattern. In the course of the campaign the anti-imperialist league engaged in widespread agitation and propaganda, both through printed material and the speeches of its leaders, and all this activity was carried on either independently of the Democrats, but in support of their candidate, or in direct cooperation with the party of Bryan and under its auspices. (Thus when, some two months later, Bryan wrote Erving Winslow to thank the league for its endorsement, he had reason.) The action of the Liberty Congress gave final and effective form to the alliance between

---

* While avoiding this in the campaign of 1900, Bryan, in 1901, openly expressed a white supremacist position, causing T. W. Higginson to break with him. (T. W. Higginson to W. J. Bryan, November 27, 1901, T. W. Higginson Papers, Houghton Library.)

the anti-imperialist league and the Democratic Party in 1900, between that middle-class, anti-war, protest movement led predominantly by Eastern Mugwumps, and one of the country's major political parties led by a Westerner of Populist sympathies, and this alliance gave the elections of 1900 a special character.[69]

Gamaliel Bradford initiated the organized movement against imperialism and first called for a popular alliance around the Democratic Party on this issue. William Jennings Bryan carried the Democratic Party nationally onto anti-imperialist ground and made this alliance possible. It was the cooperation of the organizations represented by these men that carried the movement begun June 1898 in Boston to the peak of its influence.

15

The Victory of Imperialism

In July 1899 the pro-Administration *Boston Journal* wrote of the coming elections:

> Mr. Bryan and his lieutenants are already proclaiming far and wide that American intervention in the Philippines is a device of the monopolists and gold bugs, and we observe that our Boston Anti-Imperialist League is innocently lending this idea its valuable endorsement.[1]

Anti-imperialists considered this identity of views concerning monopoly as the source of imperialism a most important reason for supporting Bryan. In June a prominent anti-imperialist in Western Massachusetts advocated Bryan's candidacy since the latter was "essentially correct" in his "general view" that "imperialism is mainly an outgrowth of greedy commercialism." Herbert Welsh, the Philadelphia leader, was even more specific in his advocacy. The anti-imperialists, said Welsh, fully agreed with Bryan in thinking that the power of "organized and conscienceless" wealth was one of the greatest menaces to the United States. "We think with him that this power is that which supports imperialism."[2]

In March 1900 Bryan himself declared that "imperialism had its inspiration in the desire of the syndicates to extend their commerce by conquest." This was in fact to be the central thesis of his campaign, and in August the Democratic candidate officially opened his second bid for the presidency with his acceptance speech, widely acclaimed, that spelled the idea out in some detail:

> Imperialism would be profitable to the army contractors; it would be profitable to the shipowners, who would carry live soldiers to the Philippines and bring dead soldiers back; it would be profitable to those who would seize upon the franchises, and it would be profitable to the of-

ficials whose salaries would be fixed and paid there; but to the farmer and the laboring man, and to the vast majority of those engaged in other occupations, it would bring expenditures without returns and risks without reward.

He asked:

> If in this country, where the people have the right to vote, the republican leaders dare not take the side of the people against the great monopolies which have grown up within the last few years, how can they be trusted to protect the Filipinos from the corporations which are waiting to exploit the islands?[3]

During the campaign Bryan hammered away at this theme, often citing, by way of example, the Republican chairman of the Army Committee of the House of Representatives, who was, at the same time, president of the Philippine Lumber and Development Company. Bryan quoted the Development Company's prospectus to the effect that it had "already secured . . . valuable timber rights," and that "no other company" could "compete with this one in getting a first foothold in the islands," — where, the prospectus noted, cheap Asian labor prevailed. Bryan said that "the capitalist may see an advantage in militarism and imperialism, but," he demanded, "where is the working man's share? He will furnish sons for the army, and will help pay the expenses of war, but he has no part in the profits . . . his lot is to 'Die for the dividends of Dives.' "[4]

Drawing attention to the Republican boast that the country had now begun to export capital, Bryan asked why a man should invest abroad when the money could be used in this country. He gave an answer to this question as he summed up the imperialist argument for the Philippines: " . . . it is our duty to keep them. God commands it, and it will pay."[5]

Bryan told the voters that the imperialists needed militarism not only to protect foreign investment, but to threaten the common people at home, recalling the use of the army against striking workers. The emphasis he placed upon the menace imperialism offered to American democracy was particularly welcome to Gamaliel Bradford, who, of all the Massachusetts men, was most aroused over the possibility of repression and military dictatorship implicit in the imperialist development. Speaking for Bryan in Maine, Bradford said, "The rich in this country are beginning to distrust the multitude and get ready

"Imperialism would be profitable to the army contractors . . . it would be profitable to those who would seize upon franchises . . . but to the farmer and the laboring man . . . it would bring expenditures without returns and risks without reward." William Jennings Bryan making his acceptance speech at Indianapolis, August 8, 1900.

the sword for their protection. The danger of violence is not from below, but from above."[6]

The emergence of imperialism, with its burden of militarism and arms, posed in a new way another domestic problem — the allocation of the resources at the disposal of the national government. Herbert Myrick, the Massachusetts anti-imperialist, asked, in the chain of farm journals edited by him, whether the millions allocated to the army and navy might not be better spent on improving the postal service for the nation's farmers. A New Bedford correspondent of the *Springfield Republican* thought rural roads more important than new battleships. Bryan denounced the Republicans for pouring funds into the military establishment rather than the nation's schools and said the money spent on the Philippine war could be much better used in building reservoirs to irrigate the arid West. "But," he added, "the republicans would rather waste blood than save water."[7]

As the campaign got under way, F. B. Sanborn wrote of it:

> The present political contest is that of aggregated, aggravating and entrenched capital, in millionaires, railroads, bankers, iron-mills, sugar trusts, Standard oil tanks, coal mines, steamship syndicates, newspaper ownership, etc., against the poor and middling classes at home and the feeble nations abroad.[8]

Time and again Bryan declared that the 1900 elections represented the marshalling of democracy against plutocracy, the man against the dollar, republic against empire.[9] Most Massachusetts anti-imperialists accepted this description of the contest.

President McKinley seemed to agree with Bryan and the anti-imperialists that foreign policy was the central issue, making a full-fledged defense of his Philippine course in both his speech and letter of acceptance. Since the President was not otherwise active, these documents constituted his major intervention in the campaign, the letter of acceptance being printed in 10 million copies and 14 languages.[10]

However in 1900 the chief issue for the Republicans — set not by McKinley, but by his campaign manager, Mark Hanna — was the nation's prosperity. This was the Republican's strongest ground (on foreign policy they were more vulnerable) and Hanna put the election in the simplest terms. Did the working people wish to keep the jobs and wages they now enjoyed under the Republicans, or did they wish to return to the dark days of the Democrat Cleveland by way of Bryan and his dangerous financial schemes? With this as his battle-cry, Hanna ordered thousands of campaign buttons showing McKinley's face and a full dinner pail.[11]

The approach to the elections of those two more ideologically committed imperialists, Roosevelt and Lodge, differed markedly from Hanna's. Electioneering in the West, Roosevelt, who served as McKinley's surrogate in the campaign, created a commotion by charging that the Democrats were utter cowards in foreign policy. Gold Democrats friendly to McKinley were aggrieved, and Hanna felt obliged to warn Roosevelt against excessive statements.[12]

As Roosevelt inveighed against Bryan's "communistic doctrines" in the West, Senator Lodge introduced the theme of "law and order" to voters in Massachusetts. (Roosevelt did not campaign here, reportedly to the relief of some state Republican leaders, who worried about the effect of his jingoism on the Massachusetts electorate.) Returning from a stint of electioneering with Roosevelt, the Senator told the Republican state convention that a crowd of miners had broken up a Roosevelt meeting in Victor, Colorado, with shouts of "Coeur d'Alene, Coeur d'Alene, Bryan, Bryan." The miners had prevented Roosevelt from speaking and had booed off the stage a member of Roosevelt's entourage, a general of the United States army, in full uniform, who had just returned from the Philippines. This display of anarchy was Bryanism in practice, cried Lodge. The "solid respectability of Massachusetts . . . shivered and resolved to have none of it," wrote the *Springfield Republican*.[13]

Lodge was not the state's most persuasive Republican campaigner. His arguments were for those already convinced of the Administration's course. But, while no one expected the Democrats to carry Massachusetts, whatever danger there was to the Republicans lay in the effect of the anti-imperialists upon sympathetic Republicans, wavering Gold Democrats and independent voters. To counter-act this, Senator Hoar, only recently the Administration's chief critic in party ranks, proved very useful.[14]

In the spring of the year, while signalling his intent to support McKinley in the fall, Hoar had roundly condemned the influence of organized wealth as the source of imperialist policy, and by implication, Senator Hanna as the agent of that influence in the Republican Party. But in August, when Hanna came to Boston on a fund-raising mission and met with leading financiers and industrialists, Senator Hoar attended and gave this meeting an unconditional pledge of loyalty to the Republican Party.*

Hoar's abasement was Hanna's vindication. Small wonder that Hanna lost no time in relating this episode to a Midwestern audience, in what the press called a "capital and much-lauded election speech." As for Hoar, he went from the meeting to tell the voters of Massachusetts that organized wealth presented no threat to the country; nor was there anything to fear from the re-election of McKinley — Republican anti-imperialists like himself would take care of that.[15]

Whatever might be said of Hoar's devotion to principle, of his prudence there can be no doubt. The Senator was soon coming up for re-election, and his submission insured return to Washington without opposition from the party leadership. Hoar's Western counterpart, Senator Pettigrew from South Dakota, was also up for re-election in 1900, but Pettigrew was consistent in his anti-imperialist opposition to McKinley and campaigned for Bryan. Hanna did all he could to destroy Pettigrew in 1900; Hoar got Republican support.[16]

He earned what he got. The Senator spoke throughout the state to large and enthusiastic audiences, attacking the Bryan anti-imperialist coalition at its weakest points, attempting to split anti-imperialist votes away from the Democratic candidate and toward McKinley (while Lodge drummed up the state's imperialist vote.) [17] Hoar redoubled his outcry against Bryan and his allies for Southern Democratic suppression of black rights and especially for the disfranchisement then in progress. Throwing back the charge of big business domination of the Republicans, Hoar pointed to corporate influence in the Democratic Party, citing the complicity of Tammany's boss Croker in the recently exposed "ice-trust" in New York City. He denied that the Democrats and Republicans were far apart in Philippine policy, since neither party platform promised the immediate independence the anti-imperialists demanded. (On the other hand,

---

* At this meeting were Eben Draper, the textile machinery manufacturer, William B. Plunkett, the textile manufacturer, Oakes Ames, the shovel manufacturer, President Lucius Tuttle of the Boston and Maine railroad, James P. Stearns of the Shawmut National Bank, Frank G. Webster of Kidder, Peabody & Co., stockbrokers, Robert A. Boit, president of the associated board of trade, etc. (*Springfield Daily Republican,* August 10, 1900; *Boston Post* quoted in *Boston Evening Transcript,* September 18, 1900.)

Lodge was sure that Bryan would "scuttle and run," and Lodge's Boston associate, Curtis Guild, warned that Bryan would turn "the white women and children of the city of Manila" over to the half-breed Aguinaldo and his followers.) [18] Hoar denied that Bryan could be trusted as an anti-imperialist, pointing to his support of the peace treaty, and maintaining that imperialists in the Democratic Party, especially in its Southern wing, would prevent him from carrying out an anti-imperialist policy even if he proved sincere and was elected.

In the course of the campaign the anti-imperialists responded to the issues Hoar raised. Not only did they repeat their charge that McKinley's imperial policy stimulated domestic racism, but their mouthpiece, the *Springfield Republican,* more than once challenged Bryan to take a stand in defense of black rights (which he just as consistently evaded.) [19] The anti-imperialists did not deny big business influence in the Democratic Party, but thought it ironic that Bryan should be blamed for it, when the Democratic politicians associated with this influence were his chief foes in the party. (Croker himself had insured Bryan's defeat in New York state, the anti-imperialists maintained, by engineering the Democratic nomination of an imperialist-minded machine politician for governor in place of a widely-supported reformer who was anti-imperialist.[20]) Leading anti-imperialists declared their belief in Bryan's sincere intent to stop the war and grant the Filipinos independence. Moreover, said the anti-imperialists, if McKinley and his policies were decisively repudiated at the polls, and then Bryan faltered, the people would be in a better position to carry on the fight than if McKinley were elected, with the appearance, at least, of a national vote of confidence. Despite their disagreements with him, and what they saw as his shortcomings, Boston anti-imperialists thought Bryan the best means available at the moment to check the growth of empire.[21]

Accordingly, whatever their difficulties with the Democrats, emphasized by the dialogue with Hoar, the leaders of the New England Anti-Imperialist League devoted their most intense efforts to the campaign of 1900. The Boston office continued as the most important center of funds and propaganda for the Anti-Imperialist League nationally.[22] During the campaign the New England organization issued some 400,000 pieces of literature, which it distributed both to anti-imperialist and Democratic organizations. Boston sent large quantities to South Dakota, Ohio, West Virginia, New York, Pennsylvania, Kansas, Indiana, Michigan, Nebraska, Illinois, Wisconsin and the other New England states.[23] Chairman Jones of the Democratic National Committee asked Patrick A. Collins to speak for the party in New Jersey, and arrangements were made for other Massachusetts leaders to speak in other states, East and West, at meetings organized both by Democrats and anti-imperialists.[24]

Relations with the Democrats presented a series of problems to the anti-imperialists, but the most serious weakness of the campaign was the failure to win the participation of organized labor in the anti-imperialist coalition, despite frequent attempts. In January 1900 at an anti-imperialist league meeting attended by Gompers and other trade union leaders, President Boutwell made a special plea to working men to join in the struggle against McKinley and empire; later in the campaign he repeated this appeal.[25] Bryan similarly exhorted labor more than once.[26] Despite these entreaties the leadership of the organized labor movement failed to support the Bryan campaign in any decisive way.

About a month before the voting day a vice president of the American Federation of Labor wrote president Gompers: "I have been watching this Political campaign with great interest and I believe if half a dozen prominent Labor men would take hold politically that Bryan could surely win." Gompers vetoed this suggestion in his reply, urging a policy of neutrality upon the labor movement as between the two major parties.[27]

Gompers had urged such a policy on labor in the election of 1896 but depression-inspired pressure from the rank and file had forced A. F. of L. leadership throughout the country into considerable pro-Bryan activity over Gompers' opposition.[28] But prosperity had returned and economic pressures had subsided. "There has been a great improvement among the working people," said Gompers in a speech just before the election, and the A. F. of L. president faced no such revolt from his organization's leadership over Bryan's candidacy in 1900 as he had in 1896.[29]

Coupled with Gompers' refusal to participate in the Bryan campaign of 1900 was a slackening of his anti-imperialism, which had always been longer on declaration than on practice. But in 1900 even these declarations came to an end, the last being made in December 1899.[30] In March and July 1900 the A. F. of L. executive council issued statements reviewing the conditions facing American workers and in neither of these was there any mention of imperialism or the Philippine war.[31]

Indicative of what lay behind Gompers' policies in 1900 was the position he had taken the previous fall at a Chicago conference on the trust problem. There the press reported that Gompers "did not attack the trusts." Instead he condemned those who wished to legislate against them and urged trust magnates to be more friendly to organized labor.[32] It was this policy of conciliation with big business that influenced Gompers' withdrawal from the anti-imperialist struggle and his negative attitude to the Bryan campaign in 1900. For in this campaign the anti-imperialist movement took on a more pronounced anti-monopoly thrust than heretofore. Its coalition with Bryan was predicated on a mutually shared antagonism to the trusts.

Spurred by the anti-imperialism of Patrick A. Collins, the *Boston Post* and the *Boston Pilot,* the Irish-American working class was the backbone of the Bryan vote in Boston in 1900, and contributed to it heavily in the rest of the state. But George E. McNeill and Henry Lloyd were the only labor leaders in Massachusetts to participate actively in the Bryan campaign. Several Boston trade union leaders publicly announced support for Bryan, some declared themselves neutral, and a few spoke out for McKinley.[33]

Elsewhere the Cleveland Federation of Labor turned down Bryan's request to speak at its Labor Day rally; the Chicago Federation invited both Roosevelt and Bryan to speak at its rally; and in Indiana the labor movement came out for McKinley. While there was unquestionably support for Bryan among working people in 1900, the nation's organized labor movement generally did not participate in the Democrat's campaign.[34]

Massachusetts anti-imperialists also made special appeals to the nation's blacks. During the period of the election campaign, the white supremacist offensive against their voting rights was accompanied by bloody attacks against blacks in New Orleans, Akron and New York City. The *Springfield Republican* related this racist mob-violence "to the overbearing and contemptuous career of force and blood pursued by the nation for two years past toward the 'niggers' of the Spanish islands."[35] The connection between the worsening condition of the blacks at home and McKinley's war in the Philippines was the gist of the two pamphlets issued in thousands of copies by the New England

Anti-Imperialist League, one written by a black intellectual leader, Professor Kelley Miller of Howard University, the other by G. S. Boutwell, T. W. Higginson and W. L. Garrison, who described themselves as "trained from youth in the strictest school of anti-slavery conviction."[36]

Most active was the black anti-imperialist leader, Rev. W. H. Scott, who lived in Woburn, a suburb of Boston. Traveling for the League during the campaign, he wrote and issued in his own name a call to the blacks to break with the McKinley Administration. In this folder he directed his sharpest attack upon the main figure in the Republican campaign, Theodore Roosevelt, for his attribution of cowardice to black soldiers at San Juan Hill.[37]

Scott's concern with anti-imperialism and the defense of black rights brought him into direct conflict with the policies of Booker T. Washington during the elections. In the face of the offensive against the black vote, Washington was urging his people to forget politics and concentrate on economic self-advancement. To further these policies Washington proposed to organize a National Negro Business League at a conference to be held in Boston at the end of August.

But a week before the National Negro Business League met, Scott and other Boston blacks held a meeting to protest Washington's program. There they condemned the Southern racist offensive, McKinley's complicity and Booker T. Washington's submission. Anti-Imperialist League President Boutwell sent this meeting a message of support.[38]

Moreover echoes of the militant black protest in which Scott was prominent broke through Washington's quietist restrictions at the National Negro Business League meeting.[39] The greatest demonstration of the conference was staged by delegates in support of a young veteran of San Juan Hill who defended the bravery of black soldiers in that battle and condemned Roosevelt for maligning the race, despite Washington's ban on political discussion.*

---

* There was also expression of indignation over Roosevelt's attitude in the white community. The anti-imperialist and Democratic Congressman Naphen, running for re-election from South Boston, made the charge that Roosevelt slandered black soldiers part of his case against the Republicans. (*Boston Sunday Globe*, September 2, 1900.)

Further disagreement with Washington's policies was shown in Boston early in October when Scott joined that other black anti-imperialist, C. H. Plummer, in speaking at a meeting of blacks that filled Faneuil Hall and passed a resolution urging black voters, particularly in those states where they held the balance of power, to vote against the Republican Administration. (Here W. L. Garrison also spoke and pledged to carry the fight for black rights to Bryan's doorstep should Bryan be elected and the need arise.) [40]

Ten days after the Faneuil Hall meeting, six prominent black Bostonians, led by Archibald H. Grimké (of the abolitionist family), urged all members of their race to vote for Bryan, or at least to abstain from voting for McKinley. "Scratch the skin of Republican leaders like Hanna, Lodge, Roosevelt and McKinley," said Grimké and his friends, "and you will find race prejudice underneath, an invincible belief on their part in the divine right of the Anglo-Saxon to govern the republic and subjugate darker races." Further, they maintained, the current suppression of black rights was in reality part of a larger attack by a "plutocracy" against the entire American people, that unless checked, "would ultimately convert the republic into an empire . . . into a government of by and for vast syndicates of wealth."[41]

But in Boston, as elsewhere, some black citizens voiced support for McKinley, and the black community appeared to be divided.[42] O'Brien expressed the opinion in the *Transcript* that nationally the black vote would be overwhelmingly Republican, because of Democratic disfranchisement in the South. But Bishop H. M. Turner of the African Methodist Episcopal Church (commissioned by Lincoln as the first black chaplain in the United States Army), Captain John L. Waller (in the United States consular service under Harrison) and other nationally known blacks broke with McKinley over imperialism, and the *Boston Globe* reported that grave concern was felt at Washington over the extent of defection of colored Republicans.[43]

"I pray for his victory," wrote William James from abroad of Bryan's candidacy to banker Henry Lee Higginson, a McKinley man. Charles Eliot Norton joined his friend in Bryan's support, but the majority of Harvard's faculty, led by President Eliot, declared for McKinley.[44] In Massachusetts few educators or clergymen came out for Bryan. Rabbi Charles Fleischer did campaign actively for him, as did a Protestant minister, Rev. R. E. Bisbee, who got into serious difficulty with his congregation as a result.[45]

Hoar's arguments influenced voters of anti-imperialist sympathies, especially the conservatives repelled by Bryan's domestic views. Edward Atkinson, the anti-imperialist leader closest to Hoar, all but gave his blessing to McKinley, while Charles Francis Adams flatly declared his support for the President (in a letter to Carl Schurz, who had finally decided to vote for Bryan). Besides Adams and Atkinson, other Massachusetts businessmen previously identified with the Anti-Imperialist League announced their intention of voting for McKinley.[46]

However, both Adams and Atkinson joined their pro-Bryan friends in calling for the election of anti-imperialist and Democratic Congressmen. In Massachusetts two such Representatives were running for re-election — Henry F. Naphen from South Boston and John R. Thayer from Worcester.[47] Henry Cabot Lodge set the defeat of these men as a special goal for the Massachusetts Republican Party, while the anti-imperialist league did what it could to help them.[48] But the local candidacy that really stirred Boston anti-imperialists was that of Moorfield Storey.

An eminent attorney, former president of the American Bar Association, Storey was a man whose convictions had been set by his early experience as assistant to the Massachusetts anti-slavery leader, Senator Charles Sumner. Visiting Storey in June, John Jay Chapman came away with the impression that the Boston man was capable of giving up all his worldly goods to stop the Philippine War and the slaughter of the Philippine people.[49] Storey's personal commitment, sensed by Chapman, was demonstrated in the fall.

Declaring for Bryan after the third party movement collapsed in September, Storey then announced his intention of running for Congress as a Democrat on a platform of peace and anti-imperialism.[50] Storey was given a fighting chance to win. Brookline, the base of the 11th District where he was running, was the original home of the Mugwump movement; Storey had the approval of members of the Democratic State Committee, and the Republican candidate was an undistinguished supporter of the Administration.[51]

All went well until the Democratic district nominating convention was held. Then the nomination was taken from Storey by William F. Baker, a local Democrat, with the aid, it was rumored, of Republican plants to tip the votes.[52]

Storey's friends made a great effort to get Baker to withdraw, Bryan himself intervening on Storey's behalf, to no avail.[53]

It was agreed on all sides that Baker, who had already been beaten twice in running for Congress, had little chance against his Republican rival. But Boston papers charged that the Republicans promised Baker a local office, which he wanted and they controlled, if he would keep Storey from the Democratic nomination. Moreover, he was encouraged in this course by the imperialist-minded Gold Democrat Nathan Matthews, Jr., who, like the Republicans, had no desire to see Storey in Congress.[54]

The result was that Storey ran as an independent in a three-way race and his chances of winning were drastically reduced. In Massachusetts, as in New York, the imperialist-minded and the hack politicians in the Democratic Party joined hands with the McKinley Republicans against the coalition of Bryan and the anti-imperialists.

The Bryan campaign in Massachusetts did get aid, however, from unexpected sources. As has been noted, the national committee of the Gold Democratic Party was solidly for McKinley. But the main organization of the Gold Democrats in Massachusetts, the Young Men's Democratic Club, was split down the middle. Men like Gamaliel Bradford and Patrick A. Collins were for Bryan, and those like Nathan Matthews, Jr., and Charles A. Conant were for McKinley. As a result the organization decided to take no stand.[55] In further contrast to the sentiment of the national committee, Massachusetts' outstanding Gold Democrat, Richard Olney, early in September declared outright for Bryan with a statement of his views that had a national impact.

Olney condemned the Philippine War, intervention in China and McKinley's vision of the United States as an Asian power, though his imperialist proclivities, made evident during the Venezuelan crisis, reappeared in his call for the retention of Cuba. But this was incidental to the statement's main emphasis, wherein lay its most damaging effect. Olney claimed that to vote for McKinley was to vote for a "syndicated presidency," an administration totally subservient in both domestic and foreign policies "to the clamor of special pecuniary interests." This lent damning support to Bryan's contention, for Olney was no raggle-taggle Midwestern Populist; he was a solidly entrenched member of the Eastern establishment, close to the national centers of power, presumably in a position to know the facts.[56]

Olney's pronouncement irritated the more conservative Gold Democrats, one of whose number, a prominent Boston banker, dismissed it as "addressed to the lower classes." But it gave McKinley a bad fright. The day after Olney spoke out, "a loud noise of warning was sounded from the white house . . . in articles wired to administration organs all over the country."[57]

Later in the campaign, the Bryan candidacy got a boost from the other end of the political spectrum, from members of the Social Democratic Party. This aid was also out of the ordinary, since the official position of the Social Democrats in the elections of 1900 was that both the Democratic and Republican parties were equally to be condemned as parties of capital.[58] They differentiated between the two only in their description of the Bryan campaign (especially in its anti-trust aspects) as a middle class movement trying to turn the clock back. Occasionally they condemned the Philippine war, but more often they disregarded the question of imperialism in favor of what they saw as the most important issue, socialism versus capitalism. The Social Democratic campaign tended to drain the Bryan vote from the left, and in the Midwest the press reported that the Socialists were making headway in the factories and mines with, it was said, some encouragement from anti-Bryan employers. The Democratic leadership was concerned about this development, particularly since Hanna was effectively bringing the Republican message of prosperity to industrial workers in this region.[59]

A number of Social Democratic locals in Chicago, however, were supporting Bryan, as was Toledo's socialist mayor, Samuel ("Golden Rule") Jones.[60] But the fullest, most striking expression of support for Bryan in Social Democratic ranks came in the last days of the campaign in a statement issued at Boston. Since that city was the national center of anti-imperialist sentiment, it was not surprising that three of the four men who signed this pro-Bryan document were Bostonians. All the signers were prominent, middle class members of the Social Democratic Party and personal friends of Eugene Debs, their party's presidential candidate.* Their statement took the form

---

* Signers were: Dr. George W. Galvin, founder of the Boston Emergency Hospital, B. O. Flower, founder of the magazine *The Arena*, Frank Parsons, lecturer at Boston University Law School and president of the National Public Ownership League, all from Boston, and Eltweed Pomeroy, president of the National Direct Legislation League, from New Jersey.

of an open letter to Debs urging him to withdraw in favor of Bryan. Reinforcing the Bryan-anti-imperialist analysis from the left as Olney had from the right, they declared: "The actual issue that will be decided in this campaign is monopoly versus the people. Imperialism itself is simply monopoly showing its teeth on foreign soil. The war of conquest in the Philippines is merely to give the trusts more markets." The Republican Party was "owned and controlled by the monopolies," while the Democrats represented mainly "the farmers and artisan classes, the small merchants and the masses of the common people." The Boston men called for a practical as well as an agitational approach to their party's distinctive socialist goal, and they advanced the thought that "a vote for Bryan is a vote for the first practicable step toward the cooperative commonwealth, though neither Bryan nor the democratic party may realize that fact." They echoed the plea of the anti-imperialists for unity against the main threat, pointing out that "if the radicals act with the mild progressives, the forces of retrogression can be vanquished." On the other hand they warned that if Debs persisted in his campaign and so drew votes from Bryan, the socialists would in fact help elect McKinley, the tool of the trusts.[61]

The statement was well-publicized in the press of Massachusetts, where it was especially advantageous to the Democratic campaign, since in 1900 the Social Democrats were stronger in the eastern part of that state than anywhere else, having elected there two mayors and a state representative.[62] Whatever the effect the appeal for Bryan may have had on the socialist vote in Massachusetts, it had none on Debs. He publicly refused to withdraw.[63]

Throughout 1900 the Filipino insurgents waged guerrilla war without cease. Because its battles were small and indecisive McKinley's campaign orators tried to dismiss the conflict from view, asserting that the American military effort was merely the suppression of "robber bands." But Massachusetts anti-imperialists were persistent in calling attention to this new phase of the Philippine War and in demanding that the United States desist.[64]

In mid-October representatives of Aguinaldo approached the Democratic and anti-imperialist leadership with a proposal they hoped might help the Bryan cause. The Filipinos offered immediately to announce, in Aguinaldo's name, that their countrymen would stop fighting if Bryan were elected. The Democratic leadership, fearing treason charges from the Republicans, refused to have anything to do with the envoys, and the Boston men likewise discouraged negotiations. But a few days before the elections G. S. Boutwell, as President of the Anti-Imperialist League, issued a statement that, in effect, brought the Filipino offer to the attention of the American people. Without fully revealing the reason for his confidence, he asserted the belief that the Filipinos would cease hostilities at once in case of Bryan's election. In this final appeal before the voting, the anti-imperialists called on the American people to oust McKinley and put an end to the criminal Philippine War.[65]

In the election McKinley got a popular vote of 7,238,543 while Bryan got 6,360,796. The President held all the states he had won in 1896 — and gained Washington, Utah, South Dakota, Kansas, Wyoming and Nebraska. But his pluralities were reduced in the Eastern and Middle states. Erving Winslow noted that in New England, New York, New Jersey, Maryland, Pennsylvania and Illinois, taken together, the Republican plurality was down some 400,000 votes from 1896. McKinley gained in the West where the return of farm prosperity was important, and Bryan gained in the East where anti-imperialism was strong.[66]

In Massachusetts McKinley's plurality of 80,000 in 1900 was less than half of the 173,000 he had in 1896, a reduction which accounted for nearly one quarter of the total loss in McKinley's Eastern vote. Boston was the banner Bryan city in the country. Bryan carried it by some 8,000 votes, where McKinley had won it by 18,000 in 1896. This suggested that many from the middle class, who had voted for McKinley in 1896, in 1900 joined the city's Irish working people in support of Bryan.[67] The *Hartford Times* thought that the anti-imperialists could be especially proud of their work in Massachusetts. The Democratic candidate was evidently of the same opinion; ten days after the election he wrote Thomas Wentworth Higginson, who had served as a presidential elector on the state Democratic ticket: "If all the states had done as well as Mass. we would have won a sweeping victory."[68]

Bryan thought the main cause of his defeat was the prosperity issue and many others agreed.[69] Whether he had adequately dealt with it during the campaign was questionable. The day before the elections a Boston anti-imperialist had thrown the whole question into sharp relief when he asked how many American and Filipino lives a "full dinner-pail" was worth. During the campaign the *Springfield Republican* had called the nation's heightened economic activity "fire-arm" prosperity and had persistently reminded readers that it was caused in good part by the war policies of the government.[70] The country's prosperity, however, had remained a powerful electoral argument, so that the war economy, one of the by-products of imperial policy, itself brought a degree of mass support for that policy. Clearly, the election results indicated that American imperialism, at this early stage, carried with it a measure of political stability.

Within the over-all Republican victory certain campaigns stood out. Chairman Hanna was most pleased with the defeat of Senator Pettigrew. And Senator Lodge was so impressed with Senator Hoar's contribution that he called upon the Massachusetts legislature to re-elect his senior colleague with the biggest vote ever. In the 11th District Moorfield Storey lost to the Republican candidate, as expected. But Lodge was distressed that the anti-imperialists Naphen and Thayer were returned to Congress from South Boston and Worcester and scolded the Republicans for permitting this.[71]

The pro-McKinley *Boston Journal* foresaw "the early disappearance of 'anti-imperialism.' "[72] The anti-imperialists, on the other hand, insisted that the election results were no endorsement of McKinley's foreign policies, pointing out that many voted for McKinley with anti-imperialist reservations, or because they did not support Bryan's currency doctrines, that many didn't vote at all. The issue, moreover, had not been clearly placed before the majority of the voters since the overwhelming bulk of the nation's press was pro-imperialist.[73] This was all cold comfort. When they had argued against Hoar's position in the election campaign the anti-imperialists had said that no matter how many Republicans had voted for McKinley with anti-imperialist reservations, the Administration, if returned to office, would regard the victory as approval of its program, and so it happened.[74]

Senator Lodge claimed that the results were a particular endorsement of the Administration's Philippine policies, and the McKinley cabinet acted as if it thought the same. The day after the election, the War Department instructed General MacArthur to proceed with the ruthless and systematic extermination of the Philippine guerrillas.[75] (Before the elections, Washington had given prominence to the claim of the Taft Commission, then in the islands, that Philippine resistance would collapse on Bryan's defeat; evidently the Administration was taking no chances on its own predictions.) [76]

Victory in hand, the Republicans also gave the green light to the political offensive against the blacks at home. Shortly after the voting it was reported that the McKinley Administration (with the full agreement of Senator Lodge) had no intention of trying to reduce Southern representation in Congress because of the black disfranchisement taking place. There had been a decline in the Bryan vote in the South, and manufacturers of that region were giving valuable support to the new foreign policy. The Administration had hopes of creating a new, white man's Republican Party in the South.[77]

During the campaign Senator Lodge had defended the "much-abused Standard oil trust," in an effort to throw back the attack on monopoly. After the elections Charles Flint declared the vote to be a popular endorsement of the trusts, and, in fact, the organization of new monopolies was accelerated. The talk had been that if Bryan won, capitalists would withdraw funds and depression would ensue. With McKinley in, there was a stock market boom; the Standard Oil declared a new dividend — and a rise in prices.[78]

The international implications of the elections were important. It had been said before the vote that Bryan's election would interfere with the United States' assumption of a place as the world's financial center, would put in question the recently acquired influence in Asia and the possibilities of investment in China.[79] McKinley's election removed these worries. The United States' new role in the world as a leading contender for imperialist hegemony was made secure.

For the anti-imperialists the election campaign of 1900 was the climax of their struggle of the past two years, first against the treaty, then against the war. By means of their coalition with Bryan, they had brought the issue of imperialism's conflict with democracy to millions of Americans, far beyond all their previous efforts. A Boston observer, commenting on the election campaign in the *Atlantic Monthly,* wrote that the "instinct and passion of American democracy" was "to distrust all power that is in any way hidden, to seek to put one's hands on the secret springs of the great machine," and he praised the Bryan campaign as a manifestation of this democratic spirit.[80] Certainly the campaign of 1900 exposed the "secret springs" of modern United States foreign policy, insofar as these lay in the economic interests of the nation's big corporations and banks, in a manner and on a scale not done before, nor since. In 1896 Bryan had voiced the revulsion of the common people at the hold plutocracy was getting on the country and its institutions, using the currency issue as a vehicle. In 1900 Bryan carried forward the attack on plutocracy, bringing into focus its influence on the new role the United States was assuming in world affairs. But the chief inspiration and stimulation for this massive effort at public education and arousal in 1900 was the anti-imperialist leadership of Massachusetts.

The anti-imperialists, however, did not believe the essential significance of the elections of 1900 was to be measured in terms of their own accomplishment. They compared this contest with 1800 and 1824, when Jefferson and Jackson had led the embattled democracy against aristocracy, special privilege and wealth. They equated it as well with 1864, when, in the midst of the Civil War, Northern sympathizers of the slaveholders had challenged Lincoln's policies.[81] They thought this election as fundamental a turning point as the anti-slavery crisis. The difference was that in 1900 democracy lost and reaction won.

16

Against Atrocities: The Last Campaign

On the eve of the elections of 1900 the resistance of the Philippine guerrillas reached such a pitch that General Young in northern Luzon recommended the use of "European methods against rebellious Asiatics." General MacArthur refused for fear of arousing public opinion in the United States; the General was afraid of Congressional investigation (so Philippine Commissioner Taft complained to Secretary Root).[1] As it turned out, MacArthur was overruled by the highest authority; American public opinion was aroused; and Congress did investigate.

In his report for the year, submitted October 1900, General MacArthur had frankly told Washington that the success of the Philippine guerrillas was due to the "almost complete unity of action of the entire native population."[2] The guerrilla fighters, in other words, were able to sustain their warfare because they enjoyed the support of the overwhelming majority of the Philippine people. As the year closed, the problem facing the Adminstration was how to break the link between the guerrillas and the Philippine population as a whole.

Having settled accounts with the domestic opposition, the McKinley Administration addressed itself to the Filipinos. The day after the elections the cabinet met and sent orders to General MacArthur to "start a vigorous campaign at once, pressing the remnants of the Filipino army to the last extremity." Ten days later the Washington correspondents of two Boston papers gave an idea of the campaign the Administration proposed. On November 19 the *Herald* reported that Lord Kitchener's plan of operations in South

Africa, "harsh though it appears to be, appeals to officials of the war department, and during the coming campaign . . . no mercy is to be extended to those in active rebellion or who give aid and comfort to the insurgents." The next day the *Globe* said that it was Kitchener's plan of reconcentration (similar to that of Weyler in Cuba) that appealed to officials in the War Department, who explained that "unless the Filipinos are forced to leave the country districts and settle in the towns where they can be kept under the eye of the military authorities; there will be no hope of suppressing the guerrilla warfare." Moreover the *Globe*'s correspondent reported a War Department rumor that "General MacArthur had been told in somewhat plain language that his course had not been entirely satisfactory to the president and that he had apparently not pushed the campaign with the vigor . . . expected of him."[3]

MacArthur's subsequent action tended to corroborate these reports. On December 20 the General issued a proclamation to the people of the Philippines outlining what Secretary Root described as a "more rigid policy." Putting the islands under martial law, this proclamation, in effect, announced the determination of the McKinley Administration to sever the connection between the guerrilla fighters and the Philippine people as a whole. MacArthur warned that "the practice of sending supplies to insurgent troops from places now occupied by the United States, as is now the case, must cease," and that "men who participate in hostilities without being part of a regularly armed force . . . divest themselves of the character of soldiers and if captured are not entitled to the privileges of prisoners of war." The General declared that those supporting the guerrillas "had not heretofore been held responsible for their actions" because of "the solicitude of the United States to avoid all appearances of harshness in pacifying the islands." The December proclamation served notice that such was no longer the case.[4]

The United States war against the Filipinos had not lacked for harshness before this, as soldiers' letters and anti-imperialist protest had made known. Just after the war broke out reports had reached the United States that an undeclared practice of taking no prisoners was in evidence, and anti-imperialists had pointed to the Filipino battle ratio of five killed to one wounded (the reverse of the usual) as confirmation of these reports. What was new at this point was that the McKinley Administration elevated the application of extreme measures, hitherto unofficial and unacknowledged, into a policy that was official and acknowledged — from the highest cabinet level through the War Department to MacArthur and the forces in the field. In July 1901 General MacArthur reported to Washington that "the application of military methods since December 20, 1900, had been very drastic." It was against these "very drastic" methods that the Massachusetts anti-imperialists launched what was to be, in truth, their last campaign of any magnitude.[5]

A feature of the Administration's new military policies was the wholesale enlistment of native troops in the Philippines. Heretofore the United States army had recruited small bands of natives on an experimental basis, but in the new army bill debated by Congress in January 1901 Secretary of War Root proposed to enlist 12,000 of these.

In the same month Root complained of continuous pressure from service men and their families for release from Philippine duty; the war in the Philippines continued to be unpopular, and, although the United States had reduced its commitment by almost half, there were still some 40,000 troops in the islands. It followed that one of the great advantages of the enlistment of native troops was the return home of disgruntled United States volunteers.[6]

Initial opposition to "a more rigid policy" came over the use of native troops. Making a last stand in the lame-duck session of Congress, Senator Pettigrew declared that large-scale use of native troops would increase the severity of the United States war against the guerrillas. Pettigrew maintained that only the more savage peoples like the Macabebes, traditionally hostile to the majority of the Filipinos, would enlist as mercenary troops (as they had under Spain), and the Senator quoted Secretary Root to the effect that the Macabebes were prone to "murder, burn and rob" and were difficult to keep "within the lines of civilized warfare."[7]

Pettigrew's speech shook Gamaliel Bradford out of his post-election apathy, and he joined the Senator's protest. In a letter to the press Bradford charged that the Macabebes had taught American troops "the fiendish expedient of the 'water cure' for the purpose of compelling the surrender of guns concealed by the natives." The water cure, he explained, consisted of "placing a man on his back, forcing open his mouth and pouring into him a pail or more of water 'till he swells up like a toad,' and then squeezing it out again." (Anti-imperialists thought the Macabebes had learned this torture from the Spanish as it was common practice in the Inquisition.[8]) It was Bradford's contention that there was "overwhelming testimony" that our troops were using this torture against guerrilla suspects and prisoners. He asked an angry question: didn't the people of the United States know that their government was adopting savage methods of war, or didn't they care?[9]

Not long after Bradford's protest against the use of native troops, a band of Macabebe scouts, under the direction of General Funston, proved extremely useful to the American high command. Posing as guerrillas they wormed their way into Aguinaldo's hiding place, surprised and overwhelmed his guards, captured the Filipino leader and brought him back to Manila, a prisoner of the United States army. The ruse was successful, the deception complete, and the Philippine guerrillas suffered a serious loss. This operation disgusted Senator Hoar; he called the capture of Aguinaldo a "miserable and pitiful business," voicing the feeling of a number of his constituents.[10]

Before the Massachusetts anti-imperialists became seriously engaged in the campaign against the conduct of the war another development of imperial policy drew their fire. This was the Administration's proposal to establish a protectorate over Cuba (a matter of immediate urgency in the winter of 1901 because a Cuban constitutional session was then in session).

Providing background for the Administration's proposal was the penetration of Cuba by United States capital since the end of the war with Spain. Noteworthy was the formation in April 1900 of the Cuba Company, capitalized at eight million dollars, with its object "the development of Cuba by construction of railways and otherwise." Among those involved in this venture were Henry M. Flagler of the Standard Oil group, James J. Hill, the railroad capitalist, and William C. Whitney, the New York traction magnate. Secretary of War Root had the distribution of franchises in Cuba, and he had been, for years before this, attorney for both Whitney and Standard Oil, so that the group behind the Cuba Company, by this relationship, if by nothing else, had a certain entree to the field they proposed to develop.[11] Nor were Boston interests to be neglected. In the fall of 1901 Senator Lodge passed on to Secretary Root a letter from Henry Lee Higginson saying that his bank was behind a Boston contractor who was putting in a bid for paving and sewering Havana.

Lodge told Root that the banking house of Lee, Higginson and Company was "an old firm of the highest possible standing and largest resources."[12] (In this instance Lodge was displaying the same solicitude for the foreign opportunities of Massachusetts finance capital that he had already shown for the foreign markets of the state's industrial capital.)

Secretary of War Root was the author of those proposals, later embodied in the Platt Amendment, that made Cuba a virtual protectorate of the United States. They afforded the United States control of Cuban finances and foreign affairs, the right to military intervention in the island, and to naval stations therein. In the Secretary's words, one of the major purposes of his recommendations was to guarantee Cuba's "giving due protection to the lives and property of the citizens of all other countries within her borders"; obviously the investors of the United States fell within this purview.[13]

In February 1901 O'Brien, the *Transcript*'s Washington correspondent, pointed out that the McKinley Administration was preparing public opinion at home for the Cuban protectorate; and he cited as evidence a dispatch to Postmaster General Smith's *Philadelphia Press* that the Boston man considered to be "obviously inspired from Administration sources." Writing from Washington, the *Press* reporter had said that it should not be supposed that the United States would allow Cuba to make treaties with foreign governments, incur debt without limit or "do anything else it pleases regardless of our rights." The proposed constitution called for universal suffrage "which means the rule in Cuba of illiterates, principally Negroes, and in the opinion of the majority of the people here under such a constitution Cuba would soon become another Haiti." (It was the view of the imperialist press at the time, contradicted by the *Springfield Republican,* that Haiti, an all-black republic, was rapidly deteriorating).[14]

During the latter part of the winter the investment of American capital in Cuba was reported to be especially marked. In March 1901 the McKinley Administration established its political dominion over that island with the passage of the Platt Amendment by Congress, in a vote on partisan lines, Democrats opposing, Republicans (including Senator Hoar) supporting.[15]

On March 30 a crowd of Bostonians of middle age or older, one third of whom were women, filled Faneuil Hall at the Anti-Imperialist League's first public rally since election defeat. Newsmen felt a spirit of "never give up" in evidence. Held under the slogan, "Free America, Free Cuba, Free Philippines," the meeting heard speakers denounce the Platt Amendment as a betrayal of the pledge to honor Cuban independence made by the United States during the Spanish War. President Boutwell described the policy embodied in the Platt Amendment as one "by which strong states may tyrannize over the weaker ones upon the pretext of aiding and defending them," and a letter was read from a Havana newspaper editor telling of Cuban opposition to McKinley's terms.

The meeting also spoke out on current policy in the Far East. A Philippine speaker, Sexto Lopez, got the greatest applause of the evening.* He called attention to the fact that "quite recently a new and more rigorous system of warfare has been adopted in the Philippines." One after another, speakers denounced reconcentration, the water cure and the hiring of Filipino mercenaries. When Colonel Charles R. Codman told the audience that Filipino dead outnumbered Filipino wounded five to one, the hall was filled with cries of "Shame! Shame!"[16]

On July 4, 1901, after repeated urgings from the Boston organization, the Chicago, national leadership of the anti-imperialist league issued an address to the country, "showing that we are still in the fight." Moorfield Storey wrote the document, which repeated the emphases of the Boston meeting, declaring that the Cubans' submission to the "unjust requirements" of the Platt Amendment, enforced "by the presence of American troops on their soil," constituted "an example of national perfidy." Mark Twain, William Dean Howells and other prominent persons signed this, as did leaders of the anti-imperialist league in Eastern and Midwestern cities.[17]

Even as the Platt Amendment was being discussed, there were those who urged the outright annexation of Cuba on the model of Hawaii, Puerto Rico and the Philippines.[18] When the Administration brushed aside this annexationist pressure in favor of the Platt Amendment, it gave a new, unmistakable emphasis to an extremely significant shift in policy, first indicated when Hay had renounced

---

* Lopez was sponsored in the United States by the Boston anti-imperialist, Fiske Warren, who believed that "Filipino anti-imperialists and Yankee anti-imperialists should come together as such." (Fiske Warren to Carl Schurz, January 29, 1903, Fiske Warren to G. S. Boutwell, February 2, 1903, Schurz Papers, Library of Congress.)

United States appropriation of Chinese territory in favor of the Open Door and the preservation of China as "a territorial and administrative entity." The decisive imperialist group was turning from the annexations that had characterized the period of the Spanish-American War to a policy that allowed for economic penetration, political domination, and military intervention, but stopped short of direct colonial possession; the Open Door policy and the Platt Amendment showed the way.*

Meanwhile reports from the Philippines drew further protest from the anti-imperialists. In May 1901 Brigadier General James F. Bell returned to the United States from his command in Southern Luzon. While in Washington, D.C., he made what the *New York Times* called a "remarkable statement." Bell said:

> One sixth of the natives of Luzon have either been killed or have died of the dengue fever in the last few years. The loss of life by killing alone has been very great, but I think that not one man has been slain except where his death has served the legitimate purposes of war. It has been necessary to adopt what in other countries would probably be thought harsh measures . . .

Since the War Department estimated the population of Luzon at 3,727,488, and dengue fever was considered the result of war-induced famine, Bell's statement meant that in the central province of the Philippines some 616,000 people had died from the war. Under the title "Benevolent Assimilation" (McKinley's words for his Philippine policy), the New England Anti-Imperialist League reprinted the Bell interview in a folder for popular distribution.[19]

In July General MacArthur was relieved of the Philippine command and replaced by Major General Adna Chaffee. Chaffee had just returned to the Philippines from China, where he had led the United States forces in the successful operations of the imperialist powers against the Boxers. American anti-imperialists had condemned the allied campaign against the Boxers as one of unexampled brutality and ferocity; hence they denounced Chaffee's appointment to his new post.[20]

In September President McKinley died, struck down by an assassin's

---

* Especially as a result of the massive upsurge of the colonial peoples after World War II, this policy has been adopted more or less universally by the imperialist powers, and is known as "neo-colonialism."

bullet. "While," as F. B. Sanborn said, "the parsons and the more idiotic editors" accused the anti-imperialists of having incited it by their critcisms, the anti-imperialists deplored the deed and reminded the public that they had always opposed the policy, not the man. In fact, a young anarchist killed McKinley as "an enemy of the working people."[21]

The new president quickly made known his willingness to carry forward the new methods of imperial expansion marked by the Platt Amendment. Just after taking office Roosevelt confided to the Washington correspondent of the *New York Evening Post* that he was thoroughly in earnest in his desire to get out of Cuba and that he felt the same way about the Philippines although he believed that would take longer. Since, as was well known, the *Post* was close to the anti-imperialists, the word soon got back to them.[22]

Not long after Roosevelt threw out these hints to soothe the domestic opposition, the news of General Jacob Smith's activities in Samar caused Massachusetts anti-imperialists to launch a national campaign against the conduct of the war that set off a congressional investigation. In the fall of 1901 the island of Samar was one of the few areas still in active revolt, and there, in September, a company of American soldiers was taken by surprise and massacred. On November 4 the *Manila Times,* an American paper sympathetic to United States policy, published a report that

> Brigadier General Smith had been in Samar about 10 days and his strong policy was already making itself felt. He had already ordered all natives to present themselves in certain of the coast towns, saying that those who were found outside would be shot and no questions asked . . . [when] the time limit had expired . . . General Smith was as good as his word. His policy of reconcentration is said to be the most effective thing of the kind ever seen in these islands under any flag. All suspects including Spaniards and half-breeds, were rounded up in big stockades and kept under guard.

Shortly afterwards, this report was reprinted in the United States press.[23]

In the same month, the *Philadelphia Ledger,* another paper sympathetic to the Administration, carried a dispatch from its correspondent in Manila reviewing current military policy in the Philippines:

"All suspects . . . were rounded up in big stockades and kept under guard." The "pacification" of Samar by General Jacob Smith.

The present war is no bloodless, fake, opéra bouffe engagement; our men have been relentless, have killed to exterminate men, women, children, prisoners and captives, active insurgents and suspected people from lads of 10 up, an idea prevailing that the Filipino as such was little better than a dog . . . Our soldiers have pumped salt water into men to "make them talk," and have taken prisoners people who held up their hands and peacefully surrendered, and an hour later, without an atom of evidence to show that they were even insurrectos, stood them on a bridge and shot them down one by one, to drop into the water below and float down, as examples to those who found their bullet-loaded corpses . . . The new military plan of settling the trouble by setting them at each other looks promising.[24]

Early in December the anti-imperialists held a conference in Boston attended by Moorfield Storey, Carl Schurz, George S. Boutwell and others. The meeting drew up a petition to the United States Senate asking that body to investigate the conduct of the war in the Philippines (citing the reports from the *Manila Times* and the *Philadelphia Ledger* as evidence of need).[25]

Before the petition campaign got under way, however, Carl Schurz expressed last minute doubts as to its advisability, and Moorfield Storey wrote to bolster him. What troubled Storey, he told Schurz, was that the United States was committing cruelties in the Philippines worse than those of Spain in Cuba or England in South Africa, while the American people looked on with apparent acquiescence. Those who had thus far kept silent, wrote Storey, may well have been influenced by the silence of the anti-imperialists. He insisted, "The time to speak has come . . . if the people don't follow it is their fault not ours, but if no lead be given it is *our* fault." Storey's letter, the appeal of a New England conscience, convinced Schurz, and the petition went ahead, anti-imperialists in Boston, New York, Philadelphia and Chicago getting hundreds of signers, including many notables.[26]

On January 10 the *Springfield Republican* reprinted the petition in full, with an appeal for signatures. A few days later George Frisbie Hoar called upon the Senate to investigate the conduct of the war. At this point the whole issue was set before the public. Anti-imperialism, the movement the imperialists thought the elections of 1900 had safely laid away, rose up again, startling and shaking those in the seats of power. A debate opened in the Senate more turbulent, older Senators thought, than any since the discussion of the resolutions leading to the Spanish-American War.[27]

The first clash came between Senators Hoar and Lodge when Hoar introduced a resolution calling for a special committee of investigation. Recalling the existence of such a body during the Civil War and pointing to the need at present, Hoar spoke at length and earnestly. In reply Lodge sharply denied the need for any investigation; however, said the Senator, if there had to be one, surely the committee on the Philippines of which he was chairman was competent to handle it. Though of "more than ordinary vigour," the debate between Hoar and Lodge was only a taste of what lay ahead.[28]

Shortly afterwards the imperialists got another shock, administered by one of their own, and all the worse for that. The Massachusetts Reform Club held a meeting in Boston at which Herbert Welsh of Philadelphia recited army atrocities and called for an investigation. While this was not pleasing to the imperialists, even more disconcerting, because so unexpected, was the speech at this same meeting of the leading member of McKinley's first Philippine commission, President Schurman of Cornell University. He called for the eventual independence of the Philippines.[29]

Anti-imperialists thought that Schurman, a supple opportunist, was merely bending to the policy shift taking shape at the highest levels of the Administration, but his words were bitter medicine for many others. General Wheaton in the Philippines was very disturbed, telling the press that in the islands men were thrown in jail for saying less. The General hung the sign of treason round the neck of the respectable educator, and confusion overtook the imperialist camp.[30]

Uneasy and defensive, pressed by editorial support for Hoar's resolution, the Republicans in the Senate decided to give in to the anti-imperialist demand for an investigation so long as it was in charge of the Philippine committee where Lodge could keep it quiet. Hoar, as the Boston press predicted, consented "to the entombment of his resolution in that committee sooner than offend his colleague."[31] On January 28, Lodge, "much against his will, and in a very bad temper," asked the Senate to authorize his committee to conduct an investigation. The debate raged for hours, "a hurricane of bitter vituperation, of personal taunt, of ugly charges and unmodified criticism." Sensing their advantage, the Democrats took the offensive, and the excitement reached a peak when Senator Teller of Colorado, the elderly Silver Republican turned Bryan Populist, chided the Republicans for General Wheaton's intemperate remarks. Half a dozen of that party sprang to their feet in the general's defense, while Senator Lodge made a threatening rush toward the Colorado senator, and, "white to the lips," threw back the attack.[32]

On February 1 the Philippine committee opened its investigatory hearings with William Howard Taft, now Governor of the Philippines, as first witness. At the same time debate began on the Administration's legislative proposal to regulate the government of the Philippines. The Congressional Democrats opened up a wholesale attack on the Republican policy of conquest and colonialism. Senator Hoar hit at the harsh sedition laws already operative in the Philippines. The anti-imperialist press was thick with soldiers' letters detailing cruelties of the campaign in the islands. Moorfield Storey's petition had unleashed a new surge of anti-imperialist feeling, as he had hoped it would.[33]

The imperialists were dismayed. Questions they thought settled seemed again unhinged.[34] In this context, Senator Lodge wrote Secretary of War Root asking for information from the War Department about the allegations of cruelty then being made against the United States Army. Secretary Root responded by saying that a number of cases of alleged misconduct had been investigated, and in most instances the reports were unfounded or exaggerated. He closed with this ringing endorsement: "The war in the Philippines has been conducted by the American army with scrupulous regard for the rules of civilized warfare, with careful . . . consideration for the prisoner and non-combatant, with self-restraint and with humanity never surpassed . . . "[35]

If the Lodge-Root exchange was intended to take the army off the hook and quiet the growing unrest, it had the opposite effect. It drew the Administration into the anti-imperialist target, alongside the army.

Some two weeks after Root's letter the Washington correspondents of the *Boston Evening Transcript* and the *New York Evening Post* reported an interview with a Republican congressman, who preferred to remain unnamed. He had visited the Philippines the summer before and "his opportunities for observing and knowing the situation were in many ways exceptional." He told the reporters:

> You never hear of any disturbances in Northern Luzon . . . because there isn't anybody there to rebel. That country was marched over and

cleared out in a most resolute manner. The good lord in Heaven only knows the number of Filipinos that were put under the ground; our soldiers took no prisoners; they kept no records; they simply swept the country and wherever or however they could get hold of a Filipino they killed him. The women and children were spared and may now be noticed in disproportionate numbers in that part of the island.

It was the congressman's opinion that this was the only way the islands could be pacified, since every Filipino was at heart a rebel against American authority.[36]

Next the press carried news from Manila of the court martial of Major Littleton W. T. Waller, accused of shooting eleven defenseless Filipinos without trial on the island of Samar. Waller placed all blame for his actions on orders given him by General Smith:

The major said that Gen. Smith instructed him to kill and burn, and said that the more he killed and burned the better pleased he would be; that it was no time to take prisoners, and that he was to make Samar a howling wilderness. Major Waller asked Gen. Smith to define the age limit for killing, and he replied "Everything over ten."

Three officers of the marine corps testified to the truth of Waller's statements.[37]

It was then revealed that the highest ranking officer of the United States Army, General of the Army Nelson A. Miles (the Massachusetts military man who had exposed rotten beef during the Spanish War), had written Secretary of War Root protesting the "marked severity" of the war against the Filipinos. When Root replied denying the charge (in a letter personally endorsed by Roosevelt), Miles had insisted on his point and cited as evidence the report of an American official in the Philippines, Governor Cornelius Gardener of Tayabas province.[38]

Democrats on the Senate investigating committee demanded to see the Gardener report. On examining it, they found that this official had leveled serious charges against the army, including "the extensive burning of barrios [native villages] in trying to lay waste the country so that the insurgents cannot occupy it," and "the torturing of natives by so-called water-cure and other methods in order to obtain information." Appended to the Gardener report was a supplement from the secretary of the province of Batangas where General Bell had been campaigning. The secretary reported that one third of the population had been killed by military slaughter, by famine and pestilence; out of a population of three hundred thousand, some one hundred thousand had died.[39]

Finally, on April 14, after hearing Governor Taft and General MacArthur, the Senate committee turned its attention to witnesses Herbert Welsh had supplied to the Democratic minority on the committee. These were two soldiers from western Massachusetts who testified concerning the operations of the "water cure detail" under orders from a Major Edwin F. Glenn; as a result of information thus obtained a native town of ten thousand population had been burned to the ground, its inhabitants escaping only with the clothes on their backs.[40]

These exposures and the public indignation they aroused brought the greatest embarrassment to the Administration. It was clear, at the very least, that Governor Gardener's report had been in Root's hands when he publicly denied charges of cruelty and praised the army for its exemplary humanity. The *Springfield Republican* charged that Root, as a New York corporation lawyer, would not hesitate to perpetrate military outrage to carry out imperialist policy. It accused both Root and Roosevelt of concealment and bad faith. Nor was the *Republican* alone in making such charges. There was talk in Washington of Root's resignation, and much agitation at the White House.[41]

Then, on April 15, after a cabinet meeting, President Roosevelt made an abrupt about face that relieved the pressure on the Administration. He publicly ordered the court martial of General Smith and Major Glenn, and Secretary of War Root transmitted these orders to General Chaffee and informed the press. The President's move tended to deflect from Washington the thrust of the campaign against the conduct of the war and to take from it much of its force. Not long afterwards a committee of Boston clergymen called a rally to protest the military atrocities where speakers hailed the President as the leader of their fight.[42]

Boston anti-imperialist leaders took a more negative view, however. They insisted that Roosevelt and Root had known all along the way the war was going, had kept it quiet as long as they could, and had only spoken out when forced by public opinion. The *Army and Navy Journal* agreed, writing that it was nonsense to suggest that the Administration did not know and approve the harsh methods of war practiced by United States forces in the Philippines.

Roosevelt himself shed some light on this question. Just after he ordered General Smith court martialed, the President sent a letter of congratulations to General Bell on the success of his campaign in Batangas. Bell was the general who had thrown some one hundred thousand Filipinos into concentration camps and whose methods none other than Senator Lodge condemned as "cruel."[43]

In the spring of 1902, Charles Francis Adams, one of the leaders of the campaign to spur the investigation, had said: "Roosevelt proposes to please everyone; he will be very severe in words — on outrages; but no one will be punished."[44] By July the truth of the charge was apparent. Waller was acquitted by his court martial; Glenn fined $50; and Smith was "admonished." Roosevelt made a public review of the Smith case and tapped the general on the wrist, retiring him a year and half early from the army list.[45] The President had promised a thoroughgoing investigation but evidently was satisfied with what his closest friend and advisor, Senator Lodge, had done, since he proposed nothing additional.*

The Senate committee broke off its investigation in June and it was never resumed. Senator Lodge had on the whole kept the hearings under tight control, assisted by a disciplined Republican majority. Contrary to congressional custom and despite protest, Lodge had refused to admit the public and the press to the hearings, giving out information solely to three or four selected newsmen.[46] He had allowed only two categories of witnesses: high-ranking officials and military men who defended the Administration, and veterans of lower rank who testified to personal knowledge of various cruelties practiced. He had done his best to protect "friendly" witnesses from searching cross-examination by the Democratic minority and kept the witnesses put forward by the opposition down to a minimum (refusing some because they had not been to the Philippines, refusing others, who had been there, for other reasons).[47] The opposition leader on the committee, Senator Carmack of Tennessee, said of Lodge and his docile majority that they were "fugitives from information."[48]

---

* Indeed, somewhat later, at the time of the fall elections, the President seemed unhappy that matters had gone as far as they did, complaining bitterly to the *Springfield Republican*'s H. Parker Willis that "The court martial of Gen. Smith cost me votes — *votes!*" (quoted in a letter from Herbert Welsh to Carl Schurz, November 2, 1902, Schurz Papers, Library of Congress.)

For all his power, however, Senator Lodge was unable to prevent the public disclosure of the nature of the war the army conducted against the Filipinos. As the pattern finally emerged from all these revelations, shocked Americans tried to assimilate the mass of evidence and give it some meaning. Henry Loomis Nelson, Washington correspondent of the *Boston Herald,* concluded that "Our troops in the Philippines . . . look upon all Filipinos as of one race and condition, and being dark men, they are therefore 'niggers,' and entitled to all the contempt and harsh treatment administered by white overlords to the most inferior races."

The most consistent anti-imperialists had long contended that the prevalent American attitude of white supremacy was closely related to an imperialist policy of suppression of colonial people abroad. Now the flood of army disclosures, coupled with persistent domestic headlines of blacks lynched and burned at the stake, killed and wounded in racial riots, made a very strong case, and those outside anti-imperialist ranks, like Henry Loomis Nelson, saw the point.[49]

Herbert Welsh, who had played a big part in the campaign against army atrocities, also attempted to wrestle with the problem of responsibility. At the last public meeting to protest the army's conduct held by the Boston anti-imperialists he said:

> When Major Waller was brought to trial, he pointed to General Jacob Smith. And so, if General Smith were brought to a trial in this country . . . he would probably point upward to General Chaffee. And so if General Chaffee would be brought to trial, he would point upward to the War Department in Washington . . . and there is much logic to it . . . Because those men were under a pressure, for political reasons, to finish the war.

However, the ultimate responsibility, Welsh thought, lay with the highest authority of all, "the people of the United States."[50]

Something said by the Republican congressman who had visited the Philippines suggested a reason why this heavy responsibility lay on the American people. When asked by the correspondents whether he thought the moral sense of the country would stand for a policy of extermination, the congressman replied, "If American investors find property that they want in the Philippines, I do not think that they would be embarrassed by any sentiment at home against the sweeping off [of] the Filipinos."[51]

17

The Dissolution of the Movement

McKinley's victory in 1900 strengthened the hold imperialism had secured on the nation. Policy that had seemed open to question and reversal before the election, afterwards seemed decided and fixed on course. Failure in the treaty fight, lack of success in the struggle to stop the war, had only marked the stages of anti-imperialism's swell and growth, but the electoral campaign of 1900 was the crest of the wave; after that came break-up and subsidence.* In this light, the campaign against military atrocities was nothing more than a partial recovery before the final dissolution.

Besides the Republican victory, anti-imperialist activity was affected by the virtual defeat of the Filipino armed struggle, and the imperialists' retreat from a policy of colonial annexation to more indirect methods of domination in the style of Cuba and the Platt Amendment.

All these developments caused a decline in support for anti-imperialism on the part of the urban middle class, where it had been strongest, and encouraged a conservative faction to split the anti-imperialist movement by compromising with the imperialists precisely on the basis of their shift in tactics. This split gave the death-blow to anti-imperialism as a national movement.

While the conclusive break-up did not occur until 1904, the process

---

* Symptomatic was the effect of the elections on Gamaliel Bradford and John Jay Chapman. Overwrought by their campaign efforts, defeat undid them. Right after the voting, Bradford, the initiator of the anti-imperialist coalition, went into a prolonged depression, while, somewhat later, Chapman, champion of the third party tactic, suffered a complete breakdown that incapacitated him for years. (Gamaliel Bradford, letter to the editor, *Springfield Daily Republican*, February 9, 1901; M. A. DeWolfe Howe, *John Jay Chapman and his Letters*, pp. 153-162.)

of deterioration set in immediately after the elections of 1900. Tendencies that then developed gave indication of what lay ahead.

Bryan's defeat weakened the influence of the more radical anti-imperialists like Bradford, Boutwell and Sanborn, who had promoted the coalition with the Democratic leader, and strengthened the position of the more conservative, like Carl Schurz and Moorfield Storey (who had only supported the coalition at the last moment), or Charles Francis Adams (who had rejected it altogether). Similarly, in the Democratic Party, Bryan, spokesman for middle class revolt against monopoly, lost ground to Gorman, well-known as the ally of big business. Its champions weakened by defeat, the anti-monopoly coalition of 1900, tenuous and fragmentary at best, fell apart.

In the condition of Republican victory, the more conservative anti-imperialist leaders tended to limit their opposition to particular aspects of imperialist policy (military atrocities, for example) rather than to imperialism as a system of monopoly rule; in place of an attempt to win labor, blacks, and the widest popular support they sought connections with middle class and well-to-do whites, with conservative Democrats, and, above all, Republicans. Moreover men like Charles Francis Adams were of the opinion that this could best be done by making a clean break with those anti-imperialist leaders identified with the old policies, by splitting the movement, in short.

Right after the elections there was an attempt to break away from the radical "taint" of the anti-imperialist league leadership by the establishment of a Philippine Information Society to issue publications reviewing United States-Philippine relations. While Charles Francis Adams was prominent in this group's leadership, for the most part it was composed of Bostonians not previously identified with the anti-imperialist league, including the wealthy socialite, Mrs. Glendower Evans, and Albert Bushnell Hart, the Harvard historian who supported McKinley's foreign policy.[1]

Also involved was the Boston anti-imperialist Fiske Warren, a wealthy paper manufacturer. Sharing Adams' point of view, Warren thought there should be a change in the anti-imperialist leadership, or a new organization altogether. For the moment, however, he was satisfied with the Information Society, considering it fortunate that the enterprise should start without "any suspicion of being fostered by anti-imperialists," but instead should "creep around through imperialists."[2]

Warren unburdened himself in these terms to Schurz, who, like Storey, occupied something of a middle ground between the radical and conservative anti-imperialists. In reply Schurz warned that the new organization must keep "entirely clear of Administration influences which are very insidious."[3]

Schurz evidently thought his caution justified when, in the spring of 1901, the Information Society published a pamphlet that flatly exonerated the United States of provoking the outbreak of hostilities with the Filipinos.[4] Schurz protested to the society that its pamphlet was a "misleading presentation of facts," as did Erving Winslow and Herbert Welsh.[5]

As the year 1902 opened, the campaign for the army investigation and the investigation itself countered the general post-election slump in the anti-imperialist movement. Erving Winslow noted that his associates were hopeful again, "the scattering and discouragement of a few months ago having entirely disappeared." Winslow was also pleased to get at this time written assurances from Democratic leaders in Congress that they would stand firm for Philippine independence. He had been in correspondence with them to this end since the 1900 elections, but conservative Eastern Democrats, led by men like Arthur Pue Gorman, had also been at work, trying to rid the party of Bryan and Populism, and to secure acceptance of the Philippine conquest as an established fact.[6] Now, with Bryan speaking out against army atrocities, with Congressional Democrats pushing the army investigation and Senator Hoar making his voice heard, it looked as if the anti-imperialist coalition was in operation again, in vestigial form at least.

Buoyed by this upsurge, Edwin Burritt Smith, the Chicago leader, agreed to the Boston proposal for a national conference of anti-imperialists. Such a meeting, small and private, was held at the end of April 1902 in New York City.[7] Here, for a second time, activity was initiated separate and apart from the anti-imperialist league as constituted. The move was not to form a new organization, but rather to establish a committee one step removed from the league and independent in its function, in fact to provide a new leadership.

Charles Francis Adams, who considered Erving Winslow "questionable" and Gamaliel Bradford "a bore," attended the New York conference and at its morning session proposed the establishment of a committee that would "effect the full disclosure of the facts" about the conduct of the war in the Philippines, and do whatever necessary "to vindicate the national honor." The conservative and Republican orientation of this move was indicated by the nomination of Andrew Carnegie, Cornell's President Schurman, and Henry Lee Higginson to the leadership of the proposed committee. Both Schurman and Higginson refused to serve; the banker, indignant that his name had been used without permission, issued a public disavowal. As it finally stood, the committee was composed of Charles Francis Adams of Boston, Edwin Burritt Smith of Chicago, Herbert Welsh of Philadelphia, Carl Schurz and Andrew Carnegie of New York City, with Adams chosen as chairman and Storey appointed committee counsel.[8]

In the afternoon session, Winslow, persistent as ever in the effort to revive the alliance of 1900, sought to direct the group's attention to the Democrats speaking out on the anti-imperialist side. He offered, and the conference passed, a resolution instructing the committee established that morning to confer with the Democrats about a platform that might serve as a base for anti-imperialist support of congressional candidates in the fall elections.[9]

But the most significant result of the New York conference was its work in relation to military excesses. This was especially the province of one member, Herbert Welsh, whom the committee aided with moral support and funds (Carnegie donating two thousand dollars to this end). Welsh published a Philadelphia weekly, *City and State,* opposing the corruption and domination of Pennsylvania politics by big business. What distinguished him, however, among middle class reformers of his type, was a long-time devotion to the cause of the American Indian. Perhaps it was this early bent that led him to take up the cause of the Filipinos with such intensity.[10]

When the Philippine committee began its investigation, Erving Winslow made a trip to Washington to supply the Democratic members with information, but Herbert Welsh or members of his staff were in constant contact with the minority of the committee during the four months of its existence, providing the legislators with witnesses and information. The Democrats freely acknowledged the value of his activity, just as President Roosevelt did not hesitate to tell those close to him of his annoyance at it. All in all, Herbert Welsh was the central figure in the anti-imperialist campaign against the excesses of the United States army in the Philippines.[11]

In July 1902, when Congress adjourned and the Senate hearings closed down, Charles Francis Adams looked upon President Roosevelt's review of the case of General Smith as an attempt to put an end to the question that, since winter, had been a matter of national concern. His committee accordingly issued a "counterblast" to the President's review that called attention to the material in their hands and demanded further investigation. (Carnegie refused to sign this protest.) [12]

The counterblast made reference to the case of Father Augustine, a Catholic priest reported to have been murdered by the United States armed forces. The press had carried numerous accounts of Filipino priests cooperating with the guerrillas and so running afoul of the American military, but this one was particularly awful. A Boston veteran of the Philippine war claimed knowledge that American soldiers kidnapped Father Augustine and tortured him to death with the water cure. By this means the soldiers extracted information as to the hiding place of a large sum of insurgent gold, which they then confiscated. Adams declared himself to be anxious to follow up the case of the murdered priest and make the facts known.[13]

But at the same time and in a most contradictory manner, Adams began to feel strongly that his committee had accomplished its purpose, that it was time to "discontinue further agitation."[14] Adams was repeating his earlier withdrawal from anti-imperialist activity, after the treaty fight. Like Senator Hoar, Adams found it difficult to be consistent in his anti-imperialism. But Adams' waverings seemed to have been caused by a profoundly aristocratic and conservative attitude, rather than by partisanship, as was the case with Hoar.

If men like Boutwell, Bradford and Sanborn represented middle class antagonism to monopoly and the trusts, Charles Francis Adams, of all the Boston men associated with anti-imperialism, was closest to the new elite of finance capital that was becoming so important in the nation's economic and political life. A wealthy and active investor, he was, for example, a heavy stockholder and a director of Westinghouse Electric. This company shared a monopoly in the production of the nation's electrical equipment with General Electric, of which Henry Lee Higginson and J. P. Morgan were directors and major stockholders.[15]

When, after the treaty fight, the anti-imperialists began to oppose the United States war on the Filipinos, Adams had removed himself from the opposition. Similarly in the campaign against army atrocities, he was not opposing the war, only the conduct of the war. And he lent his opposition here not particularly because of the United States treatment of the Filipinos which he did not believe to be "exceptionally savage treatment of Eastern races," but rather because of the government's "hypocritical cant and lying" in denying the harsh character of its methods. This he felt to be a stain on the nation's honor and integrity. As for the Filipinos, Adams thought that they would prosper under United States domination, since "many races, and, more especially those of African descent, improve only as they come into immediate contact with Caucasians."[16] Taking everything into account, it was not surprising that Adams' anti-imperialist concern was again dwindling.

Adams' behavior once more brought him into collision with the more militant anti-imperialists, this time with Welsh, whom Adams by now had come to place in the same "questionable" category as Winslow. The rift occurred over the issue of the renewal of the Senate investigation. In June 1902, by abruptly concluding his committee's hearings on congressional adjournment, Lodge avoided calling many witnesses whom the Democrats, with Welsh's help, had waiting to testify. Later in the year, when Congress reconvened, Welsh set about stimulating a demand for the renewal of the investigation. In the first week of February 1903, he proposed, most urgently, that the Adams committee sponsor a petition to the Senate for this purpose. Adams flatly rejected Welsh's suggestion, telling him the fight was over, the issue dead, the public had lost all interest.[17]

The experience of the New York anti-imperialists suggested that Adams exaggerated the public loss of interest, for the New Yorkers were in the midst of a lively campaign for the renewal of the investigation, holding a well-attended mass meeting and securing hundreds of names on a petition to the Senate.[18]

As he demanded action from Adams, Welsh was indignant, writing, "The apathy of Massachusetts, excuse me for saying it, seems to me scandalous, and every effort ought to be made to dispel it." Adams sailed for Europe in the middle of February, and shortly thereafter Boston anti-imperialists did what they could to dispel apathy. On the afternoon and evening of March 19 they held a meeting in Faneuil Hall attended by a large audience of "businessmen, merchants, clergymen, writers, students and representatives of the prominent families," at which Welsh, Storey, Boutwell, T. W. Higginson,

Codman, Dole and others spoke.[19] Welsh presented a number of persons refused a hearing before the Senate committee, one of them a witness to the abduction of Father Augustine, another, the mother of a New York state soldier reportedly killed by an American officer using the water cure. Storey castigated Lodge for refusing to heed the petition that the investigation be re-opened. Lodge's action reminded Storey of the slave-holders' abridgements of freedom and showed that "imperialism abroad begets imperialism at home."[20]

The Boston meeting marked the end of any sustained campaign against military excesses in the Philippines. Lodge persisted in his refusal to reconvene the investigation, and Herbert Welsh, the prime mover in that demand, not long after the Faneuil Hall rally, had a nervous collapse, worn out by his efforts.[21]

The Adams committee, however, did one last piece of work. It sent H. Parker Willis, the Washington correspondent of the *Springfield Republican,* as its own investigator to the Philippine Islands. Originally the suggestion of Adams, the Willis project was carried through largely due to Storey, who took over financial responsibility after Adams withdrew support, following a drop in the value of his investments.[22]

Early in 1903 Erving Winslow thought the Adams committee might have accomplished its purpose and hoped for a revival of the anti-imperialist league at Chicago, since, in his opinion the work should not "seem to be confined to New England or to a little committee," however influential.[23] But it worked out contrary to Winslow's hopes. In March Fiske Warren met in Chicago with Edwin Burritt Smith and other local anti-imperialists and proposed the establishment of a new organization, a Philippine Independence League, that would require of its members "no declaration of principles," no adherence to "a theory of government," but only support for the specific demand of Philippine independence, "immediate or ultimate, with or without a protectorate." Warren proposed that the organization should appeal especially to those Republicans who wanted to free the islands but who were "not . . . theoretical enough to join the anti-imperialists and too good Republicans to leave their party." (The program Warren advocated was in effect a move toward accommodation with the Roosevelt regime, since the President was known to have expressed sympathy for something close to it.) Since Smith had come to the conclusion that further activity by the anti-imperialist league in Chicago was out of place, he endorsed Warren's proposal and agreed to get in touch with members of the New York anti-imperialist league known to be in favor of such a plan. He later acquainted the Boston leaders with Chicago's decision to drop out of the anti-imperialist league.[24] The third effort on the part of the more conservative anti-imperialists to split away from the more radical finished the anti-imperialist league as a national organization.

In 1903, on the other hand, United States imperialists began the fulfillment of the last of their current goals still outstanding. They secured control of a route for an isthmian canal. In that year the Roosevelt Administration decided that such a canal should go through Panama, an integral part of Colombia. When the Colombian legislature objected to the terms offered by the United States for the cession of the necessary territory, a revolution broke out in Panama. United States marines, from a warship standing by on Administration orders, prevented Colombian troops from putting down the rebellion, and the Panamanians declared themselves an independent state. The Roosevelt Administration speedily recognized the new government and the banking house of Morgan just as speedily became its financial agent (reportedly loaning that government a large sum to help pay off the bribes that eased its birth). As was expected, the new republic of Panama proved amenable to United States plans for its territory.[25]

Subverting Colombian sovereignty, the United States supported a new government in Panama, nominally free and independent, in fact subordinate to American influence. The Roosevelt Administration's part in the Panamanian coup d'etat clearly demonstrated its adhesion to the line of imperial expansion brought forward by the Platt Amendment.

While Lodge defended the Administration in the Senate, Hoar condemned the use of United States troops to thwart the Colombian government and spurned the President's efforts to win him over in a personal interview. Moorfield Storey denounced Roosevelt's action before the Reform Club, and the New England Anti-Imperialist League published his speech and those of dissenting Democratic Senators.[26]

But the anti-imperialist attempt to organize a general campaign of opposition failed completely. In New York a petition was circulated against the Panamanian intervention, but had to be given up for lack of response. In Boston the result was equally discouraging. Charles Francis Adams joined Henry Lee Higginson in refusing to sign.[27] George McNeill spoke out against the Panamanian policy, but when the national convention of the American Federation of Labor met in Boston Gompers put that organization on record in favor of the government's action, thereby extending his previously declared policy of conciliation with the trusts to an endorsement of the foreign policy with which big business was allied.[28]

Disturbed by the reluctance of many Boston citizens to protest the intervention in Panama, William James made a penetrating and prophetic comment: "The organization of slick success in our age is only equalled by the organization of political acquiescence. Between them we shall live in a new form of society."[29]

While the lack of response to the Panama affair demonstrated a serious reduction of support for the anti-imperialists in the ranks of labor and the middle class, acknowledgement came to them that their past efforts had not been without effect. In the spring of 1904, as H. Parker Willis made his way to the Philippines, he stopped in Japan at Yokohama and there interviewed United States Consul Bellows. Bellows told Willis that American capital would not go to the Philippines under present conditions "because the authorities were so unfavorable to American interests." When asked to account for this, Bellows said that among those who had been to the Philippines it was "the general impression that this attitude . . . had been forced upon the authorities by the 'old grannies' in New England who had been so much worried over affairs in the Philippines and particularly the water cure." Corroboration for this point of view came a couple of months later from William Howard Taft. In Cambridge for the Harvard graduation, Taft told reporters that the anti-imperialists had served as a check upon United States officials in the Philippines.[30]

As the 1904 presidential campaign approached, the anti-imperialists could not draw much hope from their experience in the Congressional elections of 1902, when their conservative leadership had vetoed any attempt to re-establish connections with Bryan, and Democratic candidates had given scant attention to the Philippine issue. Massachusetts had seen some anti-imperialist activity, but even here the conservative "reorganizers" had prevailed in the Democratic Party with the gubernatorial nomination of William Gaston, a Boston traction magnate close to the Morgan interests.[31]

The leaders of the Philippine Independence League took the initiative in 1904. A delegation from that organization presented the Republican national convention in June with a petition signed by some seven thousand persons, calling for the eventual independence of the Philippines on the Cuban model. Endorsing the main trend of imperialist policy, this formula put in black and white the desire for rapprochement with the Roosevelt Administration that Fiske Warren had earlier suggested. Charles Francis Adams' name was first on the list of the committee which initiated the petition of the Philippine Independence League, while the "radical extremists" of anti-imperialism, beginning with Storey and Schurz, were excluded from the sponsoring body (just as the endorsement of Cuba's treatment traversed the public position of the anti-imperialist league).

Despite their obvious desire for respectability and compromise, the leaders of the Philippine Independence League were treated with complete indifference by the Republican national convention. Nominating Roosevelt for president, the delegates passed a resolution endorsing the Philippine conquest, because, among other things, it made possible military intervention in China (Lodge's favorite theme).[32]

A delegation from the New England Anti-Imperialist League urged the Democratic national convention to declare in favor of immediate independence for the Philippines — without success. It was the Philippine Independence League, Gorman and the "reorganizers" that carried the day here. The Democrats passed a platform resolution declaring "We ought to do for the Philippines what we have already done for the Cubans," and nominated Judge Alton B. Parker of New York for president. Before his nomination was settled upon, Parker had been quizzed by a group of New York financiers, including Morgan men. Eminently "safe," his first word on nomination was for sound currency and the gold standard. As vice-president the delegates chose a cousin of Gorman, eighty-one years old.[33]

After the convention the New England Anti-Imperialist League endorsed the Democratic plank on the Philippines. Restive under this submission to the leadership of Adams and the Philippine Independence League, Secretary Winslow later urged pressure on Parker for a declaration in favor of withdrawal of troops and immediate independence for the Philippines, without protectorate. His remonstrance had no effect.

With equal lack of success Gamaliel Bradford had pushed the

nomination of General Miles as Democratic presidential candidate. He did not think Parker the man "to attract the labor element" or generate popular enthusiasm — and these, in Bradford's opinion, were all the Democrats could rely on, since the Republicans controlled the wealth.[34] But the concept of an all-embracing coalition against monopoly, which tended to be the guide-line of the Bryan-anti-imperialist alliance of 1900, was inoperative in 1904, its champions impotent in anti-imperialist ranks, defeated in Democratic. This year, to a telling degree, conservative forces had "reorganized" both Democrats and anti-imperialists.

With its petition presented to both conventions, the Philippine Independence League considered its work done. But the anti-imperialists went through the motions of a campaign. Charles Russell Codman led a delegation to Judge Parker's summer home at Esopus, New York (where Parker spent most of the campaign in dignified silence); they addressed the candidate on the Philippine issue; he dutifully replied. Schurz wrote a lengthy appeal to independent voters, and other literature was circulated, but results were meagre. Bradford observed a "melancholy want of enthusiasm."[35]

Perhaps the anti-imperialists made their sharpest intervention in the campaign when H. Parker Willis returned from the Philippines, and the Adams committee (again minus Carnegie) sent Judge Parker the findings of their investigator, which one paragraph summed up:

> We have in fact destroyed the public buildings of the country, inflicted continuous crop losses during a period of six years, ravaged and burned large sections of the country, produced conditions leading to the death of most farm animals and to serious human and animal epidemics, brought foreign trade to an unprofitable condition by our tariff legislation, inaugurated tremendously expensive government for the benefit of foreign office-holders, established a partisan judiciary, crowded the prisons and deported or sent to the gallows the best and most patriotic leaders.

The publication of these views caused a stir and drew fire from the Republicans, but it was a far cry from the anti-imperialist crusade of 1900.[36]

Indeed the elections of 1904 put many Massachusetts anti-imperialists in a quandary. Judge Parker was so obviously the candidate of those who wanted to throttle the Bryan wing of social protest and make the Democratic Party safe for big business, while, on the other hand, Roosevelt had not only hinted at second thoughts on the Philippines and condemned military atrocities, he had also made other gestures appealing to liberals and reformers. Irritating business interests, he had initiated legal proceedings against one or two trusts and expressed concern for workers' conditions in the 1902 coal strike; he had invited Booker T. Washington to dinner at the White House, horrifying racists. Without question, Roosevelt was proving to be an imperialist of a new breed — moving from open colonialism in foreign policy to more covert methods of control, preserving the status quo at home by a flexible attitude of reform and concession. While Morgan and Rockefeller contributed liberally to his campaign fund, convinced that Roosevelt was their man, to many others it was not so clear. One of the more militant Boston anti-imperialists, Edwin D. Mead, expressed the liberal puzzlement in a long letter to Storey, saying that up till the last minute he had been unable to make up his mind to vote for Parker.[37]

The elections gave Roosevelt a great majority, and Storey thought that many anti-imperialists, many Bryan followers, had voted for Roosevelt, as Edwin D. Mead was tempted to do. In Massachusetts this was the case. There the Democratic candidate for governor, who took a strong anti-imperialist position, trounced the Republican, although Roosevelt carried the state over Parker.[38]

Just before the elections Storey wrote Schurz, "I wish we could have had a campaign."[39] But that had been impossible, given the conditions. The corporate control of *both* major parties, against which Chapman had warned, had reasserted itself with a vengeance, and the anti-imperialists were paralyzed and split by a move to compromise the struggle.

Anti-imperialism was no longer represented by a nationally organized movement. With Chicago, the linch-pin of the organization in the Midwest, gone over to the Philippine Independence League, and New York City as well, with former friends falling away on all sides throughout the country, the anti-imperialist league had reverted to its original component, a small band of Boston reformers. In November 1904, the annual meeting of the New England Anti-Imperialist League formally took note of this fact, striking from its constitution all references to a national organization.[40]

Certainly the Massachusetts anti-imperialists saw a long road ahead

THE DISSOLUTION OF THE MOVEMENT 253

and felt the mounting pressure for conformity. Charles R. Codman voiced their mood in a testament he wrote for his children:

> While I . . . believe that the American people may yet do justice and . . . save the Republic from shipwreck, it is not given to me to see, or even to guess, when and how that is to be accomplished. I hope that strength will be given me to follow my conscience to the end, and not to waver in the support of what seems to me the plain and obvious principle of right, justice and Christianity. May God forgive and turn the hearts of those . . . responsible for what has been done.[41]

Afterword

The year 1904 saw the completion of two cycles of development, imperialist and anti-imperialist. Imperialist tendencies of the modern sort had developed in the United States soon after the Civil War, brought forward by the triumph of Northern industrial capital in that struggle. But it was the decade of the nineties that saw a precipitate growth of American imperialist sentiment and policies, stimulated by the heightened influence of the great industrial corporations in the nation's economy, by the failure of the home market in the crisis of '93, and by the increasing pressure of imperialist rivalry abroad (especially in Asia and Latin America). Finding prime expression in the Republican party, particularly through such leaders as Henry Cabot Lodge of Massachusetts, this imperialism, in the nineties, became conscious of itself, its needs and its goals. Indicative of this self-awareness were the speeches that the Republican publicist Charles Emory Smith gave before industrial and financial leaders in New York and Boston in 1895, outlining a program for the United States that included securing the hegemony of the Western Hemisphere, establishing military and commercial strongholds in the islands of the Caribbean and the Pacific, cutting the isthmian canal, and achieving international financial supremacy on the foundation of the industrial supremacy already gained. By such means, Smith said, the United States would win "unchallenged primacy" among the nations of the earth. There was general agreement in imperialist quarters over the goals that Smith so synthesized, for Smith projected what was, in fact, nothing less than a program for the establishment of a basic position, economic and strategic, from which the United States could make a bid for world supremacy. By 1904 this program had been substantially achieved.

What Smith had not projected, what the American imperialists had not, perhaps, foreseen, was the development of popular opposition, both at home and abroad, as the immediate obstacle to the program's fulfillment. Beginning in 1899 and continuing for more than three years, the Philippine people waged war to prevent the United States from grabbing their country as a military and commercial outpost in Asia. When the American invaders' overwhelming military superiority broke up their army, the Filipinos turned to guerrilla warfare; this the United States crushed by resorting to methods which in some applications were genocidal. In July 1902 President Roosevelt declared the Philippine war officially over (although sporadic armed resistance on the part of the Filipinos continued for years thereafter).

In the United States, expressions of opposition met the first signs of the emergence of imperialism, as Americans became alarmed at the economic monopoly and political reaction, the militarism and armaments, the war and rumor of war that the imperialist tendency seemed to drag in its train. The Venezuelan crisis and the Spanish War intensified this unrest, but the organized anti-imperialist movement in the United States was crystallized in the spring of 1898 by the revelation of the plans to appropriate the Philippines, and by the unmistakable signs of Philippine resistance to those plans. It was above all the determination of the Philippine people to affirm their national identity that recalled the American people to their own anti-imperialist traditions. That fall a small group of Boston men met to form an organization they called the Anti-Imperialist League, to oppose American imperialism and its aims (and especially the Philippine annexation). While Boston and Massachusetts remained the center of its strength, the organization spread quickly throughout the country as Americans reacted to the rapid upsurge of imperialism and monopoly. Unsuccessfully resisting the treaty to annex the Philippines, the anti-imperialist movement led a widespread opposition to the Philippine War of conquest and reached the peak of its influence in the elections of 1900, that were fought out, to a great extent, on the issue of imperialism. Defeated in 1900, the anti-imperialist movement experienced a brief revival in the struggle against the atrocities of the Philippine war, only to subside again, so that by 1904 it was reduced to its original starting point, the small Boston group (that lingered on for years, never again much more than a local sect).

As it turned out, burgeoning United States imperialism could not consolidate its position until it had broken the opposition, both at home and abroad. This it did; by 1904 both the domestic anti-imperialist movement and the Philippine resistance were effectively defeated.

Why was it that the anti-imperialist cycle ended in defeat, the imperialist in victory? Certainly central to the defeat of the Philippine people was their isolation internationally. Faced with an imperialist adversary of overwhelming military superiority, the Filipinos got no aid, military or diplomatic, from the imperialist powers that alone were capable of rendering such support effectively. None of the other imperialist powers was anxious to dispute the question with the United States, supported as she was by British imperialism.[1] The only aid the Filipinos got was moral and political support from the American anti-imperialist movement, and with its reverse in 1900 that movement lost any potential it might have had for checking the assault on Philippine independence.

The reasons for the defeat of turn-of-the-century anti-imperialism are tied up with its very character as a movement. Strongest in Boston and Massachusetts, former centers of anti-slavery activity, this anti-imperialism can best be understood as the last powerful thrust of abolitionism, the radical democratic ideology that spurred the North to victory over the slave-holders' power in the middle of the nineteenth century. As the last impulse of the anti-slavery ideal it represented a phenomenon past its prime, of ebbing strength. (This was simply a fact of life; in 1905 the national leader of the anti-imperialist movement, George S. Boutwell, died, and even before this the Annual Reports of the Anti-Imperialist League had begun to carry an extensive necrology as a regular feature — the Civil War generation, the carriers of the anti-slavery ideology, were dying off.) On the other hand, the development of United States imperialism in the same period represented the initial consolidation of a new form of economic and political power, rooted in the industrial monopolies and banks. It represented a process of first growth, of waxing and ascendant strength.

Ideology exists only in the minds of men and gains strength only so far as it moves large masses of men. The abolitionists became strong because they allied themselves with powerful social forces, in particular the Northern manufacturing class. This was how the slave power was overthrown. What were the radicals of the Civil War era to do in later years when they saw their former allies in the Northern capitalist class espouse imperialism, a system that appeared to be so directly opposed to the nation's further democratic development?

The most clear sighted of them proposed a popular coalition against imperialism and the monopolies, a coalition that would embrace labor, farmers, middle class, blacks, whites, native-born, foreign-born, all political parties and beliefs, radicals, liberals and conservatives. Anti-imperialism's moment of greatest strength, the elections of 1900, coincided with the greatest success of the coalition policy.

Whatever the efforts they made to reach other social strata, the main strength of the anti-imperialists, in Massachusetts and elsewhere, always lay in the urban middle class. But the experience of Boston, the strongest center, was that even after the first check to anti-imperialism in the treaty fight some of this middle class base began to fall away, and after the great defeat of 1900, significant elements of this leadership throughout the country began to pull in their horns and compromise the struggle with the imperialists; they split the anti-imperialist movement for this purpose, hastening its demise.

In 1902 George S. Boutwell, the chairman of the anti-imperialist league and erstwhile associate of Lincoln, concluded that the leadership of a successful struggle against imperialism was to lie in the hands of labor. He told a Boston audience of trade unionists: "The final effort for the salvation of the republic is to be made by the laboring and producing classes."[2] If this was to be the case, it was obvious that American labor, at the moment, was not ready to shoulder its responsibility, dominated as it was by men like Gompers, who were unfolding a policy of conciliation with the trusts and support for their foreign policy. Whatever the future would hold for Boutwell's belief, at the time he spoke the anti-imperialists were declining in influence; they represented an ideology without a stable and growing social base.

The failure of the anti-imperialists does not mean that they were without effect. United States officials believed that their influence modified government policy in the Philippines to some extent. Perhaps their most important immediate influence was upon the overall operation of United States imperial policy. After a rash of annexations accompanying the Spanish War, the dominant imperialist group turned away from outright colonialism to indirect forms of political domination, accompanied by economic penetration, and, on occasion, by military intervention. The anti-imperialist uprising of the American people aganst the annexation of the Philippines appears to have influenced that decision. Secretary of State Hay told a friend in the spring of 1899 that the United States could not attempt to take over a portion of Chinese territory as the other imperialist powers were doing because "we do not think that the public opinion of the United States would justify this Government in taking part in the great game of spoliation now going on."[3] Hay said this when the anti-imperialist agitation was at its height, so that this agitation evidently had much to do with the formulation of the Open Door policy, the first sign of the shift in imperialist tactics. To further imperialist ends under the guise of the freedom and independence of nations, in the manner of the Platt Amendment and the Panama coup, henceforth became the master style of United States imperialist policy. From first to last, hypocrisy was the tribute the imperialists paid to the power of the American democratic tradition and its hold upon the mass of the people.

In sharp contrast was the moral integrity of the anti-imperialists, their special strength. Calling in question the looming goal of world empire, they rejected the subjugation of the Philippines by armed force. Throughout the war they declared their own government to be in the wrong and the Filipino people to be in the right. In effect they left the time-honored ground of nationalism and moved toward a new position of internationalism wherein the democratic-minded citizens of an imperialist nation joined forces with a colonial people to resist the domination of that imperialist nation. In an age of chauvinism and greedy materialism the anti-imperialists took a principled and internationalist stand against an unjust war of conquest.

Very noteworthy was their acute criticism and analysis of United States imperialism as a system of rule by the banks and monopolies. It is true that they criticized this system most often from the viewpoint of the past, of a petty bourgeois society of merchants, farmers and small manufacturers, of free trade and individualism. But if, for the most part, they did not clearly see the future, or the way out of the problems imperialism presented, they saw those problems incisively and boldly. (They were first, for example, to point to a connection between the struggle against imperialist foreign policy and the fight for black rights at home.) That is why the anti-imperialist movement, though of brief duration, has an enduring importance; it was like a flare in the night, lasting only a minute, but laying bare the battlefield.

Most Americans alive today have never known their country except as one in which great industrial combinations and banks exercise tremendous political influence; they have not known the United States without a swollen militarism, a huge army and navy and heavy armaments, without a foreign policy of more or less active and aggressive interference, hidden or overt, in the national affairs of other peoples. Many, perhaps, have come to see all this as the American way, whether they like it or not, something to be taken for granted.

Such was not the case with the early anti-imperialists. Having known that the United States was not always imperialist, they were encouraged to believe that it would not always remain so, despite the new system's achievement of a relative stability in their own time. They regarded imperialism, like the slave power, as an historical aberration, and were confident that the American people would one day throw it off, as they had the slave power, to return the nation to its true path of development, the democratic path, the popular path.

The anti-imperialists were ultimately defeated, but most of them remained convinced that the struggle they initiated would go on, in other generations if need be, till their cause was triumphant. They said, time and again, that nothing is ever settled until it is settled right.

Two strains ran through their thought — that their movement, the anti-imperialist movement, represented an idea whose time had not yet come, and that imperialism represented a finite tendency in United States development, a certain stage, if you will, in the country's history, open to supersession. Perhaps none expressed this complex of ideas more eloquently than the *Boston Evening Transcript*'s Edward H. Clement, when he spoke to a Tufts college reunion, in these words:

> As Emerson says, "Every wrong that blossoms carries its punishment with it on the same stem." The insolence of the British aristocracy produced the democracy of America. The arrogance of the slave-holding agricultural aristocracy of the South produced the domination of the money-making manufacturing states of the North. If the money-making and manufacturing triumph proceeds to empire-making, the fate of empires which was taught us here as the A, B, C of history is before it . . . The great unseen compensating pendulum swings to and fro to keep the wheels of the universe in motion; it cannot be hurried; but it will not be behind time; it will know when the world has had enough of a given thing. The thing itself will set to pulling the pendulum back when it has loaded its evil sufficiently upon the age . . . [4]

Bibliographical Note

Republic or Empire is particularly the product of a close reading of the *Boston Evening Transcript* and the *Springfield Republican* for the years 1898 through 1900. These journals served as "house organs" for the anti-imperialist movement in the period mentioned and provided important material not available in other primary and secondary sources. In addition the papers of Carl Schurz in the Congressional Library were a valuable source of information for the years 1901-1904.

The study of the anti-imperialist movement as such began with the publication by *The Philippine Social Science Review* of Maria C. Lanzar's "The Anti-Imperialist League" in the years 1930, 1932 and 1933. Fred H. Harrington followed with "The Anti-Imperialist Movement in the United States, 1898-1900" (*Mississippi Valley Historical Review*, September, 1935) and "Literary Aspects of American Anti-Imperialism" (*New England Quarterly*, December, 1937). Twenty years later William Appleman Williams revived the discussion of the anti-imperialist movement in *The Tragedy of American Diplomacy* (The World Publishing Company, Cleveland and New York, 1959) and *The Contours of American History* (The World Publishing Company, Cleveland and New York, 1961). Williams denied that the anti-imperialists were bona fide, claiming that they opposed only the colonial, not the non-colonial, forms of imperial expansion. Endorsing this interpretation is William J. Pomeroy's *American Neo-Colonialism* (International Publishers, New York, 1970). However, Robert L. Beisner's *Twelve Against Empire,* a study of twelve anti-imperialist leaders and their ideas, denies the validity of Williams' thesis. A useful sketch of the anti-imperialist movement is that of Frank Freidel in *Dissent in Three Wars* (Harvard University Press, Cambridge, Massachusetts, 1970). E. Berkeley Tompkins' *Anti-Imperialism in the United States* (University of Pennsylvania Press, Philadelphia, 1970) contains an extensive bibliography.

Notes on the Illustrations

The photographs of anti-imperialist leaders are from books or articles by or about them, available in the Widener and Boston Public libraries. The drawing of Rev. W. H. Scott is from the *Guardian,* January 3, 1903, on microfilm at the Congregational Library, Boston. The photographs of Aguinaldo and of the Philippine dead at Santa Ana are from the National Archives, numbers 111-RB-1169 and 111-RB-1037, respectively. The photograph of Senator Hoar is from the Library of Congress. The photograph of the sentries at Santa Ana is from *Leslie's Weekly,* March 23, 1899. The drawing of the Boston anti-imperialist headquarters is from the *Boston Sunday Globe,* July 16, 1899. The photographs of Bryan's acceptance speech and of the round-up on Samar are from *Collier's Weekly,* August 25, 1900 and November 30, 1901, respectively.

Aguinaldo's statement of June 23, 1898, from which the quotation below his photograph is taken, is in H. H. Van Meter, *The Truth about the Philippines* (The Liberty League, Chicago, 1900), p. 216.

Notes

FOREWORD
1. See Richard J. Barnet, *Intervention and Revolution* (The World Publishing Company, New York and Cleveland, 1968) for a documented study of such interventions.
2. Philippe Nourry, "Camping tonight, camping tonight," translated and reprinted from *Le Figaro,* in *Atlas,* May 1968; Andrew St. George, "How the U. S. Got Che," *True,* April 1969; Marcel Niedergang, "Summer Camp For Counterinsurgents," Reprinted from *Le Monde Weekly,* by *American Report,* December 3, 1971.
3. Charles A. and Mary R. Beard, *The Rise of American Civilization,* (The Macmillan Company, New York, 1928), II, 483.
4. Dispatch from Tillman Durdin, Manila correspondent, *New York Times,* December 27, 1968.

CHAPTER 1 — Massachusetts Anti-Imperialism: The Background
1. *Boston Evening Transcript* (hereafter referred to as *BET*), June 16, 1898; diary of Charles Francis Adams, Jr., November 18, 1898, Charles Francis Adams, Jr., Papers, Massachusetts Historical Society (hereafter referred to as MHS).
2. *BET,* February 15, 1900.
3. Charles Francis Adams, Jr., memorabilia 1901-1905, February 1, 1901, Charles Francis Adams, Jr., Papers, MHS.
4. *BET,* November 25, 1898; John T. Morse, Jr., *Memoirs of Henry Lee* (Little Brown, and Company, Boston, 1905), p. 115.
5. John T. Morse, Jr., op. cit., pp. 218-219.
6. Ibid., pp. 15-17.
7. Ibid., pp. 115-116.
8. *BET,* April 4, November 10, 1898.
9. Edward Atkinson to Lyman Gage, November 25, 1898, Edward Atkinson Papers, MHS.
10. Geoffrey Blodgett, *The Gentle Reformers* (Harvard University Press, Cambridge, Massachusetts, 1964), pp. 11, 12, 14.
11. "Addison Archer's Interviews," *BET,* February, 1, 1899; *BET,* November 21, 1898.
12. Geoffrey Blodgett, op. cit., p. 98.
13. Richard Hooker, *The Story of an Independent Newspaper* (Macmillan Company, New York, 1924), p. 198.

14. A. S. Parsons to Moorfield Storey, July 28, 1898; David Greene Haskins, Jr., to Moorfield Storey, Moorfield Storey Papers, Library of Congress (hereafter referred to as LOC).
15. Report of the Secretary, *Annual Meeting of the Anti-Imperialist League*, Boston, 1899.

CHAPTER 2 — Countervailing Forces and Early Contests

1. Reginald C. McGrane, *The Economic Development of the American Nation* (Ginn and Company, Boston, 1942), p. 390.
2. "Cotton Manufactures in Massachusetts and the Southern States," Massachusetts Bureau of Statistics of Labor, *Annual Report for* 1905, (Wright and Potter Printing Co., Boston, 1906), Part II, p. 79.
3. *The Annual Statistics of Manufactures*, 1898 (Wright and Potter Printing Co., Boston, 1899), p. 164.
4. *BET*, February 17, 1899; *Springfield Daily Republican* (hereafter referred to as *SDR*), January 30, 1899; *BET*, March 16, 1899.
5. *Transactions of the New England Cotton Manufacturers' Association*, April 27-28, 1898. (Press of E. L. Barry, Waltham, Mass., 1898), p. 84.
6. Walter La Feber, *The New Empire* (Cornell University Press, Ithaca, N. Y., 1963), pp. 150, 332.
7. Editorial, "Elements of Prosperity," *Textile World*, May 1899, pp. 28-29; *BET*, January 25, 1898.
8. *Boot and Shoe Recorder*, January 8, 1896, p. 87; *Transactions of the New England Cotton Manufacturers' Association*, October 27-28, 1897, pp. 284-285, April 27-28, 1898, p. 228.
9. William Lawrence, *Henry Cabot Lodge* (Houghton Mifflin Company, Boston, 1925), p. 40.
10. Mark A. De Wolfe Howe, *Portrait of an Independent* (Houghton Mifflin Company, Boston, 1932), p. 141.
11. *Naboth's Vineyard, speech of Hon. Charles Sumner of Massachusetts on the proposed annexation of the island of Santo Domingo* (F. and J. Rives and G. A. Bailey, printers, Washington, D.C., 1870), p. 22.
12. Henry Cabot Lodge, *Oration delivered before the City Council and citizens of Boston, on the one hundred and third anniversary of the Declaration of Independence, July* 4, 1879 (Printed by order of the City Council, Boston, 1879), p. 35.
13. Henry Cabot Lodge, *Address delivered before the citizens of Nahant, Memorial Day*, 1882 (University Press, Cambridge, Mass., 1882), pp. 15, 25.
14. Mark A. De Wolfe Howe, op. cit., p. 152.
15. Walter La Feber, op. cit., pp. 46, 106; Edward Stanwood, *James G. Blaine* (Houghton Mifflin Company, Boston and New York, 1905), p. 359.
16. *Boston Herald*, January 16, 1884.
17. *Boston Daily Globe*, June 14, 1884.
18. J. E. Chamberlin, *The Boston Evening Transcript* (Houghton Mifflin Company, Boston and New York, 1930), p. 64; Thomas Wentworth Higginson, *Cheerful Yesterdays* (Houghton Mifflin Company, Boston and New York, 1898), pp. 153-154.

19. *New York Times,* October 30, 1884.
20. *BET,* October 30, 31, 1884.
21. *Selections from the Correspondence of Theodore Roosevelt and Henry Cabot Lodge* (Charles Scribner's Sons, New York, London, 1925), I, 10.
22. James G. Blaine, *The Words of James G. Blaine on the Issues of the Day* (D. L. Guernsey, Boston, 1884), p. 154.
23. U. S. Congress, House, Representative Henry Cabot Lodge speaking for the Naval Appropriations Bill, 51st Congress, 1st Sess., April 8, 1890, *Congressional Record,* XXI, 3170.
24. *BET,* April 11, 1890.
25. Ibid., April 11, 17, 19, 26, 1890.
26. Karl Schriftgiesser, *Gentleman from Massachusetts* (Little, Brown and Company, Boston, 1944), pp. 118-119.
27. U. S. Congress, Senate, Senator Henry Cabot Lodge speaking on the Revenue Bill, 53rd Congress, 2nd Sess., April 10, 1894, *Congressional Record,* XXVI, 3623.
28. Gail Hamilton, *James G. Blaine* (The Henry Bill Publishing Company, Norwich, Conn., 1895), p. 692.
29. Robert McElroy, *Grover Cleveland* (Harper Brothers Publishers, New York and London, 1923), II, 51.
30. Henry James, *Richard Olney and his public services* (Houghton Mifflin Company, Boston and New York, 1923), p. 81; Scott Nearing, *The American Empire* (The Rand School of Social Science, New York, 1921), p. 63.
31. Julius Pratt, *A History of United States Foreign Policy* (Prentice-Hall, Inc., Englewood Cliffs, N. J., 1955), p. 334.
32. John L. Stevens to John W. Foster, February 1, 1893, *Papers Relating to the Foreign Relations of the United States,* 1894 (U. S. Government Printing Office, Washington, D. C., 1895), Appendix II, 402.
33. U. S. Congress, House, Representative William F. Draper speaking on the annexation of Hawaii, 53rd Congress, 2nd Sess., February 3, 1894, Congressional Record, XXVI, 1897.
34. Henry Cabot Lodge, "Naval Policy of the United States," *Speeches and Addresses* (Houghton Mifflin Company, Boston and New York, 1909), p. 182.
35. Henry Cabot Lodge, "Our Duty to Hawaii," op. cit., p. 167.
36. Henry Cabot Lodge, "Naval Policy of the United States," op. cit., pp. 184-186.
37. U. S. Congress, House, Report #243, *Intervention of the United States Government in Affairs of Foreign Friendly Governments,* J. H. Blount to W. Q. Gresham, July 17, 1893, p. 59.
38. Henry Cabot Lodge, "Our Blundering Foreign Policy," *The Forum,* March 1895, p. 16.

CHAPTER 3 — The Venezuelan Crisis
1. Quoted in E. B. Tompkins, *The Great Debate: Anti-Imperialism in the United States, 1890-1920.* (Ph.D. dissertation, University of Pennsylvania, 1963), p. 122; *BET,* December 23, 1893.
2. Grover Cleveland, *Papers and Addresses,* edited by A. E. Bergh (The Sun Dial Classics Co., Publishers, New York, 1908), p. 316.

3. Ibid., p. 369.
4. Quoted in Robert McElroy, op. cit., II, 178.
5. *BET*, December 23, 1895.
6. Henry Cabot Lodge, "Our Blundering Foreign Policy," *The Forum*, March 1895, p. 17.
7. Henry Cabot Lodge, "England, Venezuela, and the Monroe Doctrine," *North American Review*, June 1895, p. 658.
8. Ruhl J. Bartlett, *The Record of American Diplomacy* (Alfred A. Knopf, New York, 1956), pp. 344-345.
9. Michael E. Hennessy, *Twenty-five Years of Massachusetts Politics* (Practical Politics Inc., Boston, Massachusetts, 1917), p. 58.
10. *BET*, December 21, 1895.
11. Edward Atkinson, "Jingoes and Silverites," *North American Review*, November, 1895, pp. 554-555, 560.
12. *Home Market Club Bulletin*, December 1895, p. 6.
13. *BET*, December 9, 1895.
14. J. R. Leeson to Edward Atkinson, December 10, 1895; J. Sterling Morton to Edward Atkinson, December 10, 1895, Edward Atkinson Papers, MHS.
15. *BET*, December 17, 1895.
16. Quoted in Edward Chase Kirkland, *Charles Francis Adams, Jr.* (Harvard University Press, Cambridge, Massachusetts, 1965), p. 183; Edward Atkinson to J. Sterling Morton, December 20, 1895, Edward Atkinson Papers, MHS; Henry James, op. cit., p. 181.
17. Edward Atkinson to Grover Cleveland, December 20, 1895; Edward Atkinson to George Frisbie Hoar, December 20, 1895, E. Atkinson Papers, MHS; *BET*, December 21, 1895.
18. John A. Garraty, *Henry Cabot Lodge* (Alfred A. Knopf, New York, 1953), p. 161.
19. *BET*, December 19, 1895.
20. Dana Estes to Charles Russell Codman, December 20, 1895; Dana Estes to Edward Atkinson, December 21, 1895, Edward Atkinson Papers, MHS.
21. *BET*, December 23, 28, November 13, December 21, 1895.
22. Ibid., December 21, 1895.
23. *Harvard Crimson*, December 21, 1895; *Selections from the Correspondence of Theodore Roosevelt and Henry Cabot Lodge*, I, 204-205; *Harvard Crimson*, January 7, 1896.
24. *Harvard Crimson*, January 9, 1896.
25. *The Labor Leader*, December 21, 1895.
26. *Boston Herald*, January 6, 1896.
27. *Boston Post*, January 6, 1896.
28. *BET*, December 17, 24, 1895.
29. James Ford Rhodes, *The History of the United States from Hayes to McKinley, 1877-1896* (The Macmillan Company, New York, 1919), p. 450.
30. *Transactions of the New England Cotton Manufacturers' Association*, September 22-24, 1896, pp. 240-242.
31. *BET*, January 8, 1896.

32. *BET*, November 27, 1895.

CHAPTER 4 — The Spanish War: "The Political Economy of Barbarism"
1. Henry Cabot Lodge, *Speeches and Addresses*, pp. 279-280.
2. *Selections from the Correspondence of Theodore Roosevelt and Henry Cabot Lodge*, I, 249.
3. Quoted in J. A. Garraty, op. cit., p. 182.
4. Ibid., p. 182.
5. *Speeches, correspondence and political papers of Carl Schurz*, edited by Frederic Bancroft (G. P. Putnam's Sons, New York, 1913), VI, 268, 271.
6. Karl Schriftgiesser, op. cit., p. 162.
7. Alvin F. Harlow, *Theodore Roosevelt* (J. Messner, inc., New York, 1943), pp. 162-163.
8. *The Letters of Theodore Roosevelt*, ed. by E. E. Morison (Harvard University Press, Cambridge, 1951-1954), I, 607, 622.
9. 55th Congress, 3rd Sess., House of Representatives, Document No. 1, *Papers Relating to the Foreign Relations of the United States* (Government Printing Office, Washington, D.C., 1901), p. 559; R. G. Neale, *Great Britain and United States Expansion* (Michigan State University Press, 1966), p. 53.
10. W. M. Clemens, *Theodore Roosevelt* (F. T. Neely, Publisher, New York and London, 1899), pp. 113-114; *Selections from the Correspondence of Theodore Roosevelt and Henry Cabot Lodge*, I, 278; H. K. Beale, *Theodore Roosevelt and the rise of America to world power* (John Hopkins Press, Baltimore, 1956), p. 70; J. A. S. Grenville and G. B. Young, *Politics, Strategy, and American Diplomacy* (Yale University Press, New Haven and London, 1966), p. 273; L. H. Healey and L. Kutner, *The Admiral* (Ziff-Davis publishing company, Chicago, New York, 1944), pp. 134, 136-137.
11. H. K. Beale, op. cit., p. 52; M. A. De Wolfe Howe, op. cit., p. 194.
12. *Speech of Moorfield Storey to National Democratic Convention*, Moorfield Storey Papers, LOC.
13. E. J. Benton, *International law and diplomacy of the Spanish-American War* (Johns Hopkins Press, Baltimore, 1908), p. 72.
14. *Journal of John Davis Long*, edited by M. Long (Smith, Rindge, New Hampshire, 1956), pp. 213-214; 55th Congress 2nd Sess., *Report of the Committee on Foreign Relations, United States Senate, Relative to Affairs in Cuba* (Government Printing Office, Washington, 1898), p. 491.
15. *The Letters of Theodore Roosevelt*, I, 747; *BET*, January 25, 1898.
16. William Lawrence, op. cit., pp. 110-111; *Journal of John Davis Long*, pp. 216-218.
17. H. H. Kohlsaat, *From McKinley to Harding* (C. Scribner's Sons, New York, London, 1923), pp. 66-67.
18. *Textile Record*, March 1898; *Boot and Shoe Recorder*, March 30, 1898.
19. Thomas Beer, *Hanna* (Alfred A. Knopf, New York, 1929), pp. 199-200.
20. *BET*, March 25, April 4, 5, 6, 1898.
21. *Papers of John Davis Long*, edited by G. W. Allen (Massachusetts Historical Society, 1939), p. 80.

268 REPUBLIC OR EMPIRE

22. *BET*, March 28, 1898.
23. Ibid., April 2, 1898.
24. Ibid., April 9, 1898.
25. *Boston Post*, April 9, 1898; *Advocate of Peace*, May 1898.
26. 55th Congress, 3rd Sess., House of Representatives, Document No. 1, *Papers Relating to the Foreign Relations of the United States* (Government Printing Office, Washington, 1901), p. 747; E. J. Benton, op. cit., p. 91.
27. *BET*, April 11, 1898; Henry Cabot Lodge, *Speeches and Addresses*, p. 378.
28. S. B. Griffin, *People and Politics* (Little, Brown and Co., Boston, 1923), p. 345; *Home Market Bulletin*, May 1898; *BET*, April 21, 1898.
29. 55th Congress, 2nd Sess., House of Representatives, Document No. 405, *Message of the President of the United States* (Government Printing Office, Washington, 1898), p. 8.
30. *BET*, April 25, 26, 28, May 12, 1898.
31. Ibid., April 25, 1898.
32. Ibid., April 29, 1898; Norton Papers, Houghton Library (hereafter referred to as HL); *Letters of Charles Eliot Norton* (Houghton Mifflin Company, Boston and New York, 1913), II, 458.
33. Norton Papers, HL.
34. *Letters of Charles Eliot Norton*, II, 254.
35. Quoted in *BET*, May 9, 11, 1898.
36. *American Wool and Cotton Reporter*, March 10, April 7, 1898.
37. Ibid., May 26, 1898.
38. Henry Cabot Lodge, *Speeches and Addresses*, p. 307.
39. *BET*, March 25, 1898.

CHAPTER 5 — Faneuil Hall and Aguinaldo

1. *BET*, December 17, 1897.
2. R. A. Alger, *The Spanish-American War* (Harper and bros., New York and London, 1901), p. 326.
3. *SDR*, December 18, 1899; *BET*, December 24, 1897.
4. A. Dewey, *Life and Letters of Admiral Dewey* (The Woolfall Company, New York, 1899), p. 194.
5. *Papers of John D. Long*, pp. 69-70.
6. T. M. Agoncillo and O. M. Alfonso, *A Short History of the Filipino People* (University of the Philippines, Quezon City, 1960), pp. 4, 110-111, 148; W. C. Forbes, *The Philippine Islands* (Houghton Mifflin Company, Boston and New York, 1928), I, 55-59, II, 354.
7. Article by Aguinaldo, *SDR*, January 25, 1900.
8. Nathan Sargent, *Admiral Dewey and the Manila Campaign* (Naval Historical Foundation, 1947), p. 16; L. H. Healey and L. Kutner, op. cit., pp. 157-158.
9. 55th Congress, 3rd Sess., Senate Document No. 62 (Government Printing Office, Washington, 1899), Part 2, pp. 333-334.
10. Ibid., pp. 347, 341-342.
11. *Reports of Rear-Admiral George Dewey on the Battle of Manila Bay, May 1, 1898, and on the Investment and Fall of Manila, May 1 to August 13, 1898* (Government Printing Office, Washington, 1900), p. 43.

NOTES

12. 55th Congress, 3rd Sess., Senate Document No. 62, Part 2, pp. 345-346, 431.
13. Ibid., pp. 357, 340, 345, 352.
14. L. H. Healey and L. Kutner, op. cit., p. 224; *Reports of Rear-Admiral George Dewey on the Battle of Manila Bay, May 1, 1898, and on the Investment and Fall of Manila, May 1 to August 13, 1898*, p. 43.
15. J. Barrett, *Admiral George Dewey* (Harper and Brothers, Publishers, New York and London, 1899), p. 35; General F. Greene, "Our Rule in the Philippines," *North American Review*, February 1900.
16. *BET*, May 13, 1898.
17. Sargent, op. cit., p. 53; *Reports of Rear-Admiral George Dewey on the Battle of Manila Bay, May 1, 1898, and on the Investment and Fall of Manila, May 1 to August 13, 1898*, p. 41.
18. 55th Congress, 3rd Sess., Senate Document No. 62, Part 2, pp. 338, 340, 354.
19. John A. Garraty, op. cit., p. 204; *Letters of Theodore Roosevelt*, II, 818; *Selections from the Correspondence of Theodore Roosevelt and Henry Cabot Lodge*, I, 299.
20. *BET*, June 2, 1898; John A. Garraty, op. cit., p. 197; *Selections from the Correspondence of Theodore Roosevelt and Henry Cabot Lodge*, I, 299.
21. *BET*, June 2, 1898; note in Gamaliel Bradford's handwriting in Vol. V of Gamaliel Bradford Scrapbooks, 1897-1907, Gamaliel Bradford Papers, MHS.
22. W. L. Garrison to C. E. Norton, April 27, 1898, C. E. Norton Papers, HL; *BET*, June 8, 1898.
23. *BET*, June 8, 10, 1898.
24. Note in Gamaliel Bradford's handwriting in Vol. V of Gamaliel Bradford Scrapbooks, 1897-1907, Gamaliel Bradford Papers, MHS; application in Archives, Boston City Hall.
25. Moorfield Storey to C. E. Norton, June 12, 1898, C. E. Norton Papers, HL; *Boston Advertiser, Boston Journal, BET*, June 16, 1898.
26. *BET*, June 12, 1898; note in Moorfield Storey's handwriting, Scrapbook II, 1896-1899, Moorfield Storey Papers, LOC; *Anti-Imperialism, Speeches at the Meeting in the Faneuil Hall, Boston, June 15, 1898*.
27. *Boston Record, Boston Post*, June 20, 1898.
28. Letter of George E. McNeill to *Labor Standard*, Gamaliel Bradford Papers, MHS; *Boston Herald*, June 22, 1896.
29. Autobiographical Sketch, Gamaliel Bradford Papers, MHS.
30. Gamaliel Bradford, *Lesson of Popular Government* (The Macmillan Company, New York and London, 1899), I, 508.
31. *BET*, June 16, 1898; *Boston Post*, June 19, 1898; R. M. McElroy, op. cit., II, 274-275.
32. *BET*, June 16, July 18, 1898.
33. C. Benitez, *History of the Philippines* (Ginn and Company, Boston, 1954), pp. 288-289.
34. *Reports of Rear-Admiral George Dewey on the Battle of Manila Bay, May 1, 1898, and on the Investment and Fall of Manila, May 1 to August 13, 1898*, pp. 43, 46.
35. *Selections from the Correspondence of Theodore Roosevelt and Henry Cabot Lodge*, I, 311-312; *New York Sun*, June 22, 1898.

36. *BET,* June 10, 1898.
37. Quoted in John A. Garraty, op. cit., p. 201.
38. *American Wool and Cotton Reporter,* June 30, 1898.
39. Erving Winslow, *An Epitome of Historical Events* (Government Printing Office, Washington, 1902), p. 13.

CHAPTER 6 — Aging Abolitionists, Rejuvenated Racism

1. *BET,* May 16, 19, 1898.
2. Edward H. Clement, "19th Century Journalism," *New England Magazine,* December 1906, p. 415; Edwin D. Mead, "Boston Memories of Fifty Years," *Fifty Years of Boston,* edited by E. M. Herlihy (Boston, 1932), p. 21; J. E. Chamberlin, op. cit., pp. 160-161; "Edward Henry Clement," *The Tufts College Graduate,* January 1907, p. 155.
3. *BET,* July 15, 1898; Theodore Roosevelt, *The Rough Riders* (Charles Scribner's Sons, New York, 1920), pp. 144-145; John Hope Franklin, *From Slavery to Freedom* (A. A. Knopf, New York, 1947), p. 416.
4. Theodore Roosevelt, op. cit., p. 143; *BET,* August 6, 1898; quoted in Rayford W. Logan, *The Betrayal of the Negro* (Collier Books, New York, 1967), p. 318.
5. John Hope Franklin, op. cit., pp. 418-419.
6. *BET,* May 5, 11, 1898.
7. U. S. Congress, Senate, Senator George Frisbie Hoar speaking on Hawaiian annexation, 55th Congress, 2nd Sess., July 5, 1898, *Congressional Record,* XXXI, 6661-6662-6663.
8. Frederick A. Ober, *Puerto Rico and Its Resources* (D. Appleton and Company, New York, 1899), p. 237; *Boston Herald,* July 30, 1898.
9. *Textile Record,* July 1898, p. 375.
10. *BET,* July 12, 1898.
11. Ibid., December 29, 1898.
12. Ibid., June 21, 1898.
13. Maj. Gen. Wesley Merritt, U.S.A., "The Manila Campaign," *The American Spanish War, a history by the war leaders* (Chas. A. Haskell and Son, Norwich, Conn., 1898), p. 264; George E. Dewey, *Autobiography* (C. Scribner's Sons, New York, 1913), p. 274.
14. O. K. Davis, "Dewey's Capture of Manila," McClure's Magazine, October 1899, pp. 174, 180; *SDR,* December 29, 1899.
15. O. K. Davis, op. cit., 178, 181; *Compilation of Philippine Insurgent Records* (Government Printing Office, Washington, 1903), p. 17.
16. *Reports of Admiral George Dewey on the battle of Manila Bay, May 1, 1898, and on the investment and fall of Manila, May 1 to August 13, 1898,* pp. 63-64; *Boston Herald* report quoted in *BET,* August 9, 1898.
17. *Compilation of Insurgent Records,* p. 17.
18. *SDR,* August 25, 1898; *BET,* August 29, 1898.
19. *Springfield Weekly Republican,* September 2, 1898.
20. *BET,* August 26, 1898.

CHAPTER 7 — The New England Anti-Imperialist League

1. A. S. Parsons to Moorfield Storey, July 28, 1898; D. G. Haskins, Jr., to Moorfield Storey, August 2, 1898, Moorfield Storey Papers, LOC; *BET*, September 10, November 11, 1898.
2. *Making Peace With Spain, the Diary of Whitelaw Reid*, edited by H. Wayne Morgan (University of Texas Press, Austin, 1965), p. 15.
3. Ibid., p. 15.
4. J. E. Chamberlin, op. cit., pp. 191, 196.
5. *BET*, September 17, 1898; George E. Dewey, op. cit., chapter XVII.
6. Charles Emory Smith, "McKinley in the Cabinet Room," *Saturday Evening Post*, October 11, 1902, p. 7.
7. H. Wayne Morgan, editor, op. cit., p. 58.
8. 55th Congress, 3rd Sess., House of Representatives, Document No. 1, *Papers Relating to the Foreign Relations of the United States* (Government Printing Office, Washington, 1901), pp. 901, 920-921-922.
9. *BET*, August 2, 1898.
10. *SDR*, October 26, 1898.
11. 55th Congress, 3rd Sess., House of Representatives, Document No. 1, *Papers Relating to the Foreign Relations of the United States*, pp. 933-934-935.
12. Charles Emory Smith, op. cit., p. 6; Charles S. Olcott, *William McKinley* (Houghton Mifflin Company, Boston and New York, 1916), II, 110-111.
13. *BET*, October 4, 19, 1898.
14. *BET*, October 9, 1898; *SDR*, quoted in *BET*, November 3, 1898; *BET*, November 15, 1898.
15. *BET*, November 7, 1898.
16. Ibid., November 9, 1898; *SDR*, November 10, 1898.
17. *BET*, November 10, 15, 1898; *Boston Record*, November 19, 1898.
18. Diary of Charles Francis Adams, Jr., November 18, 1898, Charles Francis Adams, Jr., Papers, MHS; *BET*, November 11, 21, 1898.
19. Edward Atkinson to Lyman Gage, November 25, 1898, Edward Atkinson Papers, MHS.
20. *BET*, November 11, 21, 1898.
21. Ibid., November 10, 1898.
22. *Transactions of the New England Cotton Manufacturers' Association*, September 27-29, 1898, p. 70.
23. *BET*, November 16, 23, 1898.
24. *Boot and Shoe Recorder*, November 23, 1898.
25. *BET*, November 10, 1898.
26. *SDR*, November 14, 1898.
27. *BET*, November 15, 1898; *Boston Advertiser*, quoted in *BET*, November 11, 1898; *SDR*, November 15, 1898.
28. H. Wayne Morgan, editor, op. cit., pp. 177-178.
29. Ibid., p. 198.
30. 55th Congress, 3rd Sess., House of Representatives, Document No. 1, *Papers Relating to the Foreign Relations of the United States*, p. 834.

CHAPTER 8 — Opposition to the Treaty

1. G. F. Hoar to E. Hale, November 14, 1898; E. Hale to G. F. Hoar, November 28, 1898; G. F. Hoar to C. Schurz, December 5, 1898, G. F. Hoar Papers, MHS.
2. E. Hale to G. F. Hoar, November 16, 1898, G. F. Hoar Papers, MHS; G. F. Hoar, *Autobiography of Seventy Years* (Charles Scribner's Sons, New York, 1903), II, 315.
3. W. F. Draper, *Recollections of a Varied Career* (Little, Brown and Company, Boston, 1909), p. 281.
4. G. F. Hoar to W. D. Sohier, December 1, 1898, G. F. Hoar Papers, MHS; *Time and the Hour*, October 22, 1898, p. 1.
5. W. D. Sohier to G. F. Hoar, November 30, December 10, 1898; G. F. Hoar to W. D. Sohier, December 1, 1898, G. F. Hoar Papers, MHS.
6. *BET*, December 8, 1898; *SDR*, December 8, 1898; G. Bradford to G. F. Hoar, December 7, 1898, G. F. Hoar to G. Bradford, December 9, 1898, G. F. Hoar Papers, MHS.
7. *Boston Globe* quoted in *BET*, December 12, 1898; W. F. Draper, op. cit., p. 378.
8. *BET*, December 14, 1898; H. A. Baron, "Anti-Imperialism and the Democrats," *Science and Society*, Summer, 1957, pp. 228-229.
9. *SDR*, December 21, 24, 1898; *BET*, December 16, 21, 1898.
10. *SDR*, December 21, 24, 1898.
11. G. F. Hoar, op. cit., II, 322-323; R. F. Pettigrew, *Imperial Washington* (Charles H. Kerr and Company, Chicago, 1922), p. 270.
12. *BET*, December 21, 1898.
13. *SDR*, December 19, 1898.
14. Ibid., December 17, 1898.
15. *BET*, December 16, 24, 1898.
16. *BET*, December 12, 1898; *SDR*, December 21, 1898.
17. John De Witt Warren to E. Atkinson, December 3, 1898, Dana Estes to E. Atkinson, December 20, 1898, E. Atkinson Papers, MHS; *SDR*, December 13, 1898; *Los Angeles Times* quoted in *BET*, December 13, 1898.
18. *BET*, November 21, 1898, *SDR*, January 27, 1899; *BET*, February 1, 1899; W. J. Pomeroy, *American Neo-Colonialism* (International Publishers, New York, 1970), p. 57; E. Berkeley Tompkins, *Anti-Imperialism in the United States* (University of Pennsylvania Press, Philadelphia, 1970), pp. 292-293.
19. *SDR*, December 5, 7, 12, 27, 1898; *BET*, December 12, 1898; *Report of the Proceedings of the 18th Annual Convention of the American Federation of Labor*, p. 94.
20. *BET*, December 16, 20, 1898, January 10, 1899.
21. *BET*, December 24, 25, 1898; *Report of Major-General E. S. Otis, U. S. Volunteers, on Military and Civil Affairs in the Philippine Islands*, 1899 (Government Printing Office, Washington, 1899), p. 56.
22. *SDR*, December 27, 30, 1898.
23. Ibid., December 29, 1898.
24. *BET*, January 4, 1899.

25. Ibid., January 5, 1899.
26. *BET*, January 5, 1899; Moorfield Storey to G. F. Hoar, January 9, 1899, G. F. Hoar Papers, MHS; *SDR*, quoted in *BET*, January 7, 1899.
27. *Report of Major-General E. S. Otis, U. S. Volunteers, on Military and Civil Affairs in the Philippine Islands*, 1899, pp. 78-79; *BET*, January 5, 13, 1899.
28. *BET*, January 3, 1899.
29. McKinley to Otis and Dewey, January 9, 1899; Otis to Adjutant General, November 27, 1898, Files of the Adjutant General's Office, National Archives.
30. G. S. Boutwell to G. F. Hoar, December 30, 1898, G. F. Hoar Papers, MHS.
31. *SDR*, January 6, 1899.
32. Ibid., January 10, 1899.
33. *Time and the Hour*, January 14, 1899; *BET*, January 9, 1899.
34. *SDR*, January 14, 1899; *BET*, January 12, 1899.
35. *Boston Herald*, January 12, 1899; *BET*, January 13, 1899.
36. *BET*, January 16, 1899.
37. *Time and the Hour*, January 17, 1899; *SDR*, January 17, 1899; *BET*, January 16, 1899.
38. *BET*, January 16, 24, 25, 1899.
39. G. F. Hoar to G. S. Boutwell, January 17, 1899, G. F. Hoar Papers, MHS.
40. *BET*, January 18, 1899.
41. Ibid., January 19, 20, 1899.
42. Ibid., January 21, 1899.
43. Ibid., January 14, February 4, 1899.
44. Ibid., January 25, 1899; G. F. Hoar to D. G. Haskins, Jr., January 30, 1899, G. F. Hoar Papers, MHS.
45. *BET*, February 6, 1899; *Review of Reviews*, March 1899, p. 267.
46. *BET*, January 21, 1899.
47. Ibid., January 21, 1899.

CHAPTER 9 — The Treaty Passes

1. *BET*, February 6, 7, 1899.
2. G. F. Hoar, op. cit., II, 110, 320; E. Berkeley Tompkins, op. cit., pp. 192-193.
3. John R. Lambert, *Arthur Pue Gorman* (Louisiana State University Press, 1953), p. 272.
4. Arthur W. Dunn, *From Harrison to Harding* (G. P. Putnam's Sons, New York and London, 1922), I, 282.
5. *Selections from the Correspondence of Theodore Roosevelt and Henry Cabot Lodge*, I, 391-392.
6. *BET*, January 26, 1899.
7. J. F. Rhodes, *The McKinley and Roosevelt Administrations* (The Macmillan Company, New York, 1922), p. 110.
8. *BET*, January 9, 1899.
9. R. F. Pettigrew, op. cit., pp. 204-205.
10. *BET*, January 25, 1899.
11. Ibid., January 25, February 6, 1899; *SDR*, February 4, 1899.
12. *Time and the Hour*, December 10, 1898; E. H. Clement to E. Atkinson, January 13, 1899, E. Atkinson Papers, MHS; G. S. Boutwell to G. F. Hoar,

December 30, 1898, G. F. Hoar Papers, MHS.
13. *BET,* January 12, February 6, 1899.
14. Ibid., December 8, 1898.
16. *Report of Major-General E. S. Otis,* 1899 (Government Printing Office, Washington, 1899), pp. 18-22.
17. 57th Congress, 1st Sess., Senate Document No. 331, Part 1, *Senate Hearings on the Philippines* (Government Printing Office, Washington, 1902), p. 772.
18. *Report of Major General E. S. Otis,* 1899, p. 38.
19. 57th Congress, 1st Sess., Senate Document No. 331, Part 3, *Senate Hearings on the Philippines,* Minutes of the Commission Meetings, pp. 2709-2751.
20. *SDR,* January 8, 14, 1899.
21. Secretary of War Alger to Major-General Otis, January 21, 1899, Files of the Adjutant-General's Office, National Archives.
22. *SDR,* January 25, 1899.
23. *BET,* January 25, 26, 1899.
24. *SDR,* January 14, 1899.
25. *Report of Major-General E. S. Otis,* 1899, p. 94; *SDR,* February 6, 1899.
26. *Compilation of Philippine Insurgent Records,* pp. 42-43; T. A. Agoncillo and O. M. Alfonso, op. cit., p. 266.
27. Speech of Lieutenant Hall at Fanueuil Hall, March 19, 1903, printed in *Mass Meetings of Protest* (New England Anti-Imperialist League, Boston, 1903).
28. 57th Congress, 1st Sess., Senate Document No. 331, Part 2, *Senate Hearings on the Philippines,* MacArthur's Testimony, pp. 898-899; 56th Congress, 1st Sess., House Document No. 2, *Report of the War Department,* 1899 (Government Printing Office, Washington, 1899), Vol. I, Part 4, p. 463.
29. Quoted in Dean C. Worcester, *The Philippines, Past and Present* (The Macmillan Company, New York, 1914), I, 149.
30. *Report of the War Department,* 1899, pp. 463-464.
31. Richard Brinsley Sheridan, *The Filipino Martyrs* (J. Lane, London and New York, 1900), p. 155.
32. *Report of the War Department,* 1899, pp. 462, 464.
33. Charles Edward Russell, *The Outlook for the Philippines* (The Century Co., New York, 1922), p. 93.
34. 57th Congress, 1st Sess., Senate Document No. 331, Part 2, *Senate Hearings on the Philippines,* MacArthur's Testimony, p. 900.
35. *Report of the War Department,* 1899, p. 464; Herbert Welsh, *The Other Man's Country* (J. B. Lippincott Company, Philadelphia, 1900), p. 126.
36. Karl Irving Faust, *Campaigning in the Philippines* (The Hicks-Judd Company, San Francisco, 1899), p. 128; *Report of the War Department,* 1899, pp. 462, 463; *SDR,* January 22, 27, 1899; *Report of Major-General E. S. Otis,* 1899, pp. 84, 91; speech of Lieutenant Hall, *Mass Meetings of Protest.*
37. *BET,* February 11, May 8, 1899.
38. 57th Congress, 1st Sess., quoted in remarks of Senator Patterson on the Philippines, May 26, 1902, *Congressional Record,* pp. 5912-5913.
39. Quoted in Richard Brinsley Sheridan, op. cit., p. 169.

40. *SDR*, February 6, 1899; Erving Winslow, *An Epitome of Historical Events*. p. 17.
41. *BET*, February 6, 1899; 55th Congress, 3rd Sess., Senator Benjamin Tillman speaking on the Philippines, February 7, 1899, *Congressional Record*, p. 1530.
42. *BET*, February 4, 1899.
43. *Report of Major-General E. S. Otis*, 1899, pp. 90, 96; Otis Testimony, *Senate Hearings on the Philippines*, p. 787.
44. See column of F. B. Sanborn, *SDR*, July 15, 1899; editorials, ibid., January 31, February 3, 1900; speech of Carl Schurz, ibid., February 24, 1900; Herbert Welsh, *The Other Man's Country*.
45. *SDR*, February 6, 1899; diary of Charles Francis Adams, Jr., January 25, 28, 31, 1899, Charles Francis Adams, Jr., Papers, MHS.
46. *Letters of Henry Adams*, edited by Worthington Chauncey Ford (Houghton Mifflin Company, Boston and New York, 1938), II, 217.

CHAPTER 10 — Against the Philippine War

1. *SDR*, February 7, 1899.
2. *BET*, February 1, 1899.
3. Ibid., April 13, 1899; *SDR*, March 6, May 17, 1899.
4. *Boot and Shoe Recorder*, February 8, 1899.
5. *Boston Post* quoted in *SDR*, February 13, 1899.
6. *BET*, February 17, 1899.
7. *SDR*, February 17, 1899.
8. Ibid., February 17, 1899.
9. *BET*, February 17, 1899.
10. Ibid., February 15, 1899.
11. Quoted in the *BET*, February 20, 1899.
12. *BET*, January 20, 1899.
13. *SDR*, February 16, 1899.
14. *BET*, February 17, 1899; *SDR*, February 19, 1899.
15. *BET*, March 1, 1890.
16. *BET*, March 10, April 10, April 20, May 9, May 31, 1899; *Boston Post*, March 7, 1899.
17. *SDR*, March 16, 1899; *BET*, April 14, 27, 1899.
18. *SDR*, February 17, 1899.
19. *BET*, March 22, 1899.
20. *SDR*, March 6, 1899.
21. Ibid., March 21, 1899.
22. Henry Lloyd to Edward Atkinson, March 24, 1899, E. Atkinson Papers, MHS.
23. *SDR*, March 19, 1899.
24. Ibid., April 5, 1899.
25. *BET*, March 31, 1899.
26. Ibid., March 30, 1899; *Springfield Sunday Republican*, March 19, 1899.
27. *BET*, February 7, 1899.
28. Ibid., April 24, 1899.
29. *Soldiers' Letters* (Anti-Imperialist League, Boston, 1899), pp. 8, 19, 5, 3, 13.
30. *SDR*, April 25, 1899.

31. Quoted by Herbert Welsh in *The Other Man's Country*, p. 134; *Soldiers' Letters*, p. 10.
32. *SDR*, April 25, 1899.
33. *BET*, March 18, 1899.
34. Ibid., March 25, April 24, 1899; *SDR*, March 15, April 24, 27, 1899.
35. *BET*, April 25, 1899.
36. *SDR*, April 25, 1899.
37. Ibid., April 25, 1899.
38. *BET*, May 10, 1899.

CHAPTER 11 — Atkinson and the Volunteers
1. *SDR*, March 6, 1899.
2. *BET*, February 10, 1899.
3. Ibid., April 27, 1899.
4. See *Farm and Home* editorials for July 1, August 15, September 1, November 15, December 1, 15, 1898; January 1, February 15, April 15, 1899.
5. *BET*, April 3, 1899.
6. Ibid., February 10, 1899.
7. Ibid., March 1, April 18, 1899.
8. *SDR*, April 27, 1899.
9. Ibid., May 3, 1899.
10. *BET*, April 22, 1899; *SDR*, April 27, 1899.
11. *BET*, April 14, 18, 1899.
12. *SDR*, April 15, 1899.
13. *BET*, March 30, 1899.
14. *SDR*, April 21, 1899.
15. *BET*, April 20, 1899.
16. Leon Wolff, *Little Brown Brother* (Doubleday, Garden City, 1961), p. 238; *SDR*, April 24, 1899.
17. *SDR*, April 13, 1899.
18. *BET*, April 18, 1899.
19. *SDR*, April 21, July 26, 1899.
20. Ibid., April 23, 1899; *Boston Herald*, April 22, 23, 24, 1899.
21. *SDR*, April 25, 1899.
22. Ibid., April 25, 1899.
23. *BET*, May 6, 1899; H. F. Williamson, *Edward Atkinson* (Old Corner Book Store, Inc., Boston, 1934), p. 228.
24. *BET*, April 27, 1899.
25. Ibid., May 5, 6, 1899.
26. *SDR*, May 6, 7, 1899.
27. *BET*, April 26, 1899; E. Winslow to E. Atkinson, April 26, 1899, E. Atkinson Papers, MHS.
28. *SDR*, March 30, June 11, 1899.
29. *BET*, May 1, 1899; speech by J. D. Long, ibid., May 2, 1899.
30. *BET*, May 4, May 24, 1899.
31. Ibid., May 17, 1899.

32. H. F. Williamson, op. cit., pp. 4, 268, 272.
33. E. A. Stowe to E. Atkinson, January 3, 1899, E. Atkinson Papers, MHS.
34. *BET*, April 8, 1899; *SDR*, May 17, 1899.
35. *SDR*, May 3, 1899.
36. See H. F. Williamson, op. cit., pp. 228-229; R. L. Beisner, *Twelve Against Empire* (McGraw Hill Book Company, New York, 1968), pp. 99-100; E. Berkeley Tompkins, op. cit., pp. 206-208.
37. W. Warren to E. Atkinson, May 3, 1899; E. Winslow to E. Atkinson, May 8, 1899, E. Atkinson Papers, MHS.
38. *SDR*, April 30, May 25, 1899.
39. E. H. Clement to E. Atkinson, May 3, 1899, E. Atkinson Papers, MHS.
40. *BET*, April 1, 1899.
41. Diary of Charles Francis Adams, Jr., April 1, 1899, Charles Francis Adams, Jr., Papers, MHS; *BET*, May 18, 19, 1899.
42. *SDR*, May 29, 1899; *BET*, April 13, 1899.
43. *SDR*, May 6, 8, 1899.

CHAPTER 12 — The Rise of Monopoly and Finance

1. *BET*, February 10, December 30, 1899.
2. Ibid., April 29, 1899.
3. Ibid., May 26, 1899.
4. *Springfield Sunday Republican*, March 19, 1899; *The Liberator*, September 1899.
5. *Springfield Sunday Republican*, July 23, 1899.
6. Ibid., June 11, 1899; *SDR*, July 7, 1899.
7. F. B. Sanborn, *SDR*, November 11, 1899; *Boston Herald*, quoted in *SDR*, June 19, 1899.
8. F. B. Sanborn, *Recollections of Seventy Years* (Richard G. Badger, Boston, 1909, I, 206-211.
9. *SDR*, March 25, 1899.
10. Ibid., May 1, 1899.
11. Ibid., June 9, July 10, 1899.
12. Charles A. Conant, "The Struggle for Commercial Empire," *The Forum*, June 1899.
13. *The National Cyclopedia of American Biography* (James T. White and Company, New York, 1910), XIV, 227; *The Dictionary of American Biography*, IV, 334-335.
14. *SDR*, May 13, 1900.
15. Ibid., July 1, 1899.
16. *BET*, July 5, 1899.
17. *Boston Post*, July 5, 1899; *SDR*, July 5, 6, 1899.
18. *Boston Globe*, July 5, 1899; *BET*, July 5, 1899; *SDR*, July 6, 1899.
19. *SDR*, July 15, 1899; *BET*, July 25, 1899.
20. *SDR*, July 8, 1899; Ida Tarbell, *The Standard Oil Company* (McClure, Phillips and Company, New York, 1904), II, 271.
21. *Boston Globe*, July 14, 1899; *BET*, October 4, 1899.

278   REPUBLIC OR EMPIRE

CHAPTER 13 — An Organization Formed, A Republic Smashed
1. *Springfield Sunday Republican,* June 25, 1899; *Boston Sunday Post,* July 16, 1899; *Boston Post,* July 17, 18, 1899.
2. *BET,* July 19, 1899.
3. *Boston Globe,* reprinted in *SDR,* June 14, 1899.
4. *SDR,* June 21, 1899.
5. *Lowell* (Mass.) *Courier,* quoted in *SDR,* June 27, 1899.
6. *SDR,* July 16, August 3, 4, 1899.
7. *Boston Record,* quoted in *SDR,* June 24, 1899.
8. *SDR,* June 22, 1899.
9. Ibid., July 3, 18, 1899.
10. Ibid., June 17, July 15, 1899.
11. *BET,* July 10, 11, 1899.
12. Ibid., June 19, 22, 1899; *SDR,* June 27, July 2, 1899.
13. *BET,* July 17, 1899; *SDR,* July 18, 19, 1899.
14. *SDR,* July 19, 1899; *Boston Herald,* July 18, 1899; *BET,* August 12, 1899.
15. *SDR,* July 20, 21, 1899; *New York Herald,* quoted in *SDR,* July 19, 1899.
16. H. L. Higginson to President McKinley, July 11, 1898, H. L. Higginson Papers, Baker Library, Harvard School of Business Administration.
17. *SDR,* July 16, August 16, 18, 1899.
18. George S. Merriam to *SDR,* June 27, 1899; G. Bradford to same, July 27, 1899; A. F. Austin to same, August 14, 1899; editorial, *SDR,* July 14, 1899; *Worcester Gazette,* August 26, 1899.
19. *Pawtucket* (R. I.) *Times,* August 29, 1899; *Boston Journal,* September 6, 1899; *Portland* (Me.) *Advertiser,* August 28, 1899; *Lewiston* (Me.) *Sun,* August 30, 1899; *SDR,* August 27, 1899.
20. *Boston Sunday Globe,* July 16, 1899; *Boston Sunday Post,* July 16, 1899.
21. *SDR,* July 12, 1899.
22. *Boston Sunday Globe,* July 16, 1899; *SDR,* July 16, 1899; *SDR,* May 10, June 1, 1899; Report of the Secretary, *Annual Meeting of the Anti-Imperialist League,* Boston, 1899.
23. *BET,* June 26, 1899; *SDR,* July 8, 24, August 18, 1899.
24. *SDR,* May 17, 1899; *BET,* July 1, 1899.
25. *SDR,* May 9, August 3, 1899.
26. Report of the Secretary, *Annual Meeting of the Anti-Imperialist League,* Boston, 1899; *BET,* October 17, 1899; *SDR,* October 23, 1899.
27. Report of the Secretary, *Annual Meeting of the Anti-Imperialist League,* Boston, 1899; *SDR,* October 18, 20, 1899.
28. *BET,* October 20, 1899.
29. Philip C. Jessup, *Elihu Root* (Dodd, Mead and Company, New York, 1938), I, pp. 183-184; *Selections from the Correspondence of Theodore Roosevelt and Henry Cabot Lodge,* I, 416.
30. *BET,* June 5, August 21, September 16, 1899; *SDR,* July 2, 1899.
31. *SDR,* October 2, 1899; *St. Louis Republican* quoted in *SDR,* November 19, 1899.
32. *BET,* July 19, 22, August 23, 1899; *SDR,* June 24, August 3, 1899.

33. *BET,* August 23, 1899; *SDR,* August 14, 1899.
34. *BET,* September 21, 22, 1899; *SDR,* September 22, 1899.
35. *BET,* September 21, 22, 1899; *SDR,* September 22, 1899.
36. *Springfield Sunday Republican,* July 9, 1899.
37. *BET,* September 21, 1899.
38. *SDR,* October 7, 10, 1899.
39. *BET,* September 5, 11, October 20, 1899; *SDR,* October 13, 20, 1899.
40. *SDR,* October 7, November 5, 1899.
41. Ibid., October 7, 8, 10, 17, November 1, 1899.
42. *SDR,* October 1, 12, 15, November 4, 7, 8, 12, 1899.
43. Ibid., November 8, 1899.
44. *Boston Post,* quoted in *BET,* November 10, 1899; *SDR,* November 8, 9, 10, 1899.
45. *BET,* October 1, 1899; *Springfield Sunday Republican,* November 12, 1899; *SDR,* November 9, 1899.
46. *SDR,* November 8, 10, 1899.
47. *BET,* September 12, October 6, November 6, 1899; *SDR,* September 18, 1899; *Harper's History of the Philippine War,* edited by Marrion Wilcox (Harper and Brothers Publishers, New York and London, 1900), p. 297.
48. William T. Sexton, *Soldiers in the Sun* (Military Service Publishing Company, Harrisburg, Pennsylvania, 1939), p. 174.
49. *Harper's History of the War in the Philippines,* p. 308.
50. *SDR,* February 9, 1900.
51. *BET,* September 22, 1899.
52. *BET,* August 9, 1899; *The Protectionist,* June 1899, December 1899; *Transactions of the New England Cotton Manufacturers' Association,* April 27-28, 1899; *BET,* October 6, 1899.

CHAPTER 14 — Forging an Anti-Imperialist Coalition

1. *BET,* October 19, 1899; *SDR,* October 20, 1899.
2. *Springfield Sunday Republican,* October 8, 1899; *SDR,* November 17, 27, 1899.
3. *SDR,* October 23, 1899.
4. Ibid., January 1, 2, April 14, 1900.
5. Ibid., February 18, August 3, 1899, March 22, 1900.
6. *Springfield Sunday Republican,* November 19, 1899; F. B. Sanborn, *SDR,* December 24, 1899; *BET,* November 27, 1899; letter of W. Warren, *SDR,* November 23, 1899.
7. *The Political Nursery,* October 17, 1898, and *The Political Nursery Supplement,* October 24, 1898.
8. Carl Hovey, *John Jay Chapman* (Columbia University Press, New York, 1959), pp. 85-86.
9. C. Schurz to E. B. Smith, December 10, 1899; E. B. Smith to C. Schurz, December 18, 1899, C. Schurz Papers, LOC; R. F. Pettigrew, *Imperial Washington,* pp. 321-322.
10. Philip S. Foner, *History of the Labor Movement in the United States* (International Publishers, New York, 1955), II, 434; R. F. Pettigrew, op. cit., pp. 322-325.

11. *SDR*, November 7, December 7, 10, 14, 1899.
12. Ibid., January 9, 18, 25, February 1, 15, 1900; *BET*, February 2, 1900.
13. *BET*, January 1, 10, February 16, 1900; *SDR*, February 15, 17, 1900.
14. *BET*, April 17, 1900.
15. Ibid., April 18, 1900.
16. *SDR*, April 20, 1900.
17. Ibid., April 18, 1900.
18. *SDR*, October 12, 1899, February 8, 1900; *Springfield Sunday Republican*, February 4, 1900; *New England Magazine*, August 1900.
19. *SDR*, February 2, March 12, August 8, 1900; *Boston Evening Globe*, August 27, 1900.
20. *SDR*, January 10, 18, February 8, 11, March 1, 1900.
21. Ibid., January 29, 1900.
22. *BET*, January 31, February 3, 6, 1900; *SDR*, January 31, February 1, 4, 1900.
23. *SDR*, February 24, 28, 1900; *Springfield Sunday Republican*, March 18, 1900.
24. E. S. Corser to Hon. J. K. Jones, February 27, 1900; E. B. Smith to E. S. Corser, March 7, 1900; E. S. Corser to W. J. Bryan, April 12, 1900, W. J. Bryan Papers, LOC.
25. *BET*, January 5, March 7, 1900.
26. *Springfield Sunday Republican*, January 8, 1900; *SDR*, January 20, 1900; *BET*, March 19, 1900; *The Autobiography of George Dewey*, Charles Scribner's Sons, New York, 1913, pp. 266, 276-277.
27. *BET*, February 20, 1900.
28. Ibid., April 24, 1900; speech of John F. Fitzgerald, ibid., January 9, 1900; *SDR*, January 29, 1900.
29. *SDR*, January 6, 19, August 9, 1900.
30. *BET*, June 7, 1900.
31. Ibid., March 16, 19, June 4, 1900.
32. Ibid., January 9, May 15, June 8, 1900; *SDR*, July 9, 1900.
33. *BET*, March 15, 1900.
34. *Springfield Sunday Republican*, March 18, 1900.
35. *BET*, March 14, 16, May 31, 1900.
36. *Springfield Sunday Republican*, June 24, 1900; *BET*, July 2, 1900; Marilyn B. Young, *American China Policy* 1895-1901 (Harvard University Press, Cambridge, Massachusetts, 1968), pp. 136, 169.
37. *SDR*, June 21, 1900.
38. Ibid., April 27, 1900; *Boston Sunday Globe*, November 25, 1900; William B. Parsons, *An American Engineer in China* (McClure, Phillips and Company, New York, 1900), p. 45.
39. *BET*, June 20, 1900.
40. Ibid., June 19, November 6, 1900; *SDR*, June 22, 1900.
41. *SDR*, June 20, 21, 1900.
42. Thomas Beer, op. cit., p. 227; *SDR*, June 21, 1900; *BET*, June 26, 1900.
43. *BET*, June 25, 1900; *SDR*, June 19, 1900.
44. Ibid., July 5, 1900; *BET*, June 26, 1900.
45. *BET*, July 10, August 13, 1900.

46. Ibid., June 26, 1900.
47. SDR, editorial, quoted in BET, June 20, 1900; SDR, June 25, 27, July 4, 1900.
48. *Springfield Sunday Republican*, August 26, 1900.
49. SDR, June 26, 1900.
50. BET, July 2, 1900; SDR, October 2, 1900.
51. *Springfield Sunday Republican*, April 8, June 24, 1900.
52. SDR, March 21, 1900; M. E. Curti, "Bryan and World Peace," Smith College Studies in History, Vol. XVI, Nos. 3-4 (Department of History of Smith College, Northampton, Mass., 1931), pp. 134-135.
53. BET, April 4, 5, 6, 1900; *New York Commercial Advertiser*, quoted in BET, April 10, 1900.
54. BET, July 2, 5, 7, 1900; SDR, July 4, 5, 6, 8, 1900.
55. SDR, July 6, 1900.
56. Ibid., July 7, 1900.
57. J. J. Chapman to his mother, June 28, 1900, to M. Storey, July 29, 1900, J. J. Chapman Papers, HL.
58. J. J. Chapman to his wife, July 25, 1900, J. J. Chapman Papers, HL.
59. J. J. Chapman to his wife, August 7, 1900, J. J. Chapman Papers, HL; SDR, August 2, 1900; BET, September 19, 1900.
60. SDR, July 26, 1900; BET, July 26, 1900.
61. M. E. Curti, op. cit., p. 132; SDR, August 10, 1900; *Boston Sunday Globe*, August 13, 1900; BET, August 10, 15, 1900.
62. BET, August 2, 1900; *Boston Evening Globe*, August 18, 1900; clipping in J. J. Chapman Papers, HL; I. H. Klein to M. Storey, August 4, 1900, M. Storey Papers, LOC.
63. M. Storey to C. Schurz, August 21, 1900, quoted in M. De Wolfe Howe, op. cit., p. 203.
64. Clipping from the *Minnesota Democrat*, M. Storey Papers, LOC.
65. BET, August 16, 1900.
66. SDR, August 17, 1900; clipping dated August 16, 1900, M. Storey Papers, LOC.
67. SDR, August 17, 1900.
68. Ibid., August 21, 1900.
69. *Boston Globe*, August 18, 1900; BET, August 18, 1900; SDR, November 1, 1900.

CHAPTER 15 — The Victory of Imperialism

1. Quoted in BET, July 14, 1899.
2. SDR, June 9, August 22, 1900.
3. Newspaper clipping, dated March 23, 1900, "Clippings Relating to the Philippine Question," Widener Library, Harvard University.
4. SDR, September 16, 1900; BET, October 2, 1900.
5. BET, September 17, October 26, 1900.
6. SDR, October 17, 1900; undated clipping in G. Bradford Papers, MHS.
7. *Farm and Home*, December 15, 1899; Charles E. Benton, New Bedford, Massachusetts, letter to editor, SDR, April 24, 1900; *Boston Globe*, October 5, 1900; SDR, October 21, 1900.
8. SDR, July 14, 1900.

9. See Bryan's article, *North American Review,* June 1900, statement at Chicago, *SDR,* November 3, 1900, etc.
10. *BET,* September 10, 11, 1900; *SDR,* September 10, October 4, 1900.
11. *SDR,* August 9, September 27, October 10, 1900.
12. *BET,* August 1, 21, 1900; *Boston Globe,* August 20, 1900; *SDR,* August 20, 1900.
13. *Springfield Sunday Republican,* October 21, 1900; *SDR,* September 7, October 3, 29, 1900; *BET,* September 27, 28, 1900.
14. *SDR,* October 29, November 4, 1900; *BET,* October 23, 1900.
15. *BET,* September 18, 1900; *SDR,* October 13, 1900.
16. Herbert Croly, *Marcus Alonzo Hanna* (Macmillan Company, New York, 1912), pp. 332-336.
17. Hoar's arguments are to be found in various speeches and letters: G. F. Hoar to E. Atkinson, July 30, 1900, E. Atkinson Papers, MHS; *BET,* July 7, 11, 23, August 10, 30, 1900; *SDR,* October 13, 18, 28, 1900.
18. *SDR,* October 2, 1900; *BET,* June 20, July 12, October 29, 1900.
19. *SDR,* October 1, 3, 23, 1900.
20. Ibid. September 5, 6, 13, 15, 16, 26, 27, October 22, 1900; *BET,* September 21, 1900; Joseph Lee, letter to editor, *BET,* September 8, 1900.
21. *SDR,* February 24, September 21, October 11, 1900; *Boston Globe,* October 25, 1900; G. Bradford, letter to editor, *SDR,* May 21, 1900; W. L. Garrison, speech at Brookline, ibid., October 27, 1900.
22. E. Winslow to E. Atkinson, January 10, 1900, E. Atkinson Papers, MHS; Boston correspondent, *SDR,* October 5, 1900.
23. *Springfield Sunday Republican,* August 5, October 7, 1900; *SDR,* August 31, October 5, 1900; *Report of the Second Annual Meeting of the New England Anti-Imperialist League,* November 24, 1900, Report of the Secretary, p. 3.
24. *SDR,* August 23, 28, October 5, 7, 14, 16, 28, 31, 1900; *Report of the Second Annual Meeting of the New England Anti-Imperialist League,* November 24, 1900, Report of the Secretary, pp. 5, 6.
25. *SDR,* January 21, October 21, 28, 1900.
26. Ibid., August 9, September 4, 1900.
27. J. B. Lennon to S. Gompers, quoted in P. S. Foner, op. cit., II, 436; S. Gompers to J. B. Lennon, October 15, 1900, quoted in P. Taft, *The A. F. of L. in the Time of Gompers* (Harpers, New York, 1951), p. 292.
28. P. S. Foner, op. cit., II, 338-339.
29. *American Federationist,* October 1900, p. 319.
30. *Report of the Proceedings of the 19th Annual Convention of the American Federation of Labor,* pp. 16, 149.
31. *Report of the Proceedings of the 20th Annual Convention of the American Federation of Labor,* pp. 69, 71.
32. *Chicago Tribune,* September 16, 1899; *SDR,* September 16, 1899; *American Federationist,* October 1899.
33. *SDR,* October 2, 1900; *Boston Sunday Globe,* October 14, 1900; *Boston Post,* November 5, 1900.
34. P. S. Foner, op. cit., II, 436; *BET,* August 21, 1900; *SDR,* September 4, 1900.

35. *BET*, July 25, August 17, 27, 1900; *SDR*, August 24, September 5, 1900.
36. *SDR*, September 7, October 4, 1900.
37. *Springfield Sunday Republican*, October 28, 1900; *Boston Post*, November 1, 1900.
38. *Boston Evening Globe*, August 16, 1900; *Boston Globe*, August 17, 1900.
39. *BET*, August 25, 1900; *SDR*, August 24, 1900.
40. *Boston Globe*, October 4, 1900.
41. Ibid., October 15, 1900.
42. *BET*, September 13, 1900; *Boston Sunday Globe*, October 7, 1900; *Boston Globe*, October 24, 1900; *Boston Herald*, October 24, 1900; *SDR*, September 25, October 13, 1900.
43. *BET*, August 13, September 21, 1900; *Boston Globe*, September 5, 1900; *SDR*, September 12, October 5, 1900.
44. Quoted in Bliss Perry, *Henry Lee Higginson* (Atlantic Monthly Press, Boston, 1921), p. 429; *SDR*, October 10, 22, 30, 1900.
45. *SDR*, quoted in *BET*, September 21, 1900; *SDR*, October 1, 31, 1900.
46. E. Atkinson to G. F. Hoar, August 13, 1900, E. Atkinson Papers, MHS; *SDR*, October 19, 31, 1900; *BET*, September 11, 1900.
47. *Boston Sunday Post*, September 2, 1900; *SDR*, October 6, 1900.
48. *SDR*, August 31, October 5, 1900; *Boston Sunday Globe*, September 2, 1900; *Report of the Second Annual Meeting of the New England Anti-Imperialist League*, November 24, 1900, Report of the Secretary, p. 6.
49. J. J. Chapman to his wife, June 17, 1900, J. J. Chapman Papers, HL.
50. *SDR*, September 21, 28, 1900; *Boston Herald*, October 27, 1900.
51. *SDR*, September 26, 29, October 10, 1900; *Boston Globe*, September 27, *Boston Sunday Globe*, September 30, 1900; *BET*, September 27, 1900; *Boston Post*, quoted in *BET*, October 12, 27, 1900.
52. *Boston Globe*, October 9, 31, 1900; *SDR*, October 10, 1900; *Boston Post*, October 11, 1900.
53. *SDR*, October 19, 24, 1900; *Boston Post*, October 28, 1900; *Boston Sunday Herald*, November 11, 1900.
54. *Boston Sunday Globe*, September 30, 1900; *SDR*, October 10, 11, 19, 1900; *Boston Herald*, October 23, 1900.
55. *BET*, October 16, 1900.
56. *SDR*, September 6, 7, 8, 1900.
57. *Boston Globe*, September 8, 1900; *SDR*, September 4, 1900.
58. *SDR*, October 4, 1900; *Boston Globe*, October 29, 1900; *BET*, October 29, 1900.
59. *SDR*, November 2, 1900; *BET*, September 19, 26, October 26, 1900.
60. *SDR*, October 17, 1900; *BET*, October 26, 1900.
61. *SDR*, November 3, 1900; *Boston Globe*, November 3, 1900.
62. Interview with Job Harriman, Social Democratic vice presidential candidate, *SDR*, October 26, 1900.
63. *BET*, November 3, 1900.
64. *BET*, April 7, 10, May 4, July 3, 1900; *SDR*, May 18, June 9, 12, October 2, 1900.

65. *SDR*, November 3, 1900, July 8, 14, 1901.
66. *SDR*, November 9, December 12, 1900; *BET*, November 21, 30, 1900.
67. *SDR*, November 7, 1900; statement of P. A. Collins, *Boston Evening Globe*, November 7, 1900; *Boston Post*, November 8, 1900.
68. *Hartford Times*, quoted in *SDR*, November 9, 1900; W. J. Bryan to T. W. Higginson, November 15, 1900, T. W. Higginson Papers, HL.
69. Editorial, *SDR*, November 7, 1900; ibid., November 9, 1900; editorial, *Boston Herald*, quoted in *BET*, November 1, 1900; statement of R. F. Pettigrew, *BET*, November 10, 22, 1900.
70. *SDR*, February 25, October 7, 17, 23, 1900; David Greene Haskins, Jr., letter to editor, ibid., November 5, 1900.
71. Ibid., November 10, 1900; *Boston Herald*, October 5, November 11, 12, 1900.
72. Quoted in *BET*, November 7, 1900.
73. *SDR*, November 14, 1900; *Boston Journal*, quoted in *BET*, November 21, 1900.
74. Editorial, *Springfield Sunday Republican*, September 21, 1900; Massachusetts Affairs Column, ibid., October 28, 1900.
75. *SDR*, November 21, 1900; *Boston Herald*, November 19, 1900.
76. *Boston Herald*, quoted in *BET*, November 30, 1900; *SDR*, November 9, 10, 1900.
77. *SDR*, November 15, 17, 1900; *BET*, November 21, 1900.
78. *Boston Globe*, November 2, 1900; *BET*, August 18, 22, November 11, 22, 1900; *SDR*, November 8, 12, 13, 17, 30, 1900.
79. *SDR*, March 12, 1900; *Boston Globe*, August 11, 1900; *Baltimore American*, quoted in *BET*, November 2, 1900; *BET*, August 22, November 7, 1900.
80. W. G. Brown, "A defense of American parties," *Atlantic Monthly*, October 1900, quoted in *SDR*, October 25, 1900.
81. *SDR*, September 7, October 6, 14, 17, 18, 1900.

CHAPTER 16 — Against Atrocities: The Last Campaign

1. H. P. Willis, *The Philippine Problem* (Henry Holt and Company, New York, 1905), p. 22; Leon Wolff, op. cit., p. 324; W. H. Taft to E. Root, November 30, 1900, E. Root Papers, LOC.
2. 56th Congress, 2nd Sess., House Document No. 2, *Report of General MacArthur for 1900* (Government Printing Office, Washington, 1900), p. 62.
3. *SDR*, November 9, 10, 1900; *Boston Herald*, November 19, 1900; *Boston Globe*, November 20, 1900.
4. 56th Congress, 2nd Sess., Senate Document No. 167, *Letter from the Secretary of War* (Government Printing Office, Washington, 1900); William T. Sexton, op. cit., p. 253.
5. M. Storey, "*Marked Severities*" (Geo. H. Ellis Co., Printers, Boston, 1902), p. 23; 57th Congress, 1st Sess., House Document No. 2, *Report of General MacArthur for 1901* (Government Printing Office, Washington, 1901), p. 100.
6. 56th Congress, 2nd Sess., House Document No. 2, *Report of the Secretary of War for 1900* (Government Printing Office, Washington, 1900), p. 53; G. Bradford, letter to the editor, *SDR*, February 9, 1901; E. Root to Mrs. John Hay, quoted in Philip C. Jessup, op. cit., I, 335.

7. R. F. Pettigrew, quoted in G. Bradford, letter to the editor, *SDR*, February 9, 1901.
8. *SDR*, April 25, 1902.
9. G. Bradford, letter to the editor, *SDR*, February 9, 1901.
10. G. F. Hoar, letter to the editor, *Troy* (N.Y.) *Press*, quoted in *SDR*, April 10, 1901.
11. *The New York Journal*, April 26, 1900, quoted in the *Bryant Democrat*, May 3, 1900, Roosevelt Collection, Widener Library.
12. H. C. Lodge to E. Root, November 1, 1901; H. L. Higginson to H. C. Lodge, October 31, 1901, E. Root Papers, LOC.
13. Philip C. Jessup, op. cit., I, 310, 313.
14. *BET*, February 1, 1901; *SDR*, February 11, 1902.
15. *SDR*, April 2, 1901; D. F. Healy, *The United States and Cuba*, 1899-1902 (University of Wisconsin Press, Wisconsin, 1963), p. 167.
16. *Boston Sunday Globe*, March 31, 1901; *Springfield Sunday Republican*, March 31, 1901; *Free America, Free Cuba, Free Philippines* (New England Anti-Imperialist League, Boston, 1901).
17. E. B. Smith to M. Storey, July 24, 1901, Storey Papers, LOC; E. B. Smith to C. Schurz, January 14, April 20, June 14, 1901, C. Schurz Papers, LOC; *SDR*, July 4, 1901.
18. P. C. Jessup, op. cit., I, 307; D. F. Healy, op. cit., p. 164; speech of Senator A. J. Beveridge at Chicago, *SDR*, September 29, 1900.
19. *New York Times*, May 2, 1901; *Boston Journal*, May 3, 1901; 57th Congress, 1st Sess., House Document No. 2, *Report of the Secretary of War for 1901* (Government Printing Office, Washington, 1901), Appendix D, pp. 157-158; M. Storey, "*Marked Severities*," p. 26; *Report of the Third Annual Meeting of the New England Anti-Imperialist League* (New England Anti-Imperialist League, Boston, 1901), Report of the Secretary.
20. W. T. Sexton, op. cit., p. 267; *SDR*, April 12, May 6, 1902; Memorandum by C. F. Adams, Vol. 147, C. Schurz Papers, LOC.
21. F. B. Sanborn, Boston letter, *SDR*, October 5, 1901.
22. F. E. L. (Francis Ellington Leupp) to O. G. Villard, September 20, 1901, C. Schurz Papers, LOC.
23. M. Storey to C. Schurz, December 18, 1901, C. Schurz Papers, LOC; *SDR*, January 10, 1902.
24. *SDR*, January 10, 1902.
25. M. Storey to C. Schurz, December 3, 18, 1901, C. Schurz Papers, LOC.
26. M. Storey to C. Schurz, December 18, 21, 1901; E. B. Smith to C. Schurz, February 1, 1902, C. Schurz Papers, LOC.
27. *SDR*, January 10, 1902; *BET*, January 14, 1902; *Boston Post*, January 29, 1902.
28. *BET*, January 14, 1902.
29. *Boston Post*, January 21, 1902.
30. F. B. Sanborn, Boston letter, *SDR*, February 1, 1902.
31. *SDR*, January 17, 29, 1902.
32. *Letters of Henry Adams*, edited by W. C. Ford (Houghton Mifflin Com-

pany, Boston and New York, 1930), II, 371; *Boston Post*, January 29, 1902; *SDR*, February 5, 1902.
33. *SDR*, January 27, February 1, 11, 13, 22, 1902.
34. Ibid., February 1, 1902; Henry Loomis Nelson, *Boston Herald*, quoted in *SDR*, February 18, 1902.
35. *BET*, February 20, 1902.
36. Ibid., March 5, 1902.
37. *SDR*, March 7, April 9, 1902; *Springfield Sunday Republican*, April 13, 1902.
38. *Springfield Sunday Republican*, March 30, 1902.
39. *SDR*, April 11, 12, 30, 1902.
40. Ibid., April 15, 1902; speech of Herbert Welsh, *Mass Meetings of Protest*.
41. *SDR*, April 7, 16, 17, 21, 1902; *Boston Post*, quoted in *SDR*, April 18, 1902.
42. *SDR*, April 16, May 23, 1902.
43. Ibid., April 21, 30, May 4, June 1, 1902; *Army and Navy Journal*, quoted in *SDR*, May 6, 1902.
44. C. F. Adams to C. Schurz, May 19, 1902, C. Schurz Papers, LOC.
45. *SDR*, April 16, May 29, June 11, July 17, 1902; M. Storey, "Marked Severities," p. 66.
46. *SDR*, March 2, 20, April 5, 8, 14, 1902.
47. Ibid., March 9, April 17, 18, 19, 22, 25, May 1, 4, 16, 1902; *Springfield Sunday Republican*, April 13, 1902.
48. *SDR*, May 2, 1902.
49. Henry Loomis Nelson, *Boston Herald*, quoted in *SDR*, May 2, 1902; *Springfield Sunday Republican*, May 18, 1902; *SDR*, May 27, 1902.
50. Speech of Herbert Welsh, *Mass Meetings of Protest*.
51. *BET*, March 5, 1902.

CHAPTER 17 — The Dissolution of the Movement

1. Prospectus of the Philippine Information Society, Bound in Philippine Information Society, First Series, 1-12, 1901, Widener Library; F. Warren to C. Schurz, November 23, 1900, C. Schurz Papers, LOC; *Boston Globe*, November 20, 1900.
2. F. Warren to C. Schurz, November 23, 1900, C. Schurz Papers, LOC.
3. C. Schurz to F. Warren, November 24, 1900, C. Schurz Papers, LOC.
4. *The Outbreak of Hostilities,* The Philippine Information Society, First Series (Philippine Information Society, Boston, Mass., 1901), VII, 12.
5. Mrs. E. G. Evans to C. Schurz, March 21, 23, April 9, 1901, C. Schurz Papers, LOC; undated clipping from the *SDR*, scrapbook, M. Storey Papers, LOC.
6. E. Winslow to C. Schurz, January 17, 20, 1902; C. Schurz to C. F. Adams, May 23, 1902, C. Schurz to E. Shepard, May 23, 1902, C. F. Adams to C. Schurz, May 26, 1902, C. Schurz Papers, LOC.
7. E. B. Smith to C. Schurz, February 1, 1902, C. Schurz to E. B. Smith, February 3, 1902, M. Storey to C. Schurz, March 7, 1902, E. Winslow to C. Schurz, March 14, 1902, C. Schurz Papers, LOC.
8. Memorandum, vol. 142, C. F. Adams to C. Schurz, April 25, 1902, J. G. Schurman to C. Schurz, May 3, 1902, C. F. Adams to C. Schurz, April 30, 1902, C. Schurz Papers, LOC.
9. Memorandum, vol. 142, C. Schurz Papers, LOC.

10. *Mass Meetings of Protest*, speech of H. Welsh; H. Welsh to G. F. Krause, May 8, 1902, C. F. Adams to C. Schurz, May 8, 1902, J. Le Roy Smith to C. Schurz, February 16, 1903, Memorandum by C. F. Adams, vol. 147, C. Schurz Papers, LOC.
11. *Report of the Fourth Annual Meeting of the New England Anti-Imperialist League* (New England Anti-Imperialist League, Boston, 1902), Report of the Secretary; Memorandum by C. F. Adams, vol. 147, M. K. Sniffen to H. Welsh, quoted in H. Welsh to C. Schurz, May 7, 1902, C. F. Adams to H. Welsh, August 4, 1902, C. Schurz Papers, LOC.
12. C. F. Adams to H. Welsh, July 10, 1902, O. G. Villard to C. Schurz, July 28, 1902, C. Schurz Papers, LOC.
13. C. F. Adams to C. Schurz, August 13, 1902, C. Schurz Papers, LOC; *SDR*, February 13, April 19, 24, 1902.
14. C. F. Adams to H. Welsh, August 4, 1902, C. Schurz Papers, LOC.
15. E. C. Kirkland, op. cit., pp. 175-176; H. C. Passer, *The Electrical Manufacturers*, 1875-1900 (Harvard University Press, Cambridge, Mass. 1953), pp. 206, 323.
16. C. F. Adams to H. Welsh, July 31, 1902, C. F. Adams to C. Schurz, May 8, August 7, 1902, C. Schurz Papers, LOC.
17. T. M. Patterson to M. K. Sniffen, June 21, 1902, C. F. Adams to C. Schurz, December 20, 1902, H. Welsh to M. Storey, February 3, 1903, C. F. Adams to H. Welsh, February 4, 1903, C. Schurz Papers, LOC.
18. E. W. Ordway to C. Schurz, February 6, 1903, C. Schurz Papers, LOC.
19. H. Welsh to M. Storey, C. F. Adams, C. Schurz, February 3, 1903, C. F. Adams to H. Welsh, February 13, 1903, C. Schurz Papers, LOC; *Boston Post*, March 20, 1903.
20. *Mass Meetings of Protest*.
21. M. K. Sniffen to C. F. Adams, June 22, 1903, M. K. Sniffen to C. Schurz, June 27, 1903, C. Schurz Papers, LOC.
22. C. F. Adams to C. Schurz, July 6, August 28, 1903, M. Storey to C. Schurz, December 19, 1903, C. Schurz Papers, LOC.
23. E. Winslow to C. Schurz, January 23, 1903, C. Schurz papers, LOC.
24. Diary of F. Warren for March 14, 1903, E. Winslow to C. Schurz, March 21, 1903, G. S. Boutwell to E. B. Smith, March 21, 1903, C. Schurz Papers, LOC.
25. U.S. Congress, Senate, despatches from M. A. Teague in Panama to *Baltimore American*, printed as an annex to the speech of Senator E. W. Carmack, 58th Congress, 2nd Sess., February 9, 1904, and Senator E. W. Carmack speaking on the Panama coup, 58th Congress, 2nd Session, February 22, 1904, *Congressional Record*, pp. 1771-77, 2202; E. P. Hoyt, *The House of Morgan* (Dodd, Mead, New York, New York, 1966), pp. 209, 278; P. B. Varilla, *Panama* (McBride, Nast & Company, New York, 1914), p. 361; H. P. Pringle, *Theodore Roosevelt* (Harcourt, Brace, and Company, New York, 1931), p. 330.
26. J. F. Rhodes, *The McKinley and Roosevelt Administrations* (The Macmillan Company, New York, 1922), pp. 273-74; *Report of the Sixth Annual Meeting of the New England Anti-Imperialist League* (New England Anti-Imperialist League, Boston, 1904), Report of the Secretary.

27. E. W. Ordway to C. Schurz, December 7, 1903, Schurz Papers, LOC; M. Storey to E. W. Ordway, December 11, 1903, E. W. Ordway Papers, New York Public Library; M. Storey to E. W. Ordway, December 17, 1903, C. Schurz Papers, LOC; William James to E. W. Ordway, December 6, 1903, E. W. Ordway Papers, New York Public Library.
28. John S. Appel, *The Relation of American Labor to United States Imperialism, 1895-1905* (Unpublished Ph.D. dissertation, University of Wisconsin, 1950), p. 304.
29. William James to E. W. Ordway, December 6, 1903, E. W. Ordway Papers, New York Public Library.
30. H. Parker Willis to M. Storey, April 25, 1904, M. Storey Papers, LOC; *Report of the Sixth Annual Meeting of the New England Anti-Imperialist League,* Secretary's Report.
31. E. B. Smith to C. Schurz, January 14, 1901; C. Schurz to E. Winslow, July 15, 1901, C. Schurz to C. F. Adams, June 15, 1902, C. Schurz Papers, LOC; *Springfield Sunday Republican,* May 11, 1902; *SDR,* May 28, 1902.
32. Petition in papers of E. W. Ordway, New York Public Library; M. Storey to C. Schurz, February 4, 1904, E. W. Ordway to C. Schurz, June 24, 1904, C. Schurz to E. W. Ordway, June 28, 1904, C. Schurz Papers, LOC.
33. E. Berkeley Tompkins, *Anti-Imperialism in the United States: The Great Debate,* 1890-1920 (University of Pennsylvania Press, Philadelphia, 1970), p. 264; M. Josephson, *The President Makers* (Harcourt, Brace and Company, New York, 1940), p. 337; C. Schurz to Judge A. B. Parker, July 11, 1904, C. Schurz Papers, LOC.
34. *BET,* August 2, 1904; E. Winslow to C. Schurz, August 24, 1904, C. Schurz Papers, LOC; *Boston Herald,* July 9, 1904.
35. G. Bradford to C. Schurz, October 7, 1904, C. Schurz Papers, LOC; *Report of the Sixth Annual Meeting of the New England Anti-Imperialist League,* Report of the Secretary.
36. *Report of the Sixth Annual Meeting of the New England Anti-Imperialist League,* Report of the Secretary.
37. M. Josephson, op. cit., p. 167; E. D. Mead to M. Storey, October 20, 1904, M. Storey Papers, LOC.
38. M. Storey to C. Schurz, November 14, 1904, C. Schurz Papers, LOC; *Report of the Sixth Annual Meeting of the New England Anti-Imperialist League,* Remarks of G. S. Boutwell and F. B. Sanborn.
39. M. Storey to C. Schurz, October 25, 1904, C. Schurz Papers, LOC.
40. *Report of the Sixth Annual Meeting of the New England Anti-Imperialist League,* recommendations of the executive committee.
41. Notes and reminiscences, C. R. Codman, C. R. Codman Papers, MHS.

AFTERWORD

1. J. A. S. Grenville and G. B. Young, op. cit., p. 284.
2. *Boston Post,* January 23, 1902.
3. J. Hay to P. Dana, March 16, 1899, quoted in W. R. Thayer, *Life and Letters of John Hay,* II, 24.
4. *SDR,* July 9, 1900.

Index

Adams, Charles Francis, 8, 33, 38, 47, 99, 249; opposes treaty, 132; withdraws, 158-159; for McKinley, 216; supports investigation, 243-244; splits movement, 242-243, 250; close to financial elite, 245; his conservatism, 245-246.
Adams, Henry, 133.
Addams, Jane, 164.
Aguinaldo, Emilio, 68, 72, 96, 113, 125, 127, 130, 184, 219; at Cavite, 70; establishes government, 78; success against Spanish, 79; supported by Philippine people, 172; urges guerrilla warfare, 187; his capture, 228.
Aldrich, Nelson W., 122, 124.
Alger, Russell A., 66, 71, 153, 178; wires Otis, 126; resigns, 174.
America-China Development Company, 168, 195.
American Anti-Imperialist League, formation, 176-177; demise, 248, 252.
American Indians, war against, 2, 32; championed by Welsh, 244.
American Wool and Cotton Reporter, 61n., 62n., and war economy, 60-61; and Open Door Policy, 80.
Ames, Rev. C. G., 39, 75.
Ames, Oliver, 28n.
Anti-imperialists and anti-monopoly sentiment, 3, 18, 161-162, 222-223, 256.
Anti-imperialists and democratic traditions, 3, 7-8, 32, 257.

Anti-imperialists and Philippine nationalism, a reciprocal alliance, in effect, 65-66, 141, 175, 230n., 256, 259; charge Aguinaldo's betrayal, 70; Charge U.S. war instigation, 132, 243.
Anti-imperialist coalition policy, 17-18, 76, 78, 203, 257-258.
Anti-imperialist decline, reasons for, 212-213, 220-221, 241-242, 248-249, 251-252, 257-258.
Anti-imperialists disagree on policy toward war, 74, 154, 174-175.
Anti-imperialist growth, reasons for, 3-4, 7-8, 10-18, 32, 65-66, 202-203, 222-223, 256-257.
Anti-imperialists on black rights, imperialism and white supremacy bolster each other, 88, 146-147, 215, 240, 259.
Anti-imperialists on imperialism, export as a factor, 24, 164-165; monopoly and export of capital as factors, 161-166, 166n., 180, 185; a threat to democracy, 157, 180, 206, 215, 247; a perversion of national resources, 208; as an historical stage, 260.
Anti-imperialist opposition, annexation Santo Domingo, 23; Blaine, 24-26; naval re-armament, 28, 40, 198; annexation Hawaii, 33, 49, 91-92, 117; Venezuelan policy, 33, 38-42; war economy, 46-47, 54, 62, 220-221;

290 REPUBLIC OR EMPIRE

Spanish War, 50-59; Puerto Rican annexation, 87; Paris treaty, 99, 105-119, 132-133; Philippine War, 135-147, 174-175, 189, 219-220, 251; Boer War, 191; Open Door policy, 194; Boxer intervention, 197, 201, 231; military atrocities, 227-228, 231-232, 234, 243-247; Platt Amendment, 228-230; Panama coup, 248-249.

Anti-imperialist third party, Chapman promotes, 120, 188, 199; New York meeting, 189; rejected by anti-imperialists, 201-202.

Atkinson, Edward, 8, 99, 100, 110, 124, 138, 159, 187, 216; and Venezuelan crisis, 37, 38, 39; calls for military insubordination, 152-154; background, 155-156.

Bayard, Thomas Francis, 35.
Beard, Charles, 4.
Bell, General James F., 231, 239.
Bisbee, Rev. R. E., 216.
Black anti-imperialists (see W. H. Lewis, Kelley Miller, Clifford Plummer, Rev. W. H. Scott, Bishop H. M. Turner), oppose B. T. Washington, 15, 214; Spanish War, 57; Hose lynching, 146; Philippine War, 172; Liberty Congress, 200-202; 1900 elections, 214-215.

Blaine, James G., trail-blazing imperialist, 24; supports export trade and naval re-armament, 24, 27; calls for annexation of Hawaii, Cuba and Puerto Rico, 29.

Boot and shoe industry (see *Boot and Shoe Recorder*), second in Massachusetts, 20; support for imperialism, 20; not adapted to monopoly, 161, 185.

Boot and Shoe Recorder, 21, 52, 101, 136.

Boston Advertiser, 26, 102.
Boston Bar Association, 53.
Boston Brahmins, role in anti-imperialist leadership, 8; split on anti-imperialism, 8, 17; Anglo-phile, 37, 77; nostalgia for the past, 9, 58-59.

Boston Central Labor Union, Venezuelan crisis, 41; condemns imperialist policy, 76.

Boston Chamber of Commerce, 52.
Boston City Council, condemns imperialism, 169, **169n.**

Boston Evening Transcript, 26, 28, 35, 42, 56, 62, 65, 71, 78, 92, 94, 101-102, 118, 145-146, 151, 173, 182, 198; leading anti-imperialist papers, 16; switches to McKinley, 157.

Boston Globe, 26, 107, 175, 215; supports McKinley's policies, 21.

Boston Herald, 24, 26, 47n., 87, 152, 173, 240; anti-imperialist, 16; supports imperialism, 124, 159.

Boston Journal, 26, 125, 181, 221; supports McKinley's policies, 21.

Boston leadership, anti-imperialism, 5, 7, 111, 175; abolitionism, 7; revolutionary war, 8; reform, 16; Mugwump revolt, 25-26; Venezuelan crisis, 38, Bryan vote, 220.

Boston merchants, resist manufacturing interests, 9; links with anti-imperialists, 8, 10; oppose McKinley foreign policies, 10, 22; Anglophile, 31; oppose Venezuelan policy, 38; accept expansion, 158; ebbing influence, 162.

Boston Merchants Association, 10, 38, 113, 139, 158; opposes Spanish War, 52; disapproves McKinley's Philippine policy, 100; promotes Open Door policy, 193.

Boston Post, 15, 26, 175, 213; opposes annexation, Philippines, Puerto Rico, Hawaii; opposes Philippine War, 138.

Boutwell, George S., 99, 114, 137, 168, 176, 181, 182, 187, 189, 192, 234, 242, 245, 246; condemns Boxer intervention, 201; denounces Platt

Amendment, 230; predicts labor's eventual leadership, 258.
Bowles, Samuel, 3, 32, 176; and anti-imperialism, 16.
Bradford, Gamaliel, 8, 18, 33, 117, 192, 206, 241n., 242, 243, 245, 250, 251; initiates anti-imperialist movement, 73-75; background, 76-77; sponsors coalition policy, 76, 78, 188, 203; calls for defeat U.S. Philippine policy, 174-175; protests "water cure," 227-228.
Bray, Howard, 128.
Brown, John, 155, 163.
Bryan, W. J., 14, 46, 48, 62, 149, 242, 243, 251, 252; against imperialism, 78; for treaty, 108, 110; resumes anti-imperialism, 188; 1900 elections, 192-193, 197-199, 200, 202, 213, 220; his critique of imperialism, 205-206, 208.

Campaign against atrocities, Pettigrew's speech, 227; Bradford's protest, 227-228; Lopez's speech, 230; pamphlet, *Benevolent Assimilation*, 231; Boston conference, 234; petition for investigation, 234; Hoar's speech, 234; General Miles' protest, 237; leadership of Welsh, 244.
Capital surplus (see export of capital), as condition of capital export, 137, 166, 167; and finance capital, 185.
Carnegie, Andrew, 14, 99, 99n., 244, 245; opposition to treaty, 132; Chinese investment, 168, supports McKinley in 1900, 189.
Casson, Rev. Herbert, 41.
Censorship, Hoar charges, 141; journalists charge, 173-174.
Chaffee, Major General Adna, 231, 238, 240.
Chapman, John Jay, 216, 241n., 252; wealth corrupts both parties, 120; promotes third party, 120, 188, 199, 201, 202.

China market, and decision to occupy Philippines, 66-67, 67n.; importance to textile industry and Standard Oil, 80.
Civil service reform, 10.
Clan-na-Gael, 167, 168.
Clement, Edward, H., opponent of racism and imperialism, 16, 84, 84n., 88, 92, 110, 124, 146; an anti-imperialist summation, 260.
Cleveland, Grover, 10, 14, 26-27, 44, 78; opposes Hawaiian annexation, 30, 31, 33; Venezuelan policy, 33-36, 38, 42; opposes treaty, 132.
Codman, Charles Russell, 8, 25, 39, 201, 230, 247, 251, 253.
Collins, Patrick A., 14, 57, 191, 192, 212, 213.
Colored Protective League, 172.
Committee of Correspondence, 75.
Conant, Charles A., 165, 166, 217.
Corser, Elwood S., 189, 192, 193.
Crane, W. Murray, 181, 182.
Croker, Richard, 179, 188, 210, 211.
Cuba Company, 228.

Davis, Cushman, 67n., 96, 118.
Day, William N., 94, 96, 102.
Debs, Eugene, 218-219.
del Pilar, General Gregor, 184, 186.
Depression of 1893, stimulates imperialist tendency, 21, 33-34, 255.
Dewey, George E., 22, 50, 59, 66-68, 70, 71, 96, 114, 125, 127.
Diaz, Abbie Morton, 16.
Dole, Rev. Charles F., 15, 39, 53, 153, 247.
Draper, Eben S., 100, 210n.; manufacturer of textile machinery, 21; director, *Boston Journal*, 21; helps Lodge become Senator, 28.
Draper, George, founder of textile machinery firm and Home Market Club, 21.
Draper, William F., senior partner, Draper firm, 30; supports Hawaiian

292 REPUBLIC OR EMPIRE

annexation, 30; Hoar's friend, 106; opposes Philippine annexation, 107.

Elections, of 1896, 14, 46, 48; of 1898, 95, 97-98; of 1899, 179-182; of 1900, preparation for, 187, 192, 197, 198, 199, 201, 202; Bryan's acceptance speech, 200; Bryan-anti-imperialist agreement on issue, 205-208; McKinley's participation, 208; Hanna and prosperity, 208-209; Roosevelt and Lodge, 209; Hoar pledges loyalty, 210; Hoar's sharp attack, 210-211; League campaign, 211-212, 220; *Republican* presses Bryan on black rights, 211; Gompers and labor, 212-213; black anti-imperialists, 213-215; Storey campaign, 216-217; Olney's blast, 217-218; Social Democrats, 218-219; Filipino guerrillas, 219-220; McKinley wins, 220; reasons for Bryan's defeat, 220-221; results of Republican victory, 221-222; anti-imperialist climax, 222; of 1902, 249; of 1904, 250-252.
Eliot, Charles W., 15, 25, 53, 132, 215.
Emerson, R. W., 15, 105, 260, 163.
Empress Dowager of China, 194, 195.
Estes, Dana, 39, 111.
Executive usurpation, 113, 197.
Exploitation of subject races, 92, 171.
Export of capital (see capital surplus), a cause of imperial policy, 165-167, 166n.; goal of U.S. financial supremacy, 20, 191, 222, 255; to South America, 43; to Puerto Rico, 87; to China, 167, 168, 193, 194, 222; to the Philippines, 125, 136, 136n., 185, 206, 240, 249; to Great Britain, 191-192; to Cuba, 228-229; to Panama, 248; condemned by *Republican*, Senator Mason, W. J. Bryan, 166, 167, 206; recommended by Lodge, 228-229.
Export of manufactured goods, a cause of imperial policy, 19, 20, 21, 24, 27, 27n., 30, 34, 43, 44, 80, 165; and Massachusetts industry, 22, 97-98; Lodge recommends, 29, 72, 73; *Boston Herald* condemns, 24.

Faneuil Hall, 26, 39, 65, 74, 229, 246, 247.
Farmers, discontent, 14; Myrick represents, 14, 111; National Grange against imperialism, 15; oppose treaty, 111; affected by prosperity's return, 220.
Father Augustine, 245.
Finance capital emerges, a Democratic notation, 185.
Fitzgerald, John F., 98, 115n.; denounces imperial policy, 178; drops opposition, 192, 192n.
Fleischer, Rabbi Charles, 15, 215.
Flint, Charles R., 163, 222.
Flower, B. O., 218n.
Foraker, Joseph B., 116-117.
Foster, Frank, 40.
Frye, William P., 94, 102; charges Merritt with deceit, 173.
Funston, General Frederick, 128, 143, 173, 228.

Galvin, George W., 218n.
Gardener, Cornelius, 237, 238.
Garrison, Wm. Lloyd, Jr., 40, 74, 138, 172, 215.
Germany, 42, 66, 95, 193.
Gillett, Frederick, H., 115n., 192n.
Glenn, Major Edwin F., 238, 239.
Gorman, Arthur Pue, 105, 114, 124, 179, 180, 242, 243, 250; calls off treaty fight, 118-119.
Gompers, Samuel, 14, 99, 111, 114, 132, 139, 175, 189, 213; urges neutrality in 1900, 212.
Grayson, Private Willie, 128.
Grant, Ulysses S., 23.
Gray, George, 94, 122.
Great Britain, 14; U. S. South American rival, 28, 34, 36, 42-43; Vene-

zuelan crisis, 33-36, 42; concedes to U. S., 42, 44; Morgan loan to, 191; Open Door policy cooperation, 193.
Grimké, Archibald, H., 215.
German-Americans (see Carl Schurz), oppose imperialism, 175-176; at Liberty Congress, 200.

Hale, Eugene, 105, 122, 192.
Hall, Lieutenant John F., 128.
Hanna, Mark, 46, 121, 209, 210, 221; sets prosperity issue, 208.
Harvard University, 15.
Hay, John, 96, 99n., 133, 193, 196, 230.
Higginson, Henry Lee, 57, 162-163, 174, 199n., 215, 228, 244, 245.
Higginson, Thomas Wentworth, 8, 25, 42, 147, 192, 202n., 214, 220, 246.
Hoar, George Frisbie, 98, 108, 114, 121-122, 124, 126, 133, 140, 147, 187, 199, 228, 229, 235, 243, 245, 248; Venezuelan crisis, 39; Hawaiian annexation, 86; background, 105-106; partisanship, 106; relations with anti-imperialists, 107; opposes Philippine annexation, 107; treaty fight, 115-116, 119; charges censorship, 141, second Philippine speech, 190-191, role in 1900 campaign, 210-211, 221; calls for investigation, 234.
Home Market Bulletin (see *The Protectionist*), 19, 21, 37, 46.
Home Market Club, 21, 37, 56; Philippine annexation, 100; McKinley banquet, 136, 137.
Horton, Rev. E. A., 39.
Howells, William Dean, 164, 230.

Imperialist rivalries, a stimulus to expansionist policy, 255.
Intellectuals, and anti-imperialism, 15.
Investigation of the war, anti-imperialist petition, 234; Senate debate, 235, 239-240, 246-247; role of Welsh, 235, 238-239, 244.

Irish-Americans (see Patrick A. Collins), 41-42, 57, 200; important in Massachusetts Democracy, 14; against U.S.-British alliance, 14; oppose Philippine War, 138; Boston rally, 167-168; Boston City Council resolve, 169; Bryan vote, 213.
Isthmian Canal, 20, 30, 248, 255.
Ireland, 14.

James, William, 15, 40, 138, 215, 249.
Johnson, Lyndon, 4, 97n.
Jones, Samuel ("Golden Rule"), 218.

Kitchener, Lord, 225, 226.

Labor anti-imperialism (see Samuel Gompers, Henry Lloyd, George E. McNeill), 14, 40, 41, 114, 115; Boston Central Labor Union opposes imperialism, 76; A. F. of L. against the treaty, 111.
Labor Leader, 40.
Lawrence, George P., 115n., 192n.
Lee, Henry, 9, 20.
Lee, Higginson and Company, 9, 229.
Leeson, J. R., 38.
Lewis, W. H., 146.
Liberal Republicans, 10, 23, 24.
Liberty Congress, 200-202.
Lloyd, Henry, 75, 97, 139, 180.
Lodge, Henry Cabot, 5, 23, 27-29, 30-32, 46, 73, 101, 120-121; breaks with reform, 24; in Congress, 27; naval re-armament, 27-29; social orientation, 22, 29, 47; Hawaiian annexation, 30, 31; U. S. tradition, 32; Venezuelan crisis, 35-36, 39, 44; war economy, 47; war with Spain, 52, 53-56, 62; treaty fight, 117, 121-122; 1900 elections, 195, 196, 209-211, 221; Boxer intervention, 196; war investigation, 235, 240, 246, 247; Panamanian intervention, 248.
Long, John Davis, 27n., 48, 49, 51-53, 56, 173.

Lopez, Sexto, 230, 230n.

McArthur, General Arthur, 127, 129, 184, 221, 225-227, 231.
McCall, Samuel W., 115n., 192n.
McKinley, William, 15, 20, 22, 46, 72, 94-95, 105, 110, 112-113, 118, 125, 126, 133, 136, 137, 151, 159, 173, 174, 181; Hawaii, 48, 49, 86; war with Spain, 50-53, 55-56; decides to occupy Philippines, 66-67, 71; "goes slow" at Iloilo, 114; endorses Otis' war, 130; elections 1900, 208, 218, 220; cabinet orders guerrilla extermination, 221, 225-227; Platt Amendment, 229-231; assassination, 231-232.
McNeill, George E., 14, 40, 75, 139, 140, 213; identifies imperialism with monopoly, 76; condemns Panama coup, 248.
Mahan, Captain Alfred Thayer, 27, 30, 49.
Mason, William E., 167, 168, 192.
Massachusetts Historical Society, 32.
Massachusetts industry, displacing commerce, 9; post-Civil War growth, 20; export need, 22; and empire, 79; not inclined to monopoly, 161; losing place to monopoly, 184-185.
Massachusetts leadership, in anti-imperialism, 5, 7, 17, 18, 211, 220; in previous democratic struggles, 7, 8.
Massachusetts Peace Society, 48, 138.
Massachusetts Reform Club, 10, 17, 18, 25, 38, 54, 93, 120, 138, 235.
Massachusetts Republican Party, industrial leadership of, 10, 20; support for imperialism, 20.
Massachusetts Sons of the American Revolution, 138.
Matthews, Nathan, Jr., 167, 168, 179, 217.
Mead, Edwin, D., 16, 53, 143, 164, 175, 252.
Memphis Commercial Appeal, 102, 108.

Merritt, General Wesley, 71, 173; testimony before Peace Commission, 95-96.
Mexico, war against, 2, 32.
Miles, General Nelson A., 139, 237, 251.
Militarism, 3; brought forward by imperialism, 27; fosters imperialism, 125.
"military-industrial complex," 3, 29, 133.
Miller, Kelley, 214.
Miller, General Marcus P., 112, 113, 125.
Monopoly, growth in '98-'99, 161; strengthens export trade, 162; cause of imperialism, 164-165; dominates Republican Party, 164.
Monroe Doctrine, and Venezuelan crisis, 36.
Moody, W. H., 97, 98.
Moral integrity of anti-imperialists, 58, 234, 259.
Morgan, J. P., 26, 189, 245, 249, 250, 252; loan to Great Britain, 191; reported lending to Panamanian Republic, 248.
Morton, J. Sterling, 38, 176.
Mugwumps, political thrust of mercantile Boston, 10; Gold Democrats in '96, 48.
Mumper, A. L., 143.
Myrich, Herbert, 14, 111, 150, 175, 208.

Naphen, Henry F., 98, 214n., 216, 221.
National Association of Manufacturers, 27n., 43, 124, 193, 195.
National Grange, against imperialism, 15.
Nelson, Henry Loomis, 240.
New England Anti-Imperialist League, 5, 10, 65, 135, 141-142, 149, 168, 197, 211-214, 229, 248, 250; middle class leadership of, 8, 17-18; fosters anti-imperialist coalition, 17-18; forma-

tion, 93-97, 99; national scope, 100, 110-111, 115, 175, 211-212; seeks labor support, 139; reaction to Atkinson case, 152, 154-155; survives national body, 252.
New England Cotton Manufacturers Association, 21, 22, 43; and Philippine annexation, 100.
New England Free Trade League, and Venezuelan crisis, 40.
New England Homestead, 15.
New England Loyal Publication League, 99.
New York Chamber of Commerce, 19, 124.
New York Evening Post, 232, 236.
New York Reform Club, 111.
New York Sun, 73, 79, 91, 163.
New York Times, 180, 231.
Norton, Charles Eliot, 8, 15, 99, 215; opposes Spanish War, 57-59, 74.

O'Brien, Robert L., 125, 127, 130, 158, 215, 229; imputes duplicity to McKinley, 94-95; on Administration's attitude to Filipino hostilities, 113-114; on Arthur Pue Gorman, 119-120.
O'Donnell, Edward, 41, 140.
Office of Naval Intelligence, 50, 51.
Olney, Richard, and Venezuelan crisis, 35-36; in elections of 1900, 217-218.
Open Door policy, 196; British cooperate in, 193; and U. S. investment in China, 193; endorsed by National Association of Manufacturers, 193; threatened by Boxer revolt, 194; anti-imperialist criticism, 194; and Democrats, 197.
Osborn, Francis A., 26, 99.
Otis, General E. S., 114, 125-127, 129, 132, 142, 173-174, 178, 184; old Indian fighter, 112; doctors President's proclamation, 125; denies war danger, 125; declares war danger, 126; orders open fire, 128; refuses peace overtures, 130, 157; claims victory, 151, 172, 184.
Outbreak of the Philippine War, 126-130; Administration version of, 130, 132; anti-imperialists' understanding of, 132, 243.

Paine, Robert Treat, 16.
Paine, Robert Treat, Jr., 8, 180.
Panamanian intervention, example of neo-colonialist policy, 248; failure of imperialist protest, 248-249; endorsed by Gompers, 249.
Paris treaty, Commission hearings, 95-96; Senate fight, 114-120; reasons for passage, 121-130, 133.
Parker, Alton B., 250, 251.
Parsons, Frank, 218n.
Parsons, Herbert, 181.
Parsons, W. Barclay, 168.
Peoples' China, 2.
Pettigrew, R. F., 114, 123-124, 149, 150, 190, 221, 227.
Philadelphia Museums, 43.
Philippine Independence League, 250-252; to compromise the struggle, 247.
Philippine Lumber and Development Company, 206.
Philippine War, 3-5, 29, 32; outbreak, 126-130; unpopularity, 172-173, 149-151; indecisive character, 178; Root prepares for offensive, 178, 182-183; success of offensive, 184; Filipinos conduct guerrilla war, 187, 219, 225; U. S. adopts "very drastic" methods, 225-228; capture of Aguinaldo, 228; Roosevelt declares war over, 256.
Pillsbury, A. E., 140, 147, 168.
Pilot, 16, 26, 41-42, 168, 213.
Platt Amendment, 230; protects U. S. investment in Cuba, 229.
Platt, Thomas C., 188.
Plummer, Clifford H., 171, 172, 215.
Plunkett, William B., 56, 124, 136, 173, 210n.

Pomeroy, Eltweed, 218n.
Pratt, E. Spencer, and Aguinaldo, 70-71.
The Protectionist (formerly *Home Market Club Bulletin*), 161, 185.

Quincy, Josiah, 8, 167, 179.

Racist attitudes, as related to imperialist viewpoint, 215; Theodore Roosevelt, 50, 85; Senator Hoar, 86; *Textile Record*, 87; surrender of Manila, 88-90; annexation of Hawaii, 91-92; economic exploitation underlying, 92; Henry Cabot Lodge, 101; *Memphis Commercial Appeal*, 102; William McKinley, 110; Arthur Pue Gorman, 119; U. S. military in the Philippines, 142-143.
Racist violence, in North and South Carolina, 101; Hose lynching, 146; in New Orleans, Akron and New York City, 213.
Reed, Thomas B., 48, 49, 53.
Reid, Whitelaw, 94.
Religious anti-imperialists (see Rev. C. G. Ames, Rev. R. E. Bisbee, Rev. C. F. Dole, Rabbi C. Fleischer, Bishop J. L. Spalding, Bishop H. M. Turner), 15, 238.
Republican National Convention of 1900, endorses McKinley and Philippine War, 195; Roosevelt nominated vice-president, 196; Lodge permanent chairman, 195.
Responsibility for atrocities, question debated, 240.
Rhodes, James Ford, 42.
Rockefeller, John D., associates H. M. Flagler and H. H. Rogers, 25; brother William Rockefeller and war with Spain, 52; funds reported in America-China Development Company, 168; mining properties, 180; ship-building syndicate, 192; associate Flagler in Cuba Company, 228;
funds for Roosevelt, 252.
Rockefeller, William, 52.
Rockhill, W. W., 193.
Roosevelt Administration and atrocities, Root's attempted whitewash, 236-237; *Republican* charges bad faith, 238; White House agitation, 238; Roosevelt's about face, 238; court martial of Smith and Glenn, 238; token punishments, 239.
Roosevelt, Theodore, 4, 27, 173, 181, 182, 237, 239, 239n.; supports Blaine in 1884, 25; Venezuelan crisis, 37, 40; Assistant Secretary of Navy, 49; Hawaiian annexation, 49; war with Spain, 50, 51, 52; telegram to Dewey, 51; Rough Rider, 72; on black troops, 84-85; blames critics for Philippine War, 173; nominated vice-president, 196; election campaign 1900, 209; shifts from annexation, 232; orders court martials, 238; a new breed of imperialist, 252.
Root, Elihu, 178, 184, 225-228, 236-239; author of Platt Amendment, 229.
Russell, William E., 37.
Russian rivalry in China, 168, 193, 194n.; "Caspian Sea petroleum" vs. Standard Oil, 168-169.

Sanborn, F. B., 140, 143, 168-169, 192, 232, 242, 245; monopoly the cause of imperialism, 164; background, 163; describes 1900 elections, 208.
Schurman, Jacob G., 235, 244.
Schurz, Carl, 48, 133, 176, 188, 189, 216, 234, 242, 243, 244, 250, 251, 252.
Scott, Rev. W. H., 39; opposes B. T. Washington, 15; fights racism in U. S. Army, 85, 85n.; in 1900 elections, 214-215.
Senate Foreign Relations Committee, 49n., 51; center of war party, 46.
Slave-system, as precedent for cor-

porate empire, 32.
Smith, Charles Emory, 97, 98, 137, 229; outlines imperialist program, 19-20, 37, 255; denies annexation result of popular demand, 95; Atkinson case, 153.
Smith, Edwin Burritt, 176, 187, 193, 197, 243, 244, 247.
Smith, General Jacob, 232, 238, 239, 239n., 240, 245.
Social Democrats, in elections of 1900, 218-219.
Soldiers' Letters, 142-143.
Southern offensive against black vote, 15, 88, 101, 199, 210, 214; Republicans give green light to, 222.
Soviet Union, 2.
Spalding, Bishop John L., 164.
Spanish-American War, 3, 4, 29; in the Caribbean, 83; in the Pacific, 59; concluded, 82.
Splitting the movement, Philippine Information Society, 242-243; the Adams Committee, 243-247; Philippine Independence League, 247-252; dissolution of national movement, 248, 252.
Springfield Republican, 1, 16, 59, 91, 98, 101, 102, 108, 110, 113, 137-138, 142, 146-147, 159, 175, 178, 181, 187, 191, 197, 211, 213, 229, 234-238, 239n., 247; declares against Philippine War, 135; leading anti-imperialist paper, 163; on export of capital, 166.
Standard Oil Trust, 67, 80, 80n., 168, 169, 178, 195, 222, 228.
Stevens, J. L., 29-30.
Storey, Moorfield, 8, 50, 51, 75, 113, 132, 180, 199, 201, 230, 242, 244, 246, 247, 250, 252; speech against Spanish War, 54, 57; opposes Puerto Rican annexation, 87; runs for Congress, 216-217, 221; calls for investigation, 234; denounces Panama coup, 248.
Stotsenberg, Colonel John M., 128, 129.

Sumner, Charles, 23, 216.

Taft, William Howard, 225, 236, 238, 249.
Talbot, Thomas Hammond, 67.
Teller, Henry M., 127, 235.
Textile industry, 161; dominant in Massachusetts economy, 20; support for imperialism, 20; South American market, 42-43; China market, 67.
Textile Record, 21; war with Spain, 52.
Textile World, 21.
Thayer, John R., 216, 221.
Thoreau, H. D., 105, 163.
Thurston, J. M., 62.
Tillman, Benjamin R., 130, 199.
Time and the Hour, 117, 166n.
Treason charges against anti-imperialists, 79, 136, 152, 156-157, 167, 190.
Treaty fight, anti-imperialist petition, 99, 110; popular opposition, 111-112, 132-133; anti-imperialists advocate vote delay, 114; McKinley calls for vote, 118; Gorman and Hoar fall in line, 119; passed by one vote, 121; business pressure, 122-124; military pressure, 125-132.
Troop withdrawal, volunteer unrest, 149-152, 227; domestic demand for, 149-152, 156-157, 227.
Turner, Bishop H. M., 215.
Twain, Mark, 230.
Twentieth Century Club, 53.

United Shoe Machinery Company, 161; presses on shoe manufacturers, 185.
U. S. imperialism, influence in South America, 4, 36, 42, 44, 80-81; influence in Asia, 4, 30, 67-68, 80-81, 222; goal of world hegemony, 20, 222, 255; turns from annexation to neo-colonialism, 230-231, 231n.; first growth and consolidation, 257.
U. S. industry, post-Civil War growth, 19-20.

U. S. intervention against Boxers, 195, 196, 197; endorsed by New York businessmen, 195; harshness of, 195; condemned by anti-imperialists, 197, 201, 231.

U. S. neo-colonialism, Open Door in China, 197, 258-259; Platt Amendment, 229-231, 241; Panamanian coup, 248; concession to anti-imperialist sentiment, 259.

U. S. Steel Company, Morgan, Carnegie and third party, 189.

U. S. traditions, twofold and conflicting, 32.

U. S. War Department, 126, 127, 151, 221, 226, 227, 231, 240.

"very drastic" methods, reasons for, 225; Cabinet decision on, 221, 225; reconcentration, 226; MacArthur's proclamation, 226; Philippine enlistment, 227; "water cure", 227-228, 238; Bell's statement and campaign, 231, 239; Smith at Samar, 232; dispatch to *Philadelphia Ledger*, 233-234; interview with Congressman, 236; Waller's court-martial, 237; Gardener's report, 237; Batangas report, 237-238.

Vietnam War, 1, 3; opposition to, 4, 5.

Volunteer unrest, 149-152, 156, 201-202, 227.

Waller, Captain John L., 215.

Weller, Major Littleton W. T. 237, 239, 240.

War economy, 38, 47, 52, 187-188, 220-221; *American Wool and Cotton Reporter* explains, 60-63.

Warren, Fiske, 230n., 242, 243, 247.

Warren, Winslow, 8, 189.

Washington, Booker T., 15, 110, 164, 252; on Hawaii, 92; National Negro Business League, 214.

Welsh, Herbert, 189, 235, 238, 240, 243, 247; leads campaign against atrocities, 244; conflict with Adams, 246.

Western anti-imperialism, role of W. J. Bryan, 78, 149, 176; Pettigrew's leadership, 149, 190; campaign for troop withdrawal, 149-150, 156, 175-176; Populists and, 150, 156, 198, 203; German-Americans, 175; Chicago's role, 176.

Weyler, General Valeriano, reconcentration policy of, 45, 226.

Wheaton, General Loyd, 235, 236.

Wildman, Edwin, 68.

Williams, George Fred, 164, 168, 182.

Willis, H. Parker, 239n., 247, 249, 251.

Wilson, Dr. W. P., 43.

Winslow, Erving, 8, 18, 74-75, 80, 99, 114, 154, 176, 182, 189, 202, 220, 243, 244, 247, 250; expresses coalition policy, 18.

Women and anti-imperialism, Abbie Morton Diaz, feminist leader, supports, 16; absence of women in League leadership, 18; participation in Faneuil Hall meeting, June 1898, 75; Cambridge women circulate nation-wide anti-war petition, 138.

Wood, William M., 162.

Wu Ting Fang, 195.

Young Men's Democratic Club of Massachusetts, 38, 138.